FISH DIVERSITY AND DAM ECOSYSTEM

FISH DIVERSITY AND DAM ECOSYSTEM

By

Dr. Sunil Eknath Shinde
(M.Sc., B.Ed., Ph.D.)
Assistant Professor
Department of Zoology
Maharaj J.P. Valvi Arts, Commerce
&
Shri V.K. Kulkarni Science College
Dhadgaon Distt. Nandurbar (India)

Dr. Pathan T.S.
(M.Sc., Ph.D., FAZI., FISST)
Assistant Professor
Department of Zoology
Kalikadevi Arts, Commerce & Science College
Shirur (K.A.), Distt. Beed (M.S.) (India)
&

Dr. Sandeep Roopsing Rathod
(M.Sc., B.Ed., Ph.D.)
Assistant Professor
Department of Zoology
K.K.M. College
Manwath Distt. Parbhani (India)

DISCOVERY PUBLISHING HOUSE PVT. LTD.
NEW DELHI-110 002

Published by:
Tilak Wasan
DISCOVERY PUBLISHING HOUSE PVT. LTD.
4383/4B, Ansari Road, Darya Ganj
New Delhi-110 002 (India)
Phone : +91-11-23279245, 43596064-65
Fax : +91-11-23253475
E-mail : discoverypublishinghouse@gmail.com
sales@discoverypublishinggroup.com
parul.wasan@gmail.com
web : www.discoverypublishinggroup.com

First Edition: **2014**

ISBN: 978-93-5056-417-2

Fish Diversity and Dam Ecosystem

Printed at:
Dynamic Printers
Delhi

DEDICATED
TO

My Father

Late Mr. EKNATH HIRAMAN SHINDE

And

My Mother

Smt. SUMAN EKNATH SHINDE

Preface

This book "Fish Diversity and Dam Ecosystem" has been designed to help the correlation study between fish diversity and water parameters, students to understand the subject easily also get the practical information about water analysis method.

The book is planned to fulfil the long felt need of Environment, Zoology student and also for research student at the graduate, post-graduate and Ph.D. levels of all Indian universities. It is written in most simple and articulate language supplemented with well-illustrated diagrams.

The book has been divided into five chapters. The first is an introductory chapter describing the terminology and general descriptions of water and fishes. Then second chapter is Study area and Sampling sites in which give the information about study area and sampling stations. Then there are two next chapters: Physico-chemical parameters and Fish Diversity. In each section have been classified and described under the following headings: Introduction, Material and Methods and Results. Then next fifth chapter is Conclusion.

This book is adequately illustrated with the line diagram of fishes and there are also specially compiled table and graph to assist the reader in readily grasping the essential points discussed in the text. In fact, no pains have been spared to make the book as attractive and appealing to the students as possible and we hope that we have been able to provide a complete guide to students, which will not only be help in their class-work but will also give them better practical study of the subject. If the book should be equally useful to teachers, laboratory of pollution department and research students, we would feel amply rewarded for his efforts.

We hope that the book in its present from will serve the research student's interest effectively.

Useful suggestions and healthy criticism to improve the book will be welcomed and thankfully acknowledged.

—Authors

Acknowledgements

I would like to express my deepest gratitude to my guide, Dr. D.L. Sonawane for his encouragement during my study. His dedications as well as his expertise, patience, and organizational skills have made all the difference in my book.

I must express my deep sense of gratitude to my Parents Late Mr. Ekanath Hiraman Shinde, Smt. Suman Ekanath Shinde, my eldest Adv. Rahul Eknath Shinde and Sister-in-law Smt. Pradyna Rahul Shinde, My elder brother Mr. Kapil Eknath Shinde and Sister in law Smt. Kushal Kapil Shinde, My Sister Poonam Shinde. I am thankful to my niece Naina Shinde to her smile face inspiration to me. I am thankful to my uncles and aunts Mr. Kishore Shinde, Mr. Nivruti Shinde, Late Sakharam Shinde, Late Baburao Shinde, Tukaram Shinde, and Late Shitaram Shinde. I am thankful to my Paternal aunt and uncle Smt. Dagadu Bhole and Mr. Babasaheb Bhole. I am thankful to my maternal Grandfather Eknath Ganpati Ghodake. I am thankful to my maternal uncles and aunts and her children's. I am thankful to my cousins and their children. I am thankful to my entire family members who have directly or indirectly helped me. I am thankful to Adv. B.G. Upade and his family.

I am also thankful to Late Maharaj J.P. Valvi, Hemantbhai Valvi and my Principal Prof. N.P. Vibhandik, all teachers colleagues and non-teaching staff of the Department of Zoology, Maharaj J.P. Valvi Arts, Commerce & Shri V.K. Kulkarni Science College, Dhadgaon Distt. Nandurbar.

Last but not the least, I my thanks to all those relatives, friends and colleagues who have directly or indirectly helped me in pursuit of this work.

—Dr. Shinde S.E.

Contents

Introduction

Water is one of the abundantly available substances in nature. It is indispensable for life both for plants and animals. It acts as a solvent for many more components than any other liquid providing ionic balance and nutrients which support life water is primary necessity of life i.e. it is the most vital resource for all animals and vegetable matters. Water is one of the most amazing compounds in nature consists of two common elements hydrogen and oxygen. Water plays an important role in environmental ecosystems. It acts as a universal solvent for many more compounds than any other liquid providing ionic balance and nutrient, which support life.

The most precious natural resource on the surface of earth is water which is 94 per cent as salt water in oceans and 6 per cent fresh water; 27 per cent of the freshwater is in glaciers, 72 per cent is underground and less than one per cent is found in rivers, streams, lakes and ponds and atmosphere. This freshwater supply is continually replenished by precipitation as rain or snow. The total annual run-off from continents is about 41,000 cubic kilometers, 32,000 km^3 of water available for human exploitation worldwide. The uneven distribution of world population and usable water make variable availability of water in some part of world. Much of the Middle East and North Africa, parts of Central America and the Western United States are already short of water. Our

entry in the year 2000, has observed scarcity of water in many countries due to increasing demand from agriculture, industry and domestic use.

The variations in water demand in different countries are due to population and the prevailing level and pattern of socio-economic development. The average per capita domestic use of water in USA is more than 70 times than in Ghana. The worldwide water use increased dramatically from about 1360 km^3 in 1950 to about 5190 km^3 in 2000. Agriculture is the main drain on water supply. Averaged globally, 69 per cent water in agriculture, 23 per cent in industry and 8 per cent for domestic purposes are the estimated withdrawals.

Freshwater is abundant worldwide. Though, every year on average of more than 7000 cubic meters per capita enters rivers and aquifers. There are 22 countries with less than 1000 m^3 per capita – a level commonly taken to indicate that water scarcity is a severe constraint. Eighteen countries have less than 2000 m^3 per capita on average. The limited renewable water resources are in the Middle East, North Africa and Sub-Saharan Africa.

Countries may sometimes have to make choices between quantity and quality. Effluents are less diluted when river flows decline. In countries with inadequate effluent treatment, water quality can often been improved only if supplies from dams are used to maintain flows for dilution rather than for other economic uses. Often the disparate agencies involved in management cannot agree on trade-offs between quantity and quality.

Water scarcity is often a regional problem. More than 200 river systems, draining over half of the earth's land are shared by two or more countries. Over pumping of groundwater aquifers that stretch under political boarders also injects international politics into the management of water scarcity. This has become routine in Indonesian regional capital of Surabaya. As industry, irrigation, and population expand, so do the economic and environmental cost of investing in additional water supply.

Access to safe water remains an urgent human need in many countries. Part of the problem is contamination, diseases that are largely conquered when adequate water supply and sewerage systems are installed cause tremendous human suffering. The problem is compounded in some places by growing water scarcity, which makes it difficult to meet increasing demand.

Human wastes pose great health risks for the many people who are compelled to drink and wash in untreated water from rivers and ponds. Data from UNEP's Global Environmental Monitoring System (GEMS) demonstrate the enormous problem of such contamination, with poor and deteriorating surface water quality in many countries. Water pollution from human wastes matters less in countries that can afford to treat all water supplies, still in some high income countries water quality has continued to deteriorate.

Decomposition of pollutants lowers the amount of O_2 dissolved in water decreasing the capacity of river to support aquatic life. Oxygen loss does not threaten health directly, but it affects on fisheries may be economically important. Human sewage and agro-industrial effluent are the main causes of this problem; nutrient runoff in agricultural areas with intensive fertilizer use is another contributor. Although inadequate levels of dissolved oxygen tend to affect shorter lengths or rivers than does faecal contamination a sample of GEMS monitoring sites in the mid 1980s found that 12 per cent had dissolved oxygen levels low enough to endanger fish populations. The problem was worst where rivers pass through larger cities or industrial centers. In China only five of 15 rivers stretches sampled near large cities were capable of supporting fish. High-income countries have seen some improvement over the past decade. Middle-income countries have, on average shown no change, and low-income ones show continued deterioration.

As surface waters near towns and cities become increasingly polluted and costly to purify, public water utilities and other urban water users have turned to groundwater as a potential source of a cheaper and a safer supply. It is often more important to prevent contamination of groundwater than of surface water. Aquifers do not have the self-cleaning capacity of rivers and once polluted, are difficult and costly to clean.

One of the principal origins of groundwater pollution is seepage from the improper use and disposal of heavy metals, synthetic chemicals, and other hazardous wastes. In Latin America, for instance, the quantity of such compounds reaching groundwater from waste dumps appears to be doubling every fifteen years. Sometimes industrial effluents are discharged directly into groundwater. In coastal areas over pumping causes self water to infiltrate freshwater aquifers. In some towns contamination occurs because of lack of sewerage systems or poor maintenance of septic tanks. High chemical inputs combined with irrigation in intensive agriculture contaminate groundwater as chemicals often leach into groundwater.

In every nation scientists and conservationists are now worried increasingly about the environmental hazards that headlong development may bring. The prices of development have included pollution problem, loss of farmland and habitats (for people as well as wild-life), and even the spread of diseases. Some environmental disruption is unavoidable concomitant of development, but the ecologists and environmentalists insist harmful effects which can often be anticipated and minimized it development is preceded by ecological studies and careful planning. Though the developing nations intend on developing goals and though the developed countries continue to encourage them in this, things are appearing that the commitment to change may become tempered with caution.

Despite substantial progress in bringing sanitation services to the world population, water quality has continued to deteriorate. Little has been done to extend the treatment of human sewage. The replacement of septic tank systems with piped sewerage systems greatly reduces the risks of groundwater pollution but leads to increased pollution of surface water unless the sewage is treated Adequate water supply is not the only problem but concern over water quality is growing since 1960's. Surface water pollution from point sources was attended first but more recently groundwater, sediment pollution and non-point sources have been found to be at least equally serious problems.

Discharge of untreated or inadequately treated waste water into rivers, lakes and reservoirs causes pollution. Another water quality problem is the increasing eutrophication of rivers and lakes caused mainly by fertilizer runoff from agriculture land. Acidification of lakes by acidic deposition is common in some European countries and in North America.

Inadequate sanitation is a major cause of the degradation of the quality of groundwater and surface water. Economic growth leads to longer discharges of waste water and solid waste. Inadequate investments in waste collection and disposal mean that large quantities of waste enter both groundwater and surface water. Groundwater contamination is less visible but often more serious because it decades for polluted aquifers to cleanse themselves and because large number of people drink untreated groundwater.

Environment is degraded more when people try to compensate for inadequate provision. The lack or unreliability of piped water causes household to sink their own wells, which often leads to over pumping and depletion. In cities such as Jakarta, where almost two thirds of the population relies on groundwater, the water table declined dramatically since the 1970's. In coastal areas this can cause saline intrusion, sometimes rendering the water permanently unfit for consumption. In Bangkok excessive pumping has also led to subsidence, cracked pavements, broken water and sewerage pipes, intrusion of sea water, and flooding.

Though, it is the most abundant and widely distributed substances in nature it is, familiar to all not only forming the oceans, lakes and rivers but as a vapour being everywhere around us and penetrating even the solid mass of the earth. Water is a renewable resource that circulates continually between the atmosphere and the earth's surface. Water is used for domestic, agricultural and industrial purposes. Most domestic water is used for waste disposal and washing, with only a small amount used for drinking. The largest consumptive use of water is for agricultural irrigation. Most industrial uses of water are for cooling and dissipating and transporting waste material.

The population explosion is increasing pressure on natural resources. Demand for water is growing rapidly as population and industrial activities are expanding and irrigated agriculture continues to increase. From the past five decades withdrawal of fresh water from rivers, lakes, and underground aquifers has increased. Future availability of water for human use depends on how water resources are managed.

The creation on this earth planet is believed to be water, which has contributed in the creation of living organisms. This is trusted that life was originated in water and sustained by it. Nearly 90 per cent of the mass of living population is composed of water. The choice of habitats of the early man was in relation to availability of water and, therefore, all early civilizations have originated, established and developed near or around water bodies, for example Babylon around Euphrates, Egypt around Nile and Indian around Indus-Ganga basin.

A study of water in view of different aspects becomes important. Although the percentage of utilization of water resources for the purposes other than irrigation is low at present, this is expected to rise appreciably in the future with increasing industrialization and power generation. The conservation and efficient utilization of available water resources need maximum emphasis. Therefore, there is need to give serious consideration while making decisions relating to water management in future.

The 70 per cent of the earth's surface is water 70 per cent is evaporated back to the atmosphere from the vegetation, forests and pastures, cropland, non-economic vegetation as well as from the lakes and water surfaces. Even though 30 per cent of the precipitation supply is left for other uses primarily domestic, agricultural, and industrial; it amounts to some 1370 million acre-feet annually.

Water is a physical substance and unique in number of aspects. It can exist easily in all three states viz., solid, liquid and gaseous at temperature found at the surface of the earth and even at the same temperature. Water is a transparent medium. Its transparency enables the penetration of light, transforming radiant energy into heat. Among liquids, water is an excellent thermal conductor. Water possesses the highest heat of fusion and heat of evaporation, collectively called latent heat, of all known substances that are liquid at ordinary temperatures. The latent heat of evaporation of water is 540 cal/gm. It has highest specific heat of all common substances. It is capable of storing tremendous quantity of heat energy with relatively small rise in temperature. Water is buoyant medium, in which, organisms can exist without specialized supportive structures such as those needed by organisms that inhabit terrestrial environments. Buoyancy of water depends upon the density and temperature of water. Water becomes denser and viscous at low temperature and gives greater buoyancy, which varies with seasonal changes. Many aquatic animals change their forms according to buoyancy. Water is a universal solvent so that pure water in nature is difficult to find. In water, practically all the minerals present in soil may be dissolved. Viscosity is the cause of the frictional resistance which water offers to the moving animal and objects. Viscosity allows organisms to swim using relatively simple movements. It also protects the aquatic animals and plants from mechanical disturbances. Water is slightly compressible with increased pressure. Pressures increase with increased depth of water at the 1 atmosphere for every 10 meters of descent. Pressure influences solubility, ionic dissociation and surface tension. The surface tension acts at the water air interface and develops a biotope. Many plants and animals and their parts are affected by surface tension in many ways depending upon weather parts of animals and plants are wettable or not. Water contains iron, sodium, potassium, calcium, magnesium manganese, silica, fluoride, carbonates, bicarbonates, nitrates, phosphates, sulphates, chlorides, etc. which, are responsible for saltiness or salinity of water. The quantity of these parts increase then they affect the body systems and cause destruction of health. Density of water is greatest at above freezing temperature; thus, as water-cools from about 4°C to the freezing point and below, the density of water becomes less. The density of large water bodies, lakes and rivers varies at different places and also at different times. These differences in the water density are due to variation in temperature and salt contents of the water.

Most gases readily dissolve in water notable those that are essential for life oxygen, nitrogen and carbon dioxide. The saturation level of any gas in water depends on several variables most notable are temperature, salinity, concentration of the gas in the atmosphere and its relative solubility in water. The greater the concentration in the atmosphere, the greater its concentration in water will tend to be depending on its relative solubility in water. The deeper layers of many bodies of water including ponds, lakes and some estuaries, may contain significant amounts of the toxic gas-hydrogen sulphide, which is released by decaying organic matter. In pure water, there are equal numbers of H^+ and OH ions; it, therefore, has neutral reaction. Some natural waters, however, acquire an excess of H^+ ions and are acidic, while others, with an excess OH ions are alkaline. A physiological background makes it quite evident that water is an important ecological factor in the life of organism. It is the medium of solutes, raw material in photosynthesis and is essential for maintenance of turgidity of cell and sometimes plays an important role in fertilization, pollution and dissemination. The list could be enlarged but it is already sufficient to show that water has a special place among physical substance.

Water pollution problem is more complex than air pollution, due to slower rate of regeneration and self-purification sources of contaminants being more diverse and contamination of water being more sensitive to propagation of life than that of air.

At present water resources have been the most exploited natural system since man strides the earth. Pollution of water bodies is increasing steadily due to rapid population growth, industrial proliferation, urbanization, increasing living standards and wide spheres of human activities.

Point source pollution is easy to identify and resolve. Non-point source of pollution such as agricultural runoff and mine drainage are more difficult to detect and control than those from municipalities or industries. Thermal pollution occurs when an industry returns heated water to its source. Temperature changes in water can alter the kinds and numbers of plants and animals that live in that area. The methods of controlling thermal pollution include cooling ponds, cooling towers and dry cooling towers; many a times, the problem with water is contamination. The contamination comes from old lead piping and solder that have been used in plumbing for years.

In India, 12 per cent of people get clean drinking water, the rest quench their thirst from polluted lakes, tanks, rivers, and wells due to which more than 3 million people get affected or die of enteric diseases every year. Water contaminated by faeces remains one of the biggest killer's worldwide, 7 per cent of all diseases and deaths globally are due to lack of adequate water, sanitation and hygiene. A diarrhea alone claim lives of some 2.5 million children every year. An immediate and most critical environmental problem facing most cities in India is lack of safe drinking water, inadequate waste management, and pollution control. In India about 163 million children in rural areas do not have access to safe drinking water, causing death of millions of children every year. Diarrhoea accounts for 8.7 per cent of death in the 0 to 1 age group, 19.7 per cent in the 1 to 4 age group and 15.2 per cent in the age group of 5 to 15. Some of the common diseases transmitted through polluted water are hepatitis, dysentery, typhoid, malaria, yellow fever, dengue, trachoma, flue and tuberculosis, malnutrition increases susceptibility to water born diseases.

Good quality of water is essential for living organisms. Hence, it is referred as most vital resource for all kinds of life on this planet. Water is required for various purposes such as drinking, cooking, washing, bathing, fire fighting, cleaning, maintenance of public gardens, swimming pools, development of industries etc. Water is a vital medicine. It can eliminate water born diseases, promote rural development and improve the quality of life. Therefore, water is an essential factor in economic, social and cultural development of community.

Among all these requirements according to National Water Policy, drinking water gets first priority and importance. Water is main source for human consumption must be free from organisms and from concentration of chemicals substances, soluble or non soluble in nature, which may be hazardous to health. If water is fit for drinking, it will be suitable for all purposes. Water is in constant demand for domestic use, animal culture, industries and agriculture. However, the limited sources, less than 1 percentage, water is available for the above purposes, hence it is treated as precious. Its judicious use is strongly recommended in all sectors including crop irrigation.

The environment is consisting of the atmosphere, hydrosphere and lithosphere. The environments change its chemical composition changes as a result of human activities, without any obvious biological consequences. From the global point of view; it would be a great interest to compare the amounts of element added to the water cycle by man's activities with the amounts which are cycled naturally. It is of primary importance that water would be available to living organism in sufficient quantity, but scarcely of less significant is the quality of water. In this connection, the pollution of many rivers looms as a problem of the first magnitude and represents wasteful misuse of water and discharge of substances produced by human population in water.

The high rate of increase in human population in India and rapid peace of its industrialization have created problems of disposal of waste products. To maintenance of harbours, industrial plants, agriculture, food develops plants, villages, town and cities discharging their domestic wastes into the water bodies. The human activities increases progressively all over the world; they exert an over growing influence on near shore and banks of these water bodies and the organisms contained therein. All the polluting components (oil products, chemical wastes, domestic sewage, radioactive substances and heated effluents form cooling systems of industrial installations and power stations) tend to enrich the water with foreign organic and inorganic components, thus, influencing, as a special investigations have shown the endemic bottom invertebrate fauna modifying its composition, pattern of distribution, biological cycles and the activities of individual species.

The earlier studies on water pollution were motivated primarily by public considerations. The physical, chemical, microbiological and biological changes that occur in unpolluted streams and streams polluted by domestic waste are adequately, not completely understood. Various aspects of these changes have been studied with the exception of the biological changes. The principle area concern today is the need for understanding the biological effects of the various industrial wastes and hazardous chemicals on the biological resources of receiving water. Many industrial wastes prove to be complicated mixtures of metals, organic substances, greases and oils derived for the lubricants used for plant machinery and any other materials most easily disposed of through a floor drain, will be discharged into water ways containing substantial amounts of toxicants or oxygen reducing substances derived from other industrial or municipal waste sources.

An animal does not exist apart from its environment, exception of some habitats such as oceanic depth and the interior of a warm blooded animal where parasites reside in relatively constant conditions. Most animals face nutritional uncertainties, marked diurnal and seasonal oscillations, which altered rates of metabolism and activities. Successful living demands continued physiological adjustments in relation to environmental variables. Precisely timed physiological process must prepare the animals for diverse activities like growth, reproduction, aestivation and migration etc.

Environmental pollution and human efforts for the betterment of living standards are the two sides of the same coin. In the wake of the industrialization consequence, urbanization and ever-increasing population, the basic amenities of life, viz., air, water and land are being polluted continuously. Industrial complexes have become focused on environmental pollution. Public interest in ecology implied a concern for air and water quality, for the increasing demand on limited natural resources in the context of increasing population. Today water resources have been the most exploited natural system since man strode the earth. Time is perhaps not too far when pure and clean water, particularly in densely populated, industrialized water scare areas may be inadequate for maintaining the normal living standards. Ground water, rivers, dams, seas, lakes, ponds and streams are finding more difficult to escape from pollution. Many rivers of the world received heavy flux of sewage, industrial effluents, domestic and agricultural wastes, which consist of substances varying from simple nutrients to highly toxic hazardous chemicals.

Hydrogen, oxygen, carbon, nitrogen, calcium and phosphorous are the elements present in greater quantity in both soil and water. They are required in larger concentrations than the other elements and most studies of the problem have focused on carbon, nitrogen and phosphorus. Hydrogen and oxygen are present in almost limitless supply, the hydrogen coming from water and the oxygen from the air. Although nitrogen is abundant in air, not readily available to living organism because of the nitrogen triple bond energy. Calcium is generally available via soluble components. An organism required the supply of nitrogen in a special form i.e. easily metabolized. Thus, the presence of certain numbers of moles of nitrogen atoms might not be a sufficient condition for the organisms continued existence. Phosphates and sulphates occur in the bottom sediments and in biological sludge, both in precipitation in organic forms and incorporated in to organic compounds where as carbonates, bicarbonates and chlorides are dissolved in water. In an aquatic ecosystem, physico-chemical environment has profound influence on its biotic components. It controls diversity, biomass and spatial distribution of biotic communities in time and space. The physical and chemical parameters exert influence both individually, collectively and their interaction produced abiotic environment which ultimately conditions the origin, development and finally succession of biotic communities. Further, biotic communities intern, continuously alter abiotic components goes in a dynamic ecosystem.

With rapidly advancing technology mans impact upon the world of living things is beginning in the environment, some of these are toxic and non toxic. Man is a basic pollutant responsible for the pollution hazards and toxic effects. The toxic chemicals are discharged by industries into air, soil and water get into human and animal food chain from the environment. Once, they enter into the biochemical process, they produce serious effects on living conditions. Man has brought great changes in the natural environment both intentionally and accidentally, with disastrous consequences. Geochemical and biological process is also involved in metal pollution together with human activities in the field of technology, which resulted in contamination of various water bodies. The problem of water pollution by heavy metal is well known to be of crucial importance all over the world and especially in developing countries like India.

After the time of industrial and green revolution, the wide spread use of heavy metals is increased in industries and agricultural fields. The discharge of untreated effluents from industries and agricultural wastes which entered in environment disturbs the biological balance. Two groups of substances have lasting effect on the natural balance in aquatic system "Nutrient" which promote unrestricted biological growth and in turn oxygen depletion and sparingly degradable synthetic chemical growth and in turn oxygen depletion and sparingly degradable synthetic chemicals and other wastes which often constitute adverse effect on aquatic ecosystem. Environmental experts estimated that industrial and domestic wastewater up to a million different pollutants into natural water. Substances such poly-cyclic aromatics, pesticides, radioactive substances and trace metals directly endanger the human life.

Natural water is extremely varied in chemical composition and factors controlling the composition include physical, chemical and biological processes. Dams are the most important source of water. Unfortunately, the dam is being polluted by indiscriminate disposal of sewage, industrial wastes and human activities through rivers. The rivers are always victims of impact of urbanization. Most water bodies become contaminated due to incorporation of untreated solid and liquid waste. Generation of hazardous waste has become an integral part of different activities of modern man. Large quantities of sewage and industrial waste find its way to river and dam water bodies. Large towns in India are situated on the river banks, their runoff and those form agricultural and lands find their way to the river making the water unfit for human use.

Physico-chemical characters becomes essential part of study and also generates baseline data regarding the extent of pollution and sources for the same. Studies on the physico-chemical characterization of single industries have been reported by various researches and the related impacts on the surrounding areas have been investigated in our country.

Extensive research has been carried out on the characteristic of rivers and dams at various stretches in India and abroad. Some of the major rivers investigated in India include Ganga, Yamuna and Godavari which are polluted mainly due to the domestic wastewater discharge. On other hand, the main sources of pollution of the river Godavari are uncontrolled and partially treated industrial effluents containing toxic metals.

Autotrophic organism by their photosynthetic or chemosynthetic activity stores some organic matter. The rate at which this organic matter is stored or accumulated in the ecosystem is referring to as primary productivity of the ecosystem. Different ecosystem has different primary production depending upon their physiochemical and abiotic environment. Most of the Indian rivers, dams and fresh water streams are seriously polluted by industrial waste or effluents which comes along with waste waters of different industries (such as petrochemicals, fertilizers factories, oil refineries and mills include metals such as copper, zinc, lead and mercury etc.), detergents, petrochemicals, acid etc. All these industrial wastes are toxic to animals and may cause death or sub-lethal pathology of the respiratory system in both invertebrates and vertebrates. The toxic substances present in the industrial wastes not only disturb the ecological balance in the receiving water but also endanger the health of animal.

Recently, aquaculture has been considered as a rapidly growing in many parts of the India as well as world. Aquaculture can play an important role in many developing countries only within the context of rural development but also as a commercial activity. Aquaculture refers to the growth maintain and management of commercially important water born animals and plants. Water parameter is very important for understanding of the metabolic events in aquatic ecosystem. Plankton constitutes the basis of nutritional cycle of an aquatic ecosystem. They form a bulk of food for fishes and other aquatic organisms.

Fish constitutes half of the total number of vertebrates in the world. They live in almost all aquatic habitats; 21,723 living species of fish have been recorded out of 39,900 species of vertebrates out of these 8411 are freshwater species and 11,650 are marine. India is one of the mega biodiversity countries in the world and occupies the ninth position in terms of freshwater mega biodiversity. In India 2500 species of fishes out of which 930 live in freshwater and 1570 are marine.

Development of fishery and allied industries has special significance because this sector is well suited to supply the protein rich food at cheaper price; it has export potential and capacity to generate employment opportunities for economically weaker sections of the society. Moreover, aquaculture represents an important source of state's revenue and also contributing to ecologically balance of water resources. Fresh water ecosystems represent an alternate avenue for culture fisheries. In India, not much progress has been made in the last few decades, though freshwater bodies and the potential to culture fish species are plenty. The freshwater sources in India are mainly contributing for augmenting the crop productivity in agriculture. Their proper utilization for aquaculture and management has not been given due consideration and attention. Contamination of water bodies might lead to a change in their trophic status and render as unsuitable for aquaculture. Several physico-chemical or biological factors could act as stressors and adversely affect fish growth and reproduction. Hence, regular monitoring of physico-chemical and biological water quality parameters is essential to determine status of water body with reference to fish culture.

The present study has been undertaken as base to determine water quality of Harsool-Savangi Dam and the survey area of water with reference to present status, survey records of topography of areas, degradation areas, altered areas, identification of water flow and human interference on dam, biological diversity indices, seasonal physico-chemical and biological characteristics of water quality and fish diversity.

The study was focused in the taxonomic composition and abundance of the macro-vertebrate's community, seasonal abundance to the macro vertebrate community and baseline water quality data, based on macro-vertebrates and several physicochemical measurements to better understand and manage the water body of the Harsool-Savangi dam.

2

Study Area and Sampling Sites

Study Area

Harsool-Savangi Dam is situated in Aurangabad District, Near Savangi village 10 km away from Aurangabad (19° 56′ 14.32″ N and 75° 21′ 30.56″ E). It is one of the minor irrigation projects in Maharashtra.

Harsool-Savangi dam built up in 19th century, Nizam Era. It has been observed, that the reservoir was constructed to fulfil need of water as a basic demand of Aurangabad. They constructed underground water channel, which open in Rozabag area. During those days water was mainly used for drinking, irrigation and washing clothes, animals etc. But now a day the stored water is used for irrigation, fish culture and washing clothes, animals etc.

This dam lies between two villages that are Harsool and Savangi, that's why dam named as Harsool-Savangi Dam. This dam is constructed on Kham River, so it is also called Kham dam. The origin of Kham River is nearby Chaukka hills. Water comes from Nayegaon and Chaukka hills meet in Savangi village.

Sampling Point

The water sampling sites for physical and chemical analysis are follows:

South site (Near the dam wall)

This sampling site situated towards south side of dam, in this area bathing, washing of cloths and animal's activities have been observed.

North site (River entry point)

This sampling site situated towards north side of dam; its River entry point in dam. It has been selected for knowledge of lotic ecosystem.

East site (Agricultural field)

This sampling site situated towards east side of Dam; this site is completely free from other human activities and having agricultural fields that's why agricultural pesticides, insectidices etc. mix in the dam water.

West site (Near the dam wall and Agricultural field)

This sampling site situated towards west side of dam, in this area bathing, washing of cloths and animals etc. activities have been observed at this site agricultural pesticides and detergents mixes along with rain water in to dam.

Morphometry

Morphometry feature of Harsool-Savangi Dam.

Particulars	Descriptions
Name	Harsool-Savangi Dam At. Savangi Tal. Aurangabad Distt. Aurangabad (M.S.)
Geographic co-ordinates	19° 56′ 14.32″ N 75° 21′ 30.56″ E
Distance (Aurangabad to dam)	10 km
River	Kham
Origin of River	Chaukka hills
Distance (Origin of River)	Chaukka hills - 11 km
Type of dam	Soil (earthan Dam)
Underground water supply	Rozabag society
No. of underground channels	10-12
Nature of catchments	Good
Maximum height of dam	24.35 m

3

Physico-chemical Parameters

Introduction

Water is one of the abundantly available substances in nature, which man has exploited more than any other resources for the sustenance of life. Water of good quality is required for living organisms. Dams are the most important water resource. Unfortunately, the dams are being polluted by indiscriminate disposal of sewage, industrial wastes and due to human activities. The dams are always the victims of the negative impacts of urbanization. Most of the water bodies become contaminated due to incorporation of untreated solid and liquid waste. Large towns in India situated near the dams, their run off from agricultural lands find their way to the River and add in dam water unfit for human use. Now-a-day due to increased human population and man made conditions, the water quality is deteriorating everywhere (Jayabhaye *et al.*, 2008).

Water quality deals with the physical, chemical and biological characteristics in relation to other hydrological properties (Chhatawal, 1998). Water quality provides current information about the concentration of various solutes at given place and time. Water quality parameters provide the basis for judging the suitability of water for its designated uses and to improve existing conditions. For optimum development and management for the beneficial uses, current information is needed which is provided by water quality programmers (Lloyd, 1992). Unequal distribution of water on the surface of the earth and fast declining availability of usable fresh water are the major concerns in terms of water quantity and quality (Boyd and Tucker, 1998).

The study of water parameters is important for understanding of the metabolic events in aquatic ecosystem. The parameters influence each other and also the sediment parameters, as well as they govern the abundance and distribution of the flora and fauna. Therefore, it becomes obligatory to analyze at least the important water parameters when ecological studies on aquatic ecosystems are carried out. Such studies carried out from time to time can indicate the favourable or unfavourable changes occurring in the ecosystem.

The physico-chemical parameters studied as abiotic components individually and collectively. Further, these parameters exhibit diurnal and seasonal variations apart from variations resulting from geographical and climatic conditions. Due to open nature, continuous exchange of matter and energy between the aquatic ecosystems and its environment apart from stress resulting due to man made activities. In general, pollution invariably alters water quality, in turn influencing biogeochemical cycles, diversity, biomass and overall tropho-dynamics. Any change in the physico-chemical environment has direct influence on biotic communities due to the fact that different species of flora and fauna exhibit great variations in their responses to the alter environment, (Watson and Jhon, 2003).

Water quality of reservoirs an important aspect of water resources management. It is a key catalyst for development and conservation because it determines the spatiotemporal dynamics of aquatic organisms and drives various water uses in aquatic ecosystems including reservoirs. The quality of water is of vital concern for mankind as it is directly linked with human welfare. The broad aspect of water quality can be visualized in terms of the physical and chemical properties within which several elements of water quality can be identified. Reservoir water is rarely pure as it contains different kinds of dissolved particulate matter including gases and solids. The entry of most ions into the aquatic ecosystems is particulate matter which is reflected by the levels of water transparency.

Quantity and quality of water are interrelated and thus one cannot be considered while overlooking other in any effective water management programmes. Acceptable or ideal water quality depends on endows of the particular water body. For example water suitable for agriculture may not be suitable for recreational purpose, water suitable for drinking may not be suitable for certain sophisticated industrial uses such as in chemical and pharmacy industries. Therefore it is essential to conserve the quality of water according to best designated use of water. There are different factors responsible for pollution viz., Domestic sewage, industrial effluents, agricultural discharge, fertilizers, detergents, toxic metals slits, oils, thermal pollutants, radioactive materials and pesticides like DDT, BHC etc.

The physico-chemical characteristics of pond water have direct impact on prevailing organisms as well as on human being using such water. Fresh waters are perhaps the most vulnerable habitats and are most likely to be changed by the activities of man. This essential resource is increasingly scarce in many parts of the world due to severe impairment of water quality. The increasing anthropogenic influences in recent years in and around aquatic systems and their catchments areas have contributed to a large extent to deterioration of water quality and declining of water bodies leading to their accelerated eutrophication (Bhatt and Negi, 1985). Several physico-chemical or biological factors could act as stressors and adversely affect fish growth and reproduction (Iwama *et al.*, 2000). Without the knowledge of water chemistry, it is very difficult to understand the biological phenomenon, because the chemistry of water reveals much about metabolism of the ecosystem and explains the general hydrobiological interrelationship (Deshmukh and Ambore, 2006). Phosphorous and nitrogen inputs from the domestic wastes and fertilizers accelerate the process of eutrophication (Rao and Valsaraj, 1984). Natural factors like dust, storm, run off and weathering of minerals are slow processes causing eutrophication (Kudari *et al.*, 2006). Lentic water bodies have tremendous importance, as they are recharging reservoirs for drinking water, domestic use and as infrastructure for pisciculture. Eutrophication has become a widely recognized problem of water quality deterioration (Kim *et al.*, 2001).The consideration of physico-chemical factors in the study of limnology is basic in understanding the trophic dynamics of that water body. Each factor plays its individual role but at the same time the final effect is really the result of interaction of all the factors (Hulyal and Kaliwal, 2008).

Keeping in mind this view present study has been undertaken to assess monthly values, standard deviation, total percentage and correlation of different parameters of the water from Harsool-Savangi Dam.

Material and Methods

The water samples were collected from Harsool-Savangi Dam, for physico-chemical analysis. The geographical coordination is 19° 56′ 14.32″ N and 75° 21′ 30.56″ E Aurangabad, (M.S) India. The four different sites (South site, East site, North site and West site) were selected. The samples were collected in the early morning between 8 a.m to 11 a.m, in the first week of every month from January 2008 to December 2009. The samples were collected in acid washed five litre plastic containers from the depth of 5-10 cm below the surface of water. Separate samples were collected for dissolve oxygen (DO) and the fixed at the site by adding alkaline iodide-azide solution. These samples were analyzed immediately in the laboratory.

Physical Parameters:

1. Atmospheric temperature
2. Water temperature
3. Turbidity
4. Transparency
5. pH
6. Electric Conductivity
7. Total solids (TS)
8. Total Dissolved Solids (TDS)
9. Total Suspended Solids (TSS)

Chemical Parameters:

10. Dissolved Oxygen (DO)
11. Biochemical Oxygen Demand (BOD)
12. Chemical Oxygen Demand (COD)
13. Alkalinity
14. Total Hardness
15. Sulphate
16. Chloride
17. Nitrate
18. Phosphate

The physico-chemical analysis of the dam water was carried out in summer, monsoon and winter according to standard methods (Trivedy and Goel, 1984; CIFE, 1998; IAAB, 1998 and APHA, 2005). The correlation coefficient was used to examine the relationships among the different environmental variables including physico-chemical parameter. The correlation model was performed using SPSS 12.0.

PHYSICAL PARAMETERS

Temperature

The temperature of samples was recorded at the four different sites at the time of sampling with the help of thermometer.

Turbidity:

1. Turbidity meter was set at 100 with 40 NTU standard suspensions. In this case, every division on the scale is equal to 0.4 NTU turbidity.
2. The sample was shaken thoroughly and retained for some time to eliminate any air bubbles.
3. For each reading, the sample was put in the Nephelometer sample tube and found out its value on the scale.
4. Whenever the sample showed more turbidity (more than 40 NTU), it was diluted in such a way that turbidity values were in the range (below 40 NTU).

Calculation:

Turbidity (NTU) = Nephelometer reading × 0.4 × Dilution factor

Transparency:

1. Lowered the Secchi disc in the water with the help of rope, unit it just disappears in water. Note the depth with help of scale.
2. Then uplifted the Secchi disc and note the depth at which it reappears again.
3. For better results, measurements have been taken during the middle of sunny days.

Calculation:

$$\text{Secchi disc Transparency} = \frac{A + B}{2}$$

Where,

A = Point where secchi disappears taken in cm.

B = Point where secchi reappears taken in cm.

pH

The pH of water samples approximated with the help of pH strips at the field and was (accurate) measured coorectectly in the laboratory with digital pH meter.

Conductivity

The conductivity of a sample is a numerical expression of its ability to carry on electric current, which, in turn, depends on the ionic strength. The ionic strength of a sample depends on ionization of solutes and other substance dissolved in it.

The conductivity (Conductance) was measured directly with the help of digital conductometer.

Calculation

Conductivity = observed conductance × cell constant × temperature factor at 25 °C

Conductivity = observed conductance × 1 × 1.02

Where,

1 = cell constant

1.02 = temperature factor at 25 °C.

Total Solids (TS)

1. An evaporating dish made up of silica in a muffle furnace for about an hour. Then it was cooled in a dessicator and weighed.
2. 100 ml unfiltered water sample was evaporated in the evaporating dish on a hot plate, maintaining temperature below 98°C.
3. The residue was heated at 103-105°C in an oven for one hour and weighed after cooling the evaporating dish in desiccators.

Calculation:

$$\text{Total solid (mg/lit)} = \frac{(A-B)\ 1000 \times 1000}{V}$$

Where,

A = Final weight of the dish in gm

B = Initial weight of the dish in gm

V = Volume of sample taken in ml.

Total Dissolved Solids (TDS)

100 ml of the filtered sample (Whatmann Filter Paper Number 1) was taken in a previously dried and weighed beaker and evaporated on hot plate to dryness and weighed again.

The amounts of total dissolved solids were calculated using following formula.

Calculation

$$TDS\ (Mg/1) = \frac{(A-B)\ 1000 \times 1000}{V}$$

Where,

A = Final weight of the dish in gm

B = Initial weight of the dish in gm

V = Volume of sample taken in ml.

Total Suspended Solids (TSS)

Total suspended solids were calculated by deducting the value of dissolved solids from total solids.

CHEMICAL PARAMETERS

Dissolved Oxygen (DO)

1. The water samples were collected in 300 ml of BOD bottles with all necessary precautions, removing air bubbles to this was added 2 ml of Winkler's 'A' solution and 2 ml of Winkler's 'B ' solution to fix oxygen in water.
2. Placed the stopper and shake the contents well by inverting the bottle repeatedly.
3. Kept the bottle for some time to settle down the precipitate.
4. Added 1-2 ml of concentrated H_2SO_4 to dissolve the precipitate, from this 100 ml solution was pipette out into a conical flask.
5. Titrated against N/40 sodium thiosulphate solution using 1 per cent starch as an indicator. At the end point initial dark blue colour turns to Colourless.

Calculation

$$\text{Dissolved Oxygen (DO) in mg/1} = \frac{0.1 \times \text{ml. Titrant} \times 1000}{100}$$

Biochemical Oxygen Demand (BOD)

1. Two sets of suitable diluted samples were taken in 250 ml BOD bottles and 2 ml phosphate buffer, magnesium sulphate, calcium chloride and ferric chloride solutions were added to both sets and shaked well and allowed the precipitate to settle.

2. From it 100 ml solution was pipette out into conical flask and titrated again N/40 sodium thiosulphate using 1 per cent starch as an indicator.
3. The second set was kept in BOD incubator at 20°C for five days. After that determined DO immediately.

Calculation

BOD = $DO_I - DO_V$ × dilution factor

Where,

DO_I= Initial value of DO in mg/l

DO_V= Final value of DO after 5 days at 20 °C in mg/l

Chemical Oxygen Demand (COD)

1. 20 ml of water sample was taken in 250-500 ml conical flask.
2. Added 10 ml of 0.25 N potassium dichromate solutions.
3. Added a pinch of Ag_2, SO_4.
4. Added 30 ml of H_2SO_4.
5. Refluxed for 2 hours in water bath or a hot plate.
6. Cooled the solution and added distilled water to make the final volume about 140 ml.
7. Added 2-3 drops of ferroine indicator mixed thoroughly and titrated with 0.01 ferrous ammonium sulphates and wine red colour indicated end point.
8. Run a blank with distilled water using same quantity of the chemicals above.

Calculation:

$$\text{COD (mg/I)} = \frac{\text{(b - a)} \times \text{N of ferrous ammonium sulphate} \times 1000 \times 8}{\text{ml sample}}$$

Where,

a = ml of Titrant with sample

b = ml of Titrant with blank.

Total Alkalinity

1. It is analyzed by taking 100 ml of sample in conical flask and added 2 drops of phenolphthalein indicator.
2. When the colour changed to pink titrated it with 0.1 N HCL until the colour disappeared at end point (PA).

3. Then added 2-3 drops of methyl orange to same sample and continued the titrations until the yellow colour changed to pink at end point. This was total alkalinity (TA).

Calculation

$$\text{Alkalinity (PA) mg/1} = \frac{(\text{A} \times \text{Normality}) \text{ of HCl} \times 1000 \times 50}{\text{ml Sample}}$$

$$\text{Alkalinity (TA) mg/1} = \frac{(\text{B} \times \text{Normality}) \text{ of HCl} \times 1000 \times 50}{\text{ml Sample}}$$

Where,

A = ml of HCl used with only phenolphthalein

B = ml of total HCl used with phenolphthalein and methyl orange

PA = phenolphthalein alkalinity

TA = Total alkalinity

Total Hardness

1. Taken 50 ml sample in a conical flask.
2. Added 1 ml of buffer solution.
3. Added a pinch of Eriochrome black- T indicator and solution turned into wine red.
4. Titrated the contents against EDTA solution and end point colour changed from wine red to blue.

Calculation

$$\text{Total hardness (mg/1)} = \frac{\text{ml of EDTA} \times 1000}{\text{ml Sample}}$$

Where,

T = Titrant in ml

V = Sample in ml.

Sulphate

1. 100 ml of sample not more than 40mg/1 of SO_4 or a suitable aliquot diluted to 100ml in 250ml conical flask was taken and 5.0 ml of conditioning reagent was added.
2. The sample was stirred on a magnetic stirrer for 1 min. and during stirring 1 mg (pinch) of barium chloride crystals were added.

3. After addition of barium chloride crystals readings were taken on a turbidometer or on a spectrophotometer at 420 mm exactly after 4 min.
4. Standard curve was prepared for 0.0 to 40.0 mg/l at the interval of 5mg/l; and a graph was plotted with absorbance against concentration.
5. For adjusting the instrument, blank was prepared using distilled water. Sulphate concentration was found out using the standard curve.

Chloride

1. 50 ml of water sample was taken in a conical flask and added 2 drops of $K_2Cr_2O_4$.
2. Titrated against 0.02 N $AgNo_3$. The end point was taken into consideration when persistent brick red colour was appeared.

Calculation:

$$\text{Chlorides (mg/1)} = \frac{V \times N \times 35.5 \times 1000}{V}$$

Where,

V = volume of titrant in ml

N = 0.02 (normality of $AgNo_3$)

v = 50 ml (Volume of the sample in ml)

Phosphate

1. In 50 ml of filtered clear sample, 2 ml of ammonium molybdate solution was added, followed by 5 drops of stannous chloride solution. Blue colour was appeared.
2. Readings were recorded after 5 minute but before 12 minute of the addition of the last reagent at 690 mm on a spectrophotometer.
3. Blank was prepared using distilled water for standard curve various dilutions at the interval of 0.1 mg phosphate/l from the standard phosphate solution were taken.
4. Graph was plotted against absorbance or transmittance against concentration.

Nitrate (NO_3 N)

1. 50 ml filtered sample was taken containing not more than 1 mg/l of NO_3 N (Phenoldisulphonic acid) in a conical flask.
2. Equivalent amount of silver sulphate solution was added to remove chlorides.
3. The sample was heated slightly and the precipitate of Hgcl was filtered.
4. The filtrate was evaporated to dryness in porcelain dish and cooled. The residue was dissolved in 2 ml phenol disulphonic acid and diluted to 50 ml. and added 6 ml of liquid ammonia to develop a yellow colour.

Absorbance of standards was measured at 410 mm after setting the blank at 100 per cent transmittance a calibration curve was prepared by plotting the absorbance or transmittance against concentration the same procedure was followed for each water sample.

Results

Temperature

Temperature is very important parameter, because it influences the biota of water body by affecting activities such as behaviour, respiration and metabolism. It is necessary to study temperature variations in water body, in animals ecophysiological and toxicological aspects because, water density and oxygen content are temperature related; hence temperature indirectly affects osmoregulation and respiration of the animal (De, 2002).

In general, air and water temperature depends on geographical location and metrological conditions such as rainfall, humidity, cloudy weather and wind velocity, etc. Particularly plankton communities constituting base of the energy cycles are get affected due to temperature influence (Khan and Zafar, 1983). Apart from limiting distribution depending on tolerance limits, temperature also control the metabolic rate in all organisms and increase the productivity (Vernberg and Liaknoich, 1965). Kaven and Bell, (1965) have reported an increase in gross productivity with an increase in temperature.

Methodology for Physico-chemical Characteristics

No.	Parameters	Method Adopted	References
1.	Air and Water Temperature	Thermometers	Central Water analysis kit
2.	Turbidity	Turbidity meter	Central Water analysis kit
3.	Transparency	Secchi disc method	Trivedy and Goel,(1984)
4.	pH	Digital pH meter	Central Water analysis kit
5.	Conductivity	Conductivity bridge	Central Water analysis kit
6.	Solids (TS,TDS and TSS)	Gravimetric method	APHA, (2005)
7.	DO	Winklers Azide	APHA, (2005)
8.	BOD	Titrometry	APHA, (2005)
9.	COD	Titrometry	APHA, (2005)
10.	Alkalinity	Titrometry	APHA, (2005)
11.	Total Hardness	Titrometry	APHA, (2005)
12.	Sulphate	Phenol disulphonic acid Turbidometric	Trivedy and Goel,(1984)
13.	Chloride	Titrometry	APHA, (2005)
14.	Nitrate	Phenol disulphonic acid Turbidometric	Trivedy and Goel,(1984)
15.	Phosphate	Phenol disulphonic acid Turbidometric	Trivedy and Goel, (1984)

(TS): Total solids; **(TDS)**: Total Dissolved Solids; **(TSS)**: Total Suspended Solids; **(DO)**: Dissolved Oxygen; **(BOD)**: Biochemical Oxygen Demand; **(COD)**: Chemical Oxygen Demand

Atmospheric Temperature

South Site

During first year study January-December 2008 at south site the atmospheric temperature ranged 20.2 ± 0.99 to 36.50 ± 2.15 °C. The maximum value recorded 36.50 ± 2.15 °C and coefficient variation was 5.89 per cent was recorded in April and minimum value recorded 20.2 ± 0.99 °C and coefficient variation was 4.90 per cent was recorded in January. In the second year study January-December 2009 the atmospheric temperature at south site ranged 19 ± 5.18 to 42 ± 2.20 °C. The maximum value recorded 42 ± 2.20 °C and coefficient variation was 5.23 per cent was recorded in April; minimum value recorded 19 ± 5.18 °C and coefficient variation was 27.26 per cent was recorded in November.

In the study January-December 2008 seasonal mean and coefficient variation values recorded 33.57 ± 2.54 °C and 7.58 per cent during summer, 26.90 ± 1.61 °C and 6.00 per cent during monsoon, 21.87 ± 1.29 °C and 5.94 per cent during winter (See fig. 3.1). In the second year study January-December 2009 seasonal mean and coefficient variation values recorded 37.02 ± 6.22 °C and 16.80 per cent during summer, 27.35 ± 3.39 °C and 12.41 per cent during monsoon, 21.62 ± 2.56 °C and 11.84 per cent during winter (See Table 3.1 and Fig. 3.2).

North Site

In the study January-December 2008 at north site atmospheric temperature ranged 20.40 ± 0.99 to 36 ± 0.50 °C. The maximum value recorded 36 ± 0.50 °C and coefficient variation was 1.38 per cent was recorded in April and minimum value recorded 20.40 ± 0.99 °C and coefficient variation was 4.85 per cent was recorded in December. In the second year study January-December 2009 the atmospheric temperature at north site ranged 19.50 ± 2.41 to 42.30 ± 2.10 °C. The maximum value recorded 42.30 ± 2.10 °C and coefficient variation was 4.96 per cent was recorded in April; minimum value recorded 19.50 ± 2.41 °C and coefficient variation was 12.35 per cent was recorded in November.

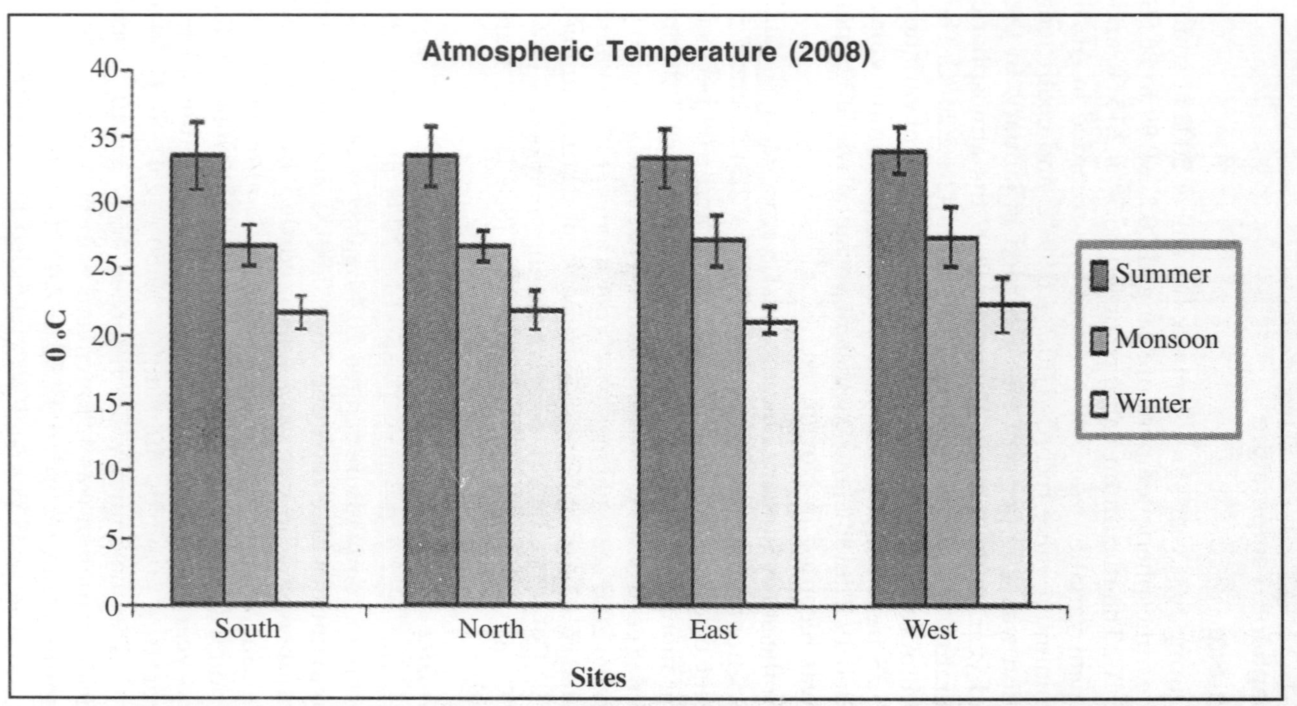

Fig. 3.1: Seasonal Variations in Atmospheric Temperature 0 °C at Different Sites of Harsool-Savangi Dam January to December 2008

Fig. 3.1: Seasonal Variations in Atmospheric Temperature (° C) at South Site, Harsool-Savangi Dam

Season	Months Jan. 2008 - Dec. 2008	Monthly Mean Values	Monthly C.V. (%)	Seasonal Mean Values	Seasonal C.V. (%)	Months Jan. 2009 - Dec. 2009	Monthly Mean Values	Monthly C.V. (%)	Seasonal Mean Values	Seasonal C.V. (%)
Summer	February	30.5±2.12	6.95	33.57±2.54	7.58	February	28±1.75	6.25	37.02±6.22	16.80
	March	32.8±1.10	3.35			March	38.1±2.41	6.32		
	April	**36.5±2.15**	5.89			April	**42±2.20**	5.23		
	May	34.5±1.81	5.24			May	40±1.19	2.97		
Monsoon	June	29±3.40	11.72	26.90±1.61	6.00	June	30±2.24	7.46	27.35±3.39	12.41
	July	27±3.72	13.77			July	26.5±3.12	11.77		
	August	26.5±1.09	4.11			August	22.9±1.14	4.97		
	September	25.1±0.90	3.58			September	30±4.12	13.73		
Winter	October	23±1.19	5.17	21.87±1.29	5.94	October	23±3.79	16.47	21.62±2.56	11.84
	November	21.5±1.20	5.58			November	**19±5.18**	27.26		
	December	22.8±1.14	5.00			December	20±1.25	6.25		
	January	**20.2±0.99**	4.90			January	24.5±2.24	9.14		

± - Mean value and Standard Deviation C.V. – Coefficient variation

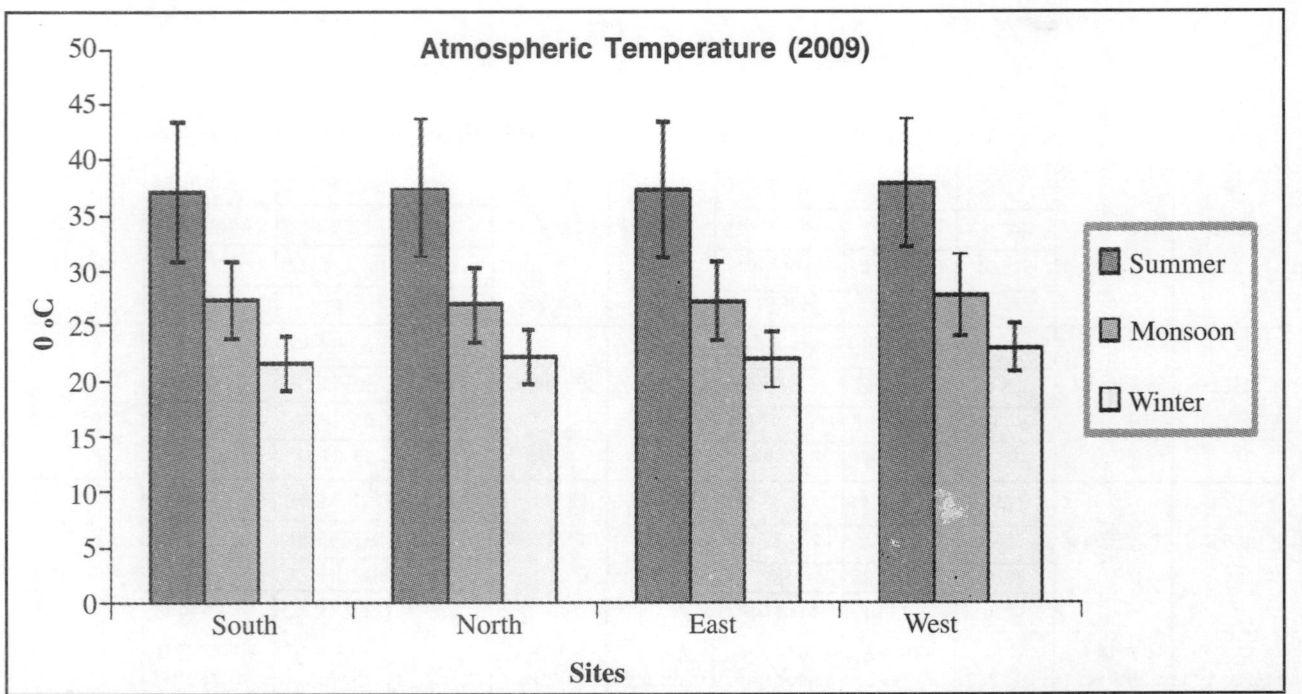

Fig. 3.2: Seasonal Variations in Atmospheric Temperature 0 °C at Different Sites of Harsool-Savangi Dam January to December 2009

In first year study January-December 2008 seasonal mean and coefficient variation values recorded 33.60 ± 2.21 °C and 6.57 per cent during summer, 26.80 ± 1.23 °C and 4.61 per cent during monsoon, 22.10 ± 1.44 °C and 6.54 per cent during winter (Fig. 3.1). In the second year study January-December 2009 seasonal mean and coefficient variation values recorded 37.47 ± 6.22 °C and 16.61 per cent during summer, 27.10 ± 3.31 °C and 12.27 per cent during monsoon, 22.30 ± 2.46 °C and 11.03 per cent during winter (Table 3.2 and Fig. 3.2).

East Site

During first year study January-December 2008 at east site the atmospheric temperature ranged 20.40 ± 1.10 to 36.00 ± 3.14 °C. The maximum value recorded 36.00 ± 3.14 °C and coefficient variation was 8.72 per cent was recorded in April and minimum value recorded 20.40 ± 1.10 °C and coefficient variation was 5.39 per cent was recorded in December. In the second year study January-December 2009 the atmospheric temperature at east site ranged 19.30 ± 1.45 to 42.50 ± 1.19 °C. The maximum value recorded 42.50 ± 1.19 °C and coefficient variation was 2.80 per cent was recorded in April; minimum value recorded 19.30 ± 1.45 °C and coefficient variation was 7.51 per cent was recorded in November.

In first year study January-December 2008 seasonal mean and coefficient variation values recorded 33.45 ± 2.14 °C and 6.40 per cent during summer, 27.27 ± 1.99 °C and 7.32 per cent during monsoon, 21.32 ± 1.03 °C and 4.83 per cent during winter (Fig. 3.1). In the second year study January-December 2009 seasonal mean and coefficient variation values recorded 37.27 ± 6.06 °C and 16.28 per cent during summer, 27.30 ± 3.47 °C and 12.71 per cent during monsoon and 22.02 ± 2.55 °C and 11.61 per cent during winter (Table 3.3 and Fig. 3.2).

West Site

In first year study January-December 2008 at west site the atmospheric temperature ranged 20.00 ± 1.19 to 36.00 ± 2.17 °C. The maximum value recorded 36.00 ± 2.17 °C and coefficient variation was 6.02 per cent was recorded in April and minimum value recorded 20.00 ± 1.19 °C and coefficient variation was 5.95 per cent was recorded in December.

Table 3.2: Seasonal Variations in Atmospheric Temperature (° C) at North Site, Harsool-Savangi Dam

Season	Months Jan. 2008 - Dec. 2008	Monthly Mean Values	Monthly C.V. (%)	Seasonal Mean Values	Seasonal C.V. (%)	Months Jan. 2009 - Dec. 2009	Monthly Mean Values	Monthly C.V. (%)	Seasonal Mean Values	Seasonal C.V. (%)
	February	31.1±0.09	0.28			February	28.4±2.19	7.71		
	March	32.5±0.10	0.30			March	38.7±1.41	3.64		
Summer	April	36±0.50	1.38	33.6±2.21	6.57	April	42.3±2.10	4.96	37.47±6.22	16.61
	May	34.8±0.24	0.68			May	40.5±1.99	4.91		
	June	28.5±2.19	7.68			June	30±2.51	8.36		
	July	26.3±1.24	4.71			July	26.9±3.34	12.41		
Monsoon	August	26.8±1.12	4.17	26.8±1.23	4.61	August	22.5±2.41	10.71	27.1±3.31	12.27
	September	25.6±0.90	3.51			September	29±2.41	8.31		
	October	23.8±1.20	5.04	22.1±1.44		October	24±3.14	13.08		
	November	21.6±1.50	6.94			November	19.5±2.41	12.35		
Winter	December	20.4±0.99	4.85	22.1±1.44	6.54	December	21±1.89	9.00	22.3±2.46	11.03
	January	22.6±1.90	8.40			January	24.7±2.09	8.46		

Table 3.3: Seasonal Variations in Atmospheric Temperature (° C) at East Site, Harsool-Savangi Dam

Season	Months Jan. 2008 - Dec. 2008	Monthly Mean Values	Monthly C.V. (%)	Seasonal Mean Values	Seasonal C.V. (%)	Months Jan. 2009 - Dec. 2009	Monthly Mean Values	Monthly C.V. (%)	Seasonal Mean Values	Seasonal C.V. (%)
Summer	February	31±1.99	6.41	33.45±2.14	6.40	February	28.6±2.47	8.63	37.27±6.06	16.28
	March	32.6±2.19	6.71			March	38±2.18	5.73		
	April	36±3.14	8.72			April	42.5±1.19	2.80		
	May	34.2±2.12	6.19			May	40±2.10	5.25		
Monsoon	June	30±2.89	9.63	27.27±1.99	7.32	June	30.5±2.75	9.01	27.30±3.47	12.71
	July	27.1±1.94	7.15			July	26.4±2.01	7.61		
	August	26.8±1.50	5.59			August	22.8±1.79	7.85		
	September	25.2±1.09	4.32			September	29.5±1.20	4.06		
Winter	October	22.8±2.10	9.21	21.32±1.03	4.83	October	23.5±1.30	5.53	22.02±2.55	11.61
	November	21.1±1.35	6.39			November	19.3±1.45	7.51		
	December	20.4±1.10	5.39			December	20.5±2.19	10.68		
	January	21±1.74	8.28			January	24.8±2.02	8.14		

In the second year study January-December 2009 the atmospheric temperature at west site ranged 20.80 ± 2.19 to 42.40 ± 2.40 °C. The maximum value recorded 42.30 ± 2.40 °C and coefficient variation was 5.66 per cent was recorded in April; minimum value recorded 20.80 ± 2.19 °C and coefficient variation was 10.52 per cent was recorded in December.

In first year study January-December 2008 seasonal mean and coefficient variation values recorded 34.02 ± 1.71 °C and 5.03 per cent during summer, 27.57 ± 2.25 °C and 8.17 per cent during monsoon, 22.50 ± 2.08 °C and 9.25 per cent during winter (Fig. 3.1). During second year study January-December 2009 seasonal mean and coefficient variation values recorded 37.95 ± 5.71 °C and 15.06 per cent during summer, 27.82 ± 3.67 °C and 13.20 per cent during monsoon, 23.12 ± 2.16 °C and 9.36 per cent during winter (Table 3.4 and Fig. 3.2).

In the present study January to December 2008 the maximum atmospheric temperature was recorded in summer season at north, east and west sites and minimum value was recorded in winter season at west site. In the second year study January-December 2009 the maximum atmospheric temperature was recorded in summer season at east site where as minimum value was recorded in winter season at south site (Table 3.1, 3.2, 3.3 and 3.4).

Water Temperature

South Site

During study January-December 2008 at south site the water temperature ranged 17.50 ± 0.70 to 32.20 ± 1.59 °C. The maximum value recorded 32.20 ± 1.59 °C and coefficient variation was 4.93 per cent was recorded in April and minimum value recorded 17.50 ± 0.70 °C and coefficient variation was 4.00 per cent was recorded in December. In the second year study January-December 2009 the water temperature at south site ranged 15.00 ± 2.24 to 37.00 ± 1.19 °C. The maximum value recorded 37.00 ± 1.19 °C and coefficient variation was 3.21 per cent was recorded in April; minimum value recorded 15.00 ± 2.24 °C and coefficient variation was 14.93 per cent was recorded in November.

Table 3.4: Seasonal Variations in Atmospheric Temperature (° C) at West Site, Harsool-Savangi Dam

Season	Months Jan. 2008 - Dec. 2008	Monthly Mean Values	Monthly C.V. (%)	Seasonal Mean Values	Seasonal C.V. (%)	Months Jan. 2009 - Dec. 2009	Monthly Mean Values	Monthly C.V. (%)	Seasonal Mean Values	Seasonal C.V. (%)
	February	32.4±0.90	2.77			February	29.6±1.14	3.85		
	March	32.8±1.12	3.41			March	39.2±1.28	3.26		
Summer	April	**36±2.17**	6.02	34.02±1.71	5.03	April	**42.4±2.40**	5.66	37.95±5.71	15.06
	May	34.9±1.29	3.69			May	40.6±1.90	4.67		
	June	30.9±2.17	7.02			June	31.2±1.50	4.80		
	July	27±2.81	10.40			July	27±2.40	8.88		
Monsoon	August	26±1.01	3.88	27.57±2.25	8.17	August	23±2.35	10.21	27.82±3.67	13.20
	September	26.4±0.40	1.51			September	30.1±1.41	4.68		
	October	25±0.90	3.60			October	24±2.75	11.45		
	November	22±1.81	8.22			November	22±1.99	9.04		
Winter	December	**20±1.19**	5.95	22.50±2.08	9.25	December	**20.8±2.19**	10.52	23.12±2.16	9.36
	January	23±1.12	4.86			January	25.7±1.50	5.83		

In study January-December 2008 seasonal mean and coefficient variation values recorded 29.67 ± 1.97 °C and 6.64 per cent during summer, 23.15 ± 1.30 °C and 5.61 per cent during monsoon, 18.62 ± 1.05 °C and 5.68 per cent during winter (Fig. 3.3). In the second year study January-December 2009 seasonal mean and coefficient variation values recorded 30.60 ± 6.40 °C and 20.94 per cent during summer, 25.25 ± 3.92 °C and 15.55 per cent during monsoon, 18.12 ± 2.59 °C and 14.31 per cent during winter (Table 3.5 and Fig. 3.4).

North Site

In the study January-December 2008 at north site the water temperature ranged 17.60 ± 1.17 to 32.00 ± 2.10 °C. The maximum value recorded 32.00 ± 2.10 °C and coefficient variation was 6.56 per cent was recorded in April and minimum value recorded 17.60 ± 1.17 °C and coefficient variation was 6.64 per cent was recorded in December. In the second year study January-December 2009 the water temperature at north site ranged 15.50 ± 2.19 to 37.20 ± 1.19 °C. The maximum value recorded 37.20 ± 1.19 °C and coefficient variation was 3.19 per cent was recorded in April; minimum value recorded 15.50 ± 2.19 °C and coefficient variation was 14.12 per cent was recorded in November.

During the study January-December 2008 seasonal mean and coefficient variation values recorded 29.80 ± 1.81 °C and 6.08 per cent during summer, 23.25 ± 1.35 °C and 5.81 per cent during monsoon, 18.67 ± 1.09 °C and 5.88 per cent during winter (Fig. 3.3). In the second year study January-December 2009 seasonal mean and coefficient variation values recorded 30.77 ± 6.47 °C and 21.05 per cent during summer, 23.72 ± 3.45 °C and 14.55 per cent during monsoon, 18.60 ± 2.57 °C and 13.81 per cent during winter (Table 3.6 Fig. 3.4).

East Site

In first year study January-December 2008 at east site the water temperature ranged 17.00 ± 0.14 to 32.8 ± 2.19 °C. The maximum value recorded 32.8 ± 2.19 °C and coefficient variation was 6.67 per cent was recorded in April and minimum

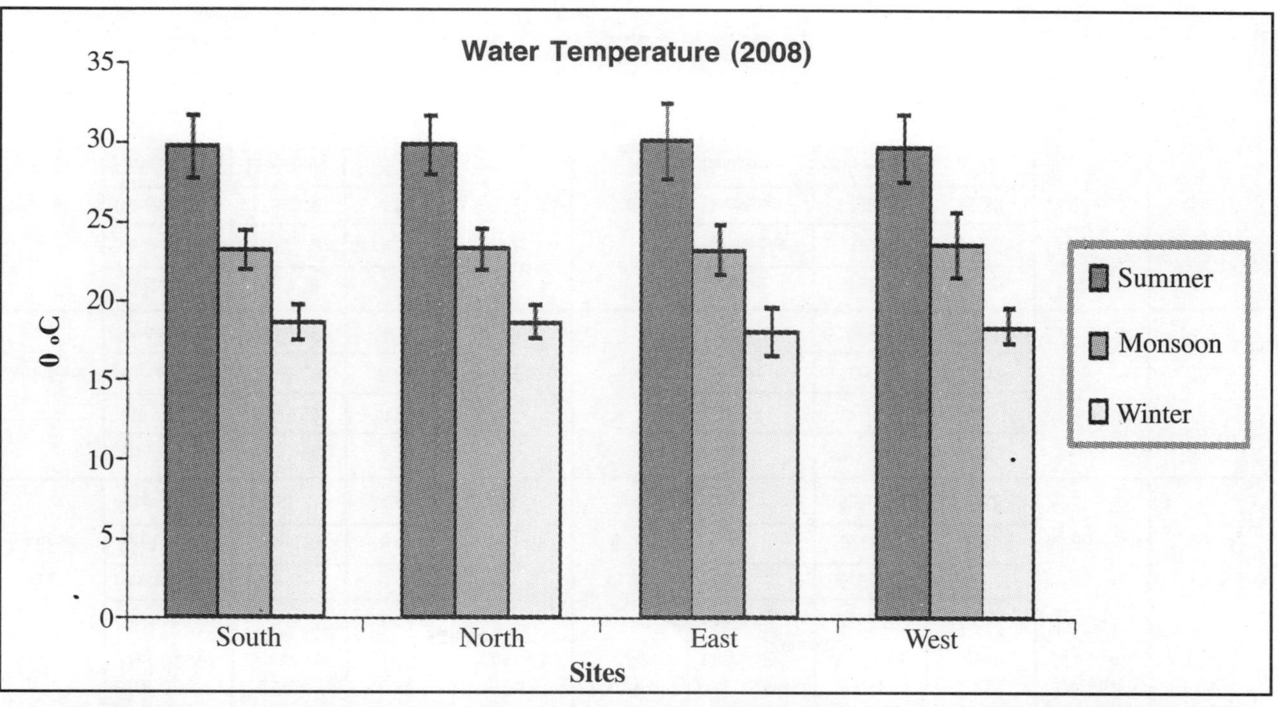

Fig. 3.3: Seasonal Variations in Water Temperature 0 °C at Different Sites of Harsoól-Savangi Dam January to December 2008

Table 3.5: Seasonal Variations in Water Temperature (° C) at South Site, Harsool-Savangi Dam

Season	Months Jan. 2008 - Dec. 2008	Monthly Mean Values	Monthly C.V. (%)	Seasonal Mean Values	Seasonal C.V. (%)	Months Jan. 2009 - Dec. 2009	Monthly Mean Values	Monthly C.V. (%)	Seasonal Mean Values	Seasonal C.V. (%)
Summer	February	27.5±1.75	6.36	29.67±1.97	6.64	February	24±2.75	11.45	30.60±6.40	20.94
	March	29±1.50	5.17			March	35.1±1.50	4.27		
	April	32.2±1.59	4.93			April	37±1.19	3.21		
	May	30±1.21	4.03			May	26.3±0.90	3.42		
Monsoon	June	25±1.14	4.56	23.15±1.30	5.61	June	27.5±0.71	2.58	25.25±3.92	15.55
	July	23±1.29	5.60			July	28±0.50	1.78		
	August	22.6±1.20	5.30			August	19.5±2.42	12.41		
	September	22±0.90	4.09			September	26±1.91	7.34		
Winter	October	20±1.19	5.95	18.62±1.05	5.68	October	20±2.19	10.95	18.12±2.59	14.31
	November	18.2±1.10	6.04			November	15±2.24	14.93		
	December	17.5±0.70	4.00			December	17±2.19	12.88		
	January	18.8±0.99	5.26			January	20.5±0.19	0.92		

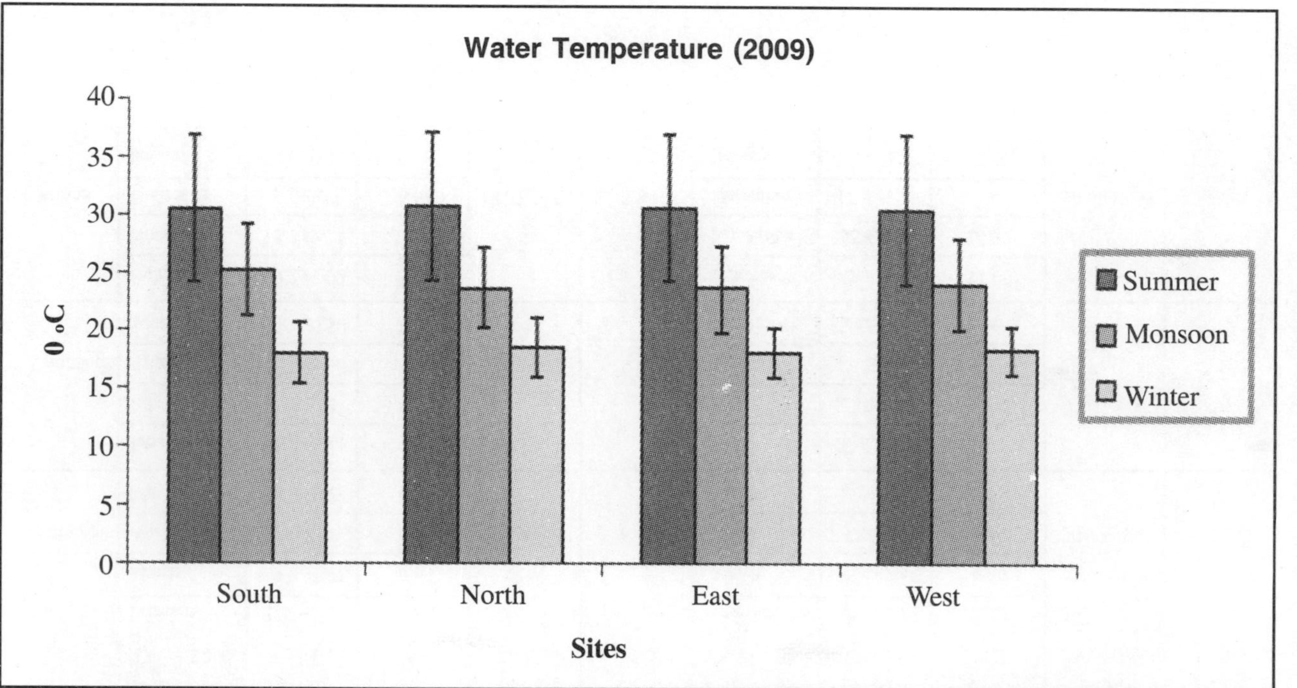

Fig. 3.4: Seasonal Variations in Water Temperature 0 °C at Different Sites of Harsool-Savangi Dam January to December 2009

Table 3.6: Seasonal Variations in Water Temperature (° C) at North Site, Harsool-Savangi Dam

Season	Months Jan. 2008 - Dec. 2008	Monthly Mean Values	Monthly C.V. (%)	Seasonal Mean Values	Seasonal C.V. (%)	Months Jan. 2009 - Dec. 2009	Monthly Mean Values	Monthly C.V. (%)	Seasonal Mean Values	Seasonal C.V. (%)
	February	27.7±1.07	3.86			February	24.2±2.01	8.30		
	March	29.2±1.91	6.54			March	35.4±2.41	6.80		
Summer	April	32±2.10	6.56	29.80±1.81	6.08	April	37.2±1.19	3.19	30.77±6.47	21.05
	May	30.3±1.29	4.25			May	26.3±2.10	7.98		
	June	25.2±2.41	9.56			June	27.4±1.99	7.26		
	July	23±1.91	8.30			July	23.3±2.44	10.47		
Monsoon	August	22.7±0.90	3.96	23.25±1.35	5.81	August	19.2±1.17	6.09	23.72±3.45	14.55
	September	22.1±0.50	2.26			September	25±2.91	11.64		
	October	20.2±1.02	5.04			October	21±2.31	11.00		
	November	18.3±2.21	12.07			November	15.5±2.19	14.12		
Winter	December	17.6±1.17	6.64	18.67±1.09	5.88	December	17.5±1.25	7.14	18.60±2.57	13.81
	January	18.6±0.96	5.16			January	20.4±2.37	11.61		

value recorded 17.00 ± 0.14 °C and coefficient variation was 0.82 per cent was recorded in January. In the second year study January-December 2009 the water temperature at east site ranged 16.00 ± 1.41 to 37.10 ± 1.21 °C. The maximum value recorded 37.10 ± 1.21 °C and coefficient variation was 3.26 per cent was recorded in April; minimum value recorded 16.00 ± 1.41 °C and coefficient variation was 8.81 per cent was recorded in November.

In the study January-December 2008 seasonal mean and coefficient variation values recorded 30.05 ± 2.42 °C and 8.06 per cent during summer, 23.20 ± 1.62 °C and 7.01 per cent during monsoon, 18.10 ± 1.43 °C and 7.95 per cent during winter (Fig. 3.3). In the second year study January-December 2009 seasonal mean and coefficient variation values recorded 30.75 ± 6.36 °C and 20.70 per cent during summer, 23.82 ± 3.49 °C and 14.68 per cent during monsoon, 18.15 ± 2.11 °C and 11.64 per cent during winter (Table 3.7 and Fig. 3.4).

West Site

In first year study January-December 2008 at west site the water temperature ranged 17.50 ± 0.90 to 32.30 ± 1.24 °C. The maximum value recorded 32.30 ± 1.24 °C and coefficient variation was 3.83 per cent was recorded in April and minimum value recorded 17.50 ± 0.90 °C and coefficient variation was 5.14 per cent was recorded in December. In the second year study January-December 2009 the water temperature at west site ranged 15.90 ± 1.12 to 37.00 ± 2.10 °C. The maximum value recorded 37.00 ± 2.10 °C and coefficient variation was 5.67 per cent was recorded in April; minimum value recorded 15.90 ± 1.12 °C and coefficient variation was 7.04 per cent was recorded in November.

During the study January-December 2008 seasonal mean and coefficient variation values recorded 29.70 ± 2.13 °C and 7.17 per cent during summer, 23.57 ± 2.07 °C and 8.80 per cent during monsoon, 18.42 ± 1.09 °C and 5.91 per cent during winter (Fig. 3.3). In the second year study January-December 2009 seasonal mean and coefficient variation values recorded 30.55 ± 6.50 °C and 21.28 per cent during summer, 24.12 ± 3.96 (°C) and 16.42 and per cent during winter 18.45 ± 2.08 °C and 11.28 per cent during winter (Table 3.8 and Fig. 3.4).

Table 3.7: Seasonal Variations in Water Temperature (° C) at East Site, Harsool-Savangi Dam

Season	Months Jan. 2008 - Dec. 2008	Monthly Mean Values	Monthly C.V. (%)	Seasonal Mean Values	Seasonal C.V. (%)	Months Jan. 2009 - Dec. 2009	Monthly Mean Values	Monthly C.V. (%)	Seasonal Mean Values	Seasonal C.V. (%)
Summer	February	27±2.01	7.44	30.05±2.42	8.06	February	24.1±2.21	9.17	30.75±6.36	20.70
	March	29.6±2.20	7.43			March	35.2±2.91	8.26		
	April	32.8±2.19	6.67			April	37.1±1.21	3.26		
	May	30.8±1.91	6.20			May	26.6±5.14	11.80		
Monsoon	June	25.5±2.31	9.05	23.20±1.62	7.01	June	27±1.10	4.07	23.82±3.49	14.68
	July	23.2±0.91	3.92			July	23.1±2.45	10.60		
	August	22.1±0.5	2.26			August	19.2±1.91	9.94		
	September	22±0.10	0.45			September	26±2.41	9.26		
Winter	October	20.1±0.12	0.59	18.10±1.43	7.95	October	19±2.09	11.00	18.15±2.11	11.64
	November	18.2±1.90	10.43			November	16±1.41	8.81		
	December	17.1±0.70	4.09			December	16.9±0.80	4.73		
	January	17±0.14	0.82			January	20.7±1.20	5.79		

Table 3.8: Seasonal Variations in Water Temperature (° C) at West Site, Harsool-Savangi Dam

Season	Months Jan. 2008 - Dec. 2008	Monthly Mean Values	Monthly C.V. (%)	Seasonal Mean Values	Seasonal C.V. (%)	Months Jan. 2009 - Dec. 2009	Monthly Mean Values	Monthly C.V. (%)	Seasonal Mean Values	Seasonal C.V. (%)
	February	27.2±1.92	7.05			February	24±2.31	9.62		
	March	29.1±2.19	7.52			March	35.2±2.01	5.71		
Summer	April	**32.3±1.24**	3.83	29.70±2.13	7.17	April	**37±2.10**	5.67	30.55±6.50	21.28
	May	30.2±1.44	4.76			May	26±2.15	8.26		
	June	26.5±1.50	5.66			June	27.1±1.15	4.24		
	July	23.6±1.66	7.03			July	23±2.70	11.73		
Monsoon	August	22.2±1.91	8.60	23.57±2.07	8.80	August	19±1.61	8.47	24.12±3.96	16.42
	September	22±0.80	3.63			September	27.4±2.55	9.30		
	October	20±1.10	5.50			October	20.2±1.92	9.50		
	November	18±1.90	10.55			November	**15.9±1.12**	7.04		
Winter	December	**17.5±0.90**	5.14	18.42±1.09	5.91	December	17.6±0.90	5.11	18.45±2.08	11.28
	January	18.2±0.80	4.39			January	20.1±1.19	5.92		

In the present study January to December 2008 the maximum water temperature was recorded in summer season at east site and minimum water temperature was recorded in winter season at east site. In the second year study January-December 2009 the maximum water temperature was recorded in summer season at north site where as minimum water temperature was recorded in winter season at south site (Table 3.5, 3.6 and 3.7).

During the study January 2008-December 2009 water temperature indicating significant positive correlation with pH, alkalinity, sulphate, chloride and fish and it indicating significant negative correlation with total solid, total dissolved solids, dissolved oxygen and phosphate (Tables 4.7 and 4.8).

In the present study, the temperature was maximum during summer and minimum during winter. Low temperature recorded in winter may be due to high water level, less solar radiation, low atmospheric temperature and high temperature in summer because of low water level, high solar radiation and clear atmosphere.

Turbidity

Suspension of particles in water interferes the passage of light is called turbidity. Turbidity is caused by wide variety of suspended matter, range in size from colloidal to coarse dispersion depending upon the degree of turbulence and also ranges from pure inorganic substances to those that are highly organic in nature. Turbid water is undesirable from aesthetic point of view in drinking water supplies.

Kaliya (1973) reported that the light penetration in lake water might be considerably reduced either as a result of high plankton density due to large quantities of suspended matter. High water clarity at shore sites may be due to low plankton populations that develop in response to low availability of phosphorous and Iron. In the Lake, however the turbidity of water is found to affect by the salts and suspended organic matter and also the humus contents, besides the heavy growth of algal blooms. Lepoid, (1968) reported that the soil erosion in the catchments and urbanization increased the turbidity. Highly turbid water causes damage to benthic community. It is recommended that in view of absence of macrophytes and poor population of insects, it may not be stocked with benthophagic species. Turbidity is a good index of Phytoplanktons population as it shows a definite positive relationship (Lal, 1981).

South Site

In the study January-December 2008 at south site the turbidity ranged 9.00 ± 0.45 to 12.10 ± 0.12 (NTU). The maximum value recorded 12.10 ± 0.12 (NTU) and coefficient variation was 0.99 per cent was recorded in September and minimum value recorded 9.00 ± 0.45 (NTU) and coefficient variation was 5.00 per cent was recorded in February. In the study January-December 2009 the turbidity at south site ranged 9.40 ± 0.10 to 12.70 ± 0.11 (NTU). The maximum value recorded 12.70 ± 0.11 (NTU) and coefficient variation was 0.86 per cent was recorded in September; minimum value recorded 9.40 ± 0.10 (NTU) and coefficient variation was 1.06 per cent was recorded in February.

During first year study January-December 2008 seasonal mean and coefficient variation values recorded 9.87 ± 0.81 (NTU) and 8.28 per cent during summer, 11.80 ± 0.40 (NTU) and 3.45 per cent during monsoon, 10.05 ± 1.02 (NTU) and 10.16 per cent during winter (Fig. 3.5). In the study January-December 2009 seasonal mean and coefficient variation values recorded 10.15 ± 0.73 (NTU) and 7.21 per cent during summer, 12.10 ± 0.60 (NTU) and 5.00 per cent during monsoon, 10.85 ± 0.97 (NTU) and 8.95 per cent during winter (Table 3.9 and Fig. 3.6).

North Site

During first year study January-December 2008 at north site the turbidity ranged 9.30 ± 0.11 to 13.50 ± 0.21 (NTU). The maximum value recorded 13.50 ± 0.21 (NTU) and coefficient variation was 1.55 per cent was recorded in September and minimum value recorded 9.30 ± 0.11 (NTU) and coefficient variation was 1.18 per cent was recorded in March. In the second year study January-December 2009 the turbidity at north site ranged 9.90 ± 0.12 to 14.60 ± 0.40 (NTU).

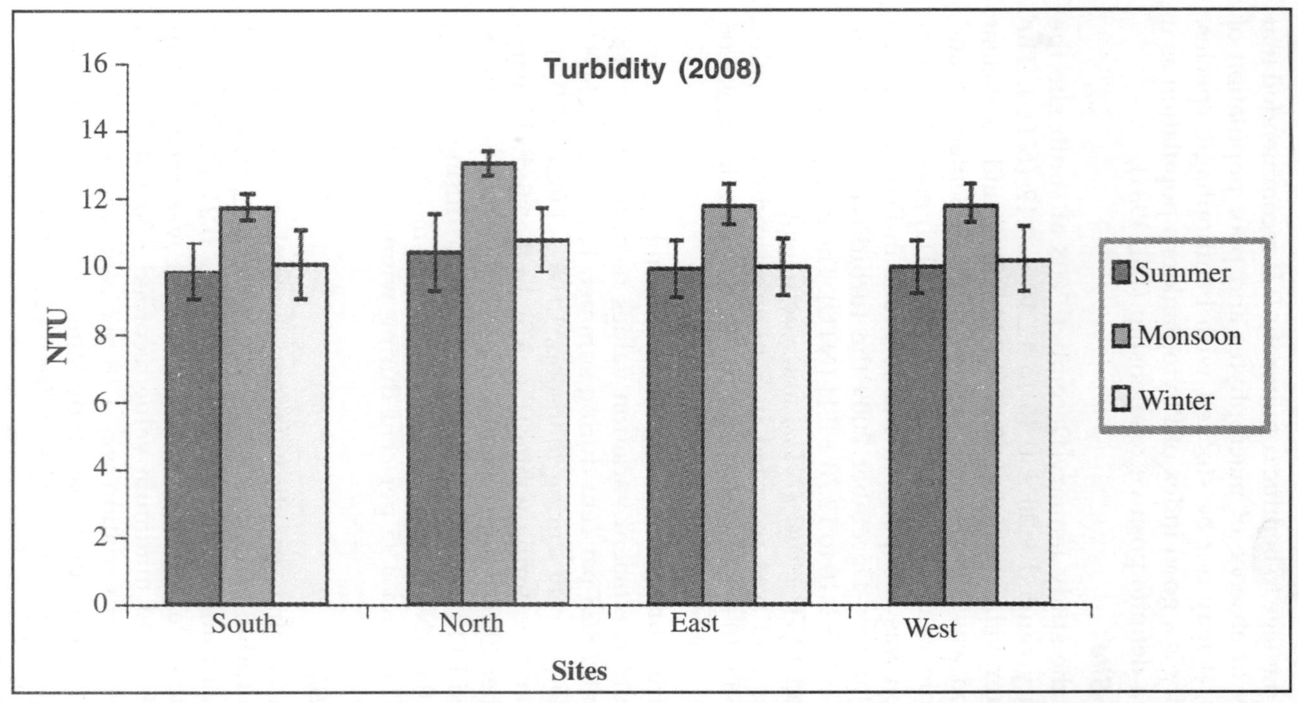

Fig. 3.5: Seasonal Variations in Turbidity (NTU) at Different Sites of Harsool-Savangi Dam January to December 2008

Table 3.9: Seasonal Variations in Turbidity (NTU) at South Site, Harsool-Savangi Dam

Season	Months Jan. 2008 - Dec. 2008	Monthly Mean Values	Monthly C.V. (%)	Seasonal Mean Values	Seasonal C.V. (%)	Months Jan. 2009 - Dec. 2009	Monthly Mean Values	Monthly C.V. (%)	Seasonal Mean Values	Seasonal C.V. (%)
Summer	February	9±0.45	5.00	9.87±0.81	08.28	February	9.4±0.10	1.06	10.15±0.73	7.21
	March	9.5±0.14	1.47			March	9.7±0.24	2.47		
	April	10.1±0.21	2.07			April	10.5±0.31	2.95		
	May	10.9±0.19	1.74			May	11±0.19	1.72		
Monsoon	June	11.2±0.71	6.33	11.80±0.40	03.45	June	11.3±0.20	1.76	12.10±0.60	5.00
	July	11.9±0.67	5.63			July	12±0.29	2.41		
	August	12±0.50	4.16			August	12.4±0.12	0.96		
	September	12.1±0.12	0.99			September	12.7±0.11	0.86		
Winter	October	11.5±0.20	1.73	10.05±1.02	10.16	October	12.1±0.50	4.13	10.85±0.97	8.95
	November	10±1.10	11.00			November	11.1±0.90	8.10		
	December	9.5±0.90	9.47			December	10.3±0.40	3.88		
	January	9.2±1.29	14.02			January	9.9±0.91	9.19		

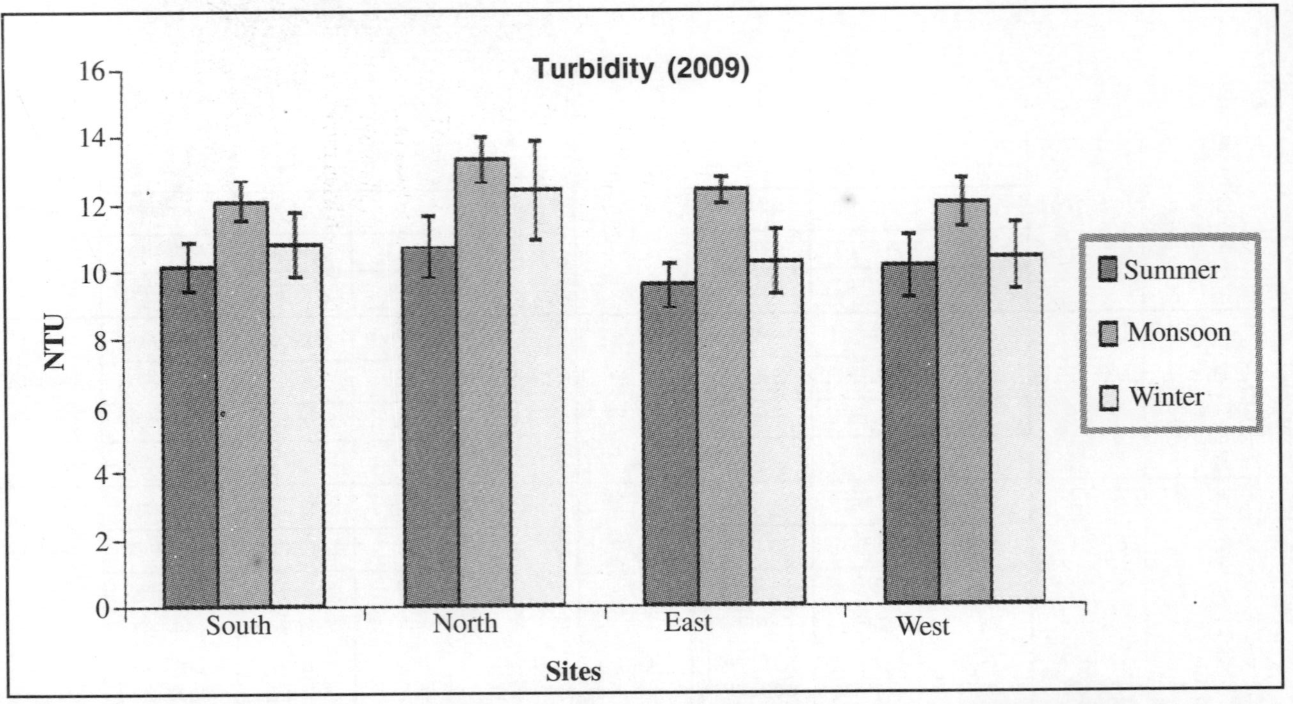

Fig. 3.6: Seasonal Variations in Turbidity (NTU) at Different Sites of Harsool-Savangi Dam January to December 2009

The maximum value recorded 14.60 ± 0.40 (NTU) and coefficient variation was 2.85 per cent was recorded in September; minimum value recorded 9.90 ± 0.12 (NTU) and coefficient variation was 1.21 per cent was recorded in March.

In first year study January-December 2008 seasonal mean and coefficient variation values recorded 10.42 ± 1.15 (NTU) and 11.11 per cent during summer, 13.07 ± 0.35 (NTU) and 2.67 per cent during monsoon, 10.82 ± 0.95 (NTU) and 8.80 per cent during winter (Fig. 3.5). In the second year study January-December 2009 seasonal mean and coefficient variation values recorded 10.72 ± 0.91 (NTU) and 8.55 per cent during summer, 13.32 ± 0.66 (NTU) and 4.99 per cent during monsoon, 12.42 ± 1.45 (NTU) and 11.72 per cent during winter (Table 3.10 and Fig. 3.6).

East Site

During first year study January-December 2008 at east site the turbidity ranged 9.00 ± 0.49 to 12.30 ± 0.19 (NTU). The maximum value recorded 12.30 ± 0.19 (NTU) and coefficient variation was 1.54 per cent was recorded in September and minimum value recorded 9.00 ± 0.49 (NTU) and coefficient variation was 5.44 per cent was recorded in February. In the second year study January-December 2009 the turbidity at east site ranged 9.00 ± 0.28 to 12.90 ± 0.25 (NTU). The maximum value recorded 12.90 ± 0.25 (NTU) and coefficient variation was 1.93 per cent was recorded in September; minimum value recorded 9.00 ± 0.28 (NTU) and coefficient variation was 3.11 per cent was recorded in March.

In first year study January-December 2008 seasonal mean and coefficient variation values recorded 9.95 ± 0.85 (NTU) and 8.58 per cent during summer, 11.85 ± 0.59 (NTU) and 3.74 per cent during monsoon, 10.00 ± 0.86 (NTU) and 8.64 per cent during winter (Fig. 3.5). In the second year study January-December 2009 seasonal mean and coefficient variation values recorded 9.57 ± 0.65 (NTU) and 6.84 per cent during summer, 12.42 ± 0.37 (NTU) and 3.03 per cent during monsoon, 10.27 ± 0.97 (NTU) and 9.48 per cent during winter (Table 3.11 and Fig. 3.6).

Table 3.10: Seasonal Variations in Turbidity (NTU) at North Site, Harsool-Savangi Dam

Season	Months Jan. 2008 - Dec. 2008	Monthly Mean Values	Monthly C.V. (%)	Seasonal Mean Values	Seasonal C.V. (%)	Months Jan. 2009 - Dec. 2009	Monthly Mean Values	Monthly C.V. (%)	Seasonal Mean Values	Seasonal C.V. (%)
Summer	February	9.9±0.12	1.21	10.42±1.15	11.11	February	10.1±0.19	1.88	10.72±0.91	08.55
	March	9.3±0.11	1.18			March	9.9±0.12	1.21		
	April	10.5±0.19	1.80			April	11±0.13	1.18		
	May	12±0.15	1.25			May	11.9±0.10	0.84		
Monsoon	June	12.9±0.10	0.77	3.07±0.35	1 02.67	June	12.5±0.20	1.60	13.32±0.66	04.99
	July	12.7±0.51	4.01			July	13.1±0.25	1.90		
	August	13.2±0.20	1.51			August	13.7±0.20	1.45		
	September	13.5±0.21	1.55			September	14.6±0.40	2.85		
Winter	October	12.1±0.4	3.30	10.82±0.95	08.80	October	14.2±0.33	2.32	12.42±1.45	11.72
	November	11±0.25	2.27			November	13±0.12	0.92		
	December	10.2±0.35	3.43			December	11.5±0.36	3.13		
	January	10±0.09	0.90			January	11±0.29	2.63		

Table 3.11: Seasonal Variations in Turbidity (NTU) at East Side, Harsool-Savangi Dam

Season	Months Jan. 2008 - Dec. 2008	Monthly Mean Values	Monthly C.V. (%)	Seasonal Mean Values	Seasonal C.V. (%)	Months Jan. 2009 - Dec. 2009	Monthly Mean Values	Monthly C.V. (%)	Seasonal Mean Values	Seasonal C.V. (%)
	February	9±0.49	5.44			February	9.1±0.21	2.30		
	March	9.6±0.26	2.70			March	9±0.28	3.11		
Summer	April	10.2±0.12	1.17	09.95±0.85	8.58	April	9.8±0.10	1.02	09.57±0.65	6.84
	May	11±0.10	0.90			May	10.4±0.11	1.05		
	June	11.3±0.19	1.68			June	12±0.19	1.58		
	July	11.7±0.14	1.19			July	12.3±0.27	2.19		
Monsoon	August	12.1±0.12	0.99	11.85±0.59	3.74	August	12.9±0.25	1.93	12.42±0.37	3.03
	September	12.3±0.19	1.54			September	12.5±0.27	2.16		
	October	11.2±0.50	4.46			October	11.6±0.12	1.03		
	November	10±0.20	2.00			November	10.3±0.14	1.35		
Winter	December	9.6±0.42	4.37	10.00±0.86	8.64	December	9.9±0.15	1.51	10.27±0.97	9.48
	January	9.2±0.29	3.15			January	9.3±0.19	2.04		

West Site

In first year January-December 2008 at west site the turbidity ranged 9.10 ± 0.10 to 12.50 ± 0.49 (NTU). The maximum value recorded 12.50 ± 0.49 (NTU) and coefficient variation was 3.92 per cent was recorded in September and minimum value recorded 9.10 ± 0.10 (NTU) and coefficient variation was 1.09 per cent was recorded in February. In the second year study January-December 2009 the turbidity at west site ranged 9.00 ± 0.19 to 12.70 ± 0.50 (NTU). The maximum value recorded 12.70 ± 0.50 (NTU) and coefficient variation was 3.93 per cent was recorded in August; minimum value recorded 9.00 ± 0.19 (NTU) and coefficient variation was 2.11 per cent was recorded in February.

During study January-December 2008 seasonal mean and coefficient variation values recorded 10.02 ± 0.81 (NTU) and 8.11 per cent during summer, 11.87 ± 0.59 (NTU) and 4.97 per cent during monsoon, 10.22 ± 0.97 (NTU) and 9.56 per cent during winter (Fig. 3.5). In the second year study January-December 2009 seasonal mean and coefficient variation values recorded 10.15 ± 0.93 (NTU) and 9.18 per cent during summer, 12.00 ± 0.74 (NTU) and 6.19 per cent during monsoon, 10.40 ± 0.98 (NTU) and 9.51 per cent during winter (Table 3.12 and Fig. 3.6).

In the present study January to December 2008 the maximum turbidity was recorded in monsoon season at north site and minimum turbidity was recorded in summer season at south and east sites. In the second year study January-December 2009 the maximum turbidity was recorded in winter season at north site where as minimum turbidity was recorded in summer season at east and west sites (Tables 3.9, 3.10, 3.11 and 3.12).

During the study January 2008 - December 2009 turbidity indicating significant positive correlation with electric conductivity, total solid, total dissolved solids, total suspended solids, biochemical oxygen demand, chemical oxygen demand, total hardness, nitrate and phosphate and it indicating significant negative correlation with transparency and fish (Table 4.7 & 4.8).

Table 3.12: Seasonal Variations in Turbidity (NTU) at West Side, Harsool-Savangi Dam

Season	Months Jan. 2008 - Dec. 2008	Monthly Mean Values	Monthly C.V. (%)	Seasonal Mean Values	Seasonal C.V. (%)	Months Jan. 2009 - Dec. 2009	Monthly Mean Values	Monthly C.V. (%)	Seasonal Mean Values	Seasonal C.V. (%)
	February	9.1±0.10	1.09			February	9±0.19	2.11		
	March	9.7±0.92	9.48			March	9.9±0.10	1.0		
Summer	April	10.3±0.19	1.84	10.02±0.81	8.11	April	10.5±0.14	1.33	10.15±0.93	9.18
	May	11±0.50	4.54			May	11.2±0.27	2.41		
	June	11.1±0.24	2.16			June	11±0.29	2.63		
	July	11.8±0.90	7.62			July	11.9±0.17	1.42		
Monsoon	August	12.1±0.56	4.62	11.87±0.59	4.97	August	12.4±0.12	0.96	12.00±0.74	6.19
	September	12.5±0.49	3.92			September	12.7±0.50	3.93		
	October	11.6±0.12	1.03			October	11.8±0.45	3.81		
	November	10.1±0.11	1.08			November	10.3±0.15	1.45		
Winter	December	9.9±0.94	9.49	10.22±0.97	9.56	December	10±0.20	2.00	10.40±0.98	9.51
	January	9.3±0.14	1.50			January	9.5±0.19	2.00		

In the present study, the turbidity values were maximum during monsoon and minimum during summer. High values of turbidity in monsoon due to influx of rain water from catchments area, muddiness, less penetration of light, washes silts, high organic matter and low transparency due to suspended inert particulate matter. However, low values of turbidity in summer due to clear atmosphere, evaporation of water and high light penetration. Particularly north site showed high transparency due to exclusive addition of River entry point results increased transparency, adversely affecting the turbidity.

Transperancy

The transparency of natural water is an indicator of productivity. The extent to which light can penetrate depends on the transparency of standing water column. Further, transparency of water is inversely proportional to turbidity, created by suspended inorganic and organic matter (Saxena, 1987). The transparency of water body get affected by the factors like planktonic growth, rainfall, position of sun in the sky, angle of incidence of rays, cloudiness, visibility and turbidity due to suspended inert particulate matter. High turbidity of water causes damage to benthic community (Anitha, 2002). Kaliya (1973) reported that high plankton density large quantities of suspended matter reduces the light penetration in a Lake.

South Site

In the first year the study January-December 2008 at south site the transparency ranged 8.00 ± 0.90 to 25.00 ± 2.34 (cm). The maximum value recorded 25.00 ± 2.34 (cm) and coefficient variation was 9.36 per cent was recorded in March and minimum value recorded 8.00 ± 0.90 (cm) and coefficient variation was 11.25 per cent was recorded in September. In the second year study January-December 2009 the transparency at south site ranged 7.00 ± 0.14 to 26.00 ± 1.57 (cm). The maximum value recorded 26.00 ± 1.57 (cm) and coefficient variation was 6.03 per cent was recorded in April;

minimum value recorded 7.00 ± 0.14 (cm) and coefficient variation was 2.00 per cent was recorded in September.

During first year study January-December 2008 seasonal mean and coefficient variation values recorded 21.10 ± 3.82 (cm) and 18.13 per cent during summer, 10.82 ± 2.76 (cm) and 25.53 per cent during monsoon, 14.27 ± 3.31 (cm) and 23.20 per cent during winter (Fig. 3.7). In the second year study January-December 2009 seasonal mean and coefficient variation values recorded 21.50 ± 3.74 (cm) and 17.42 per cent during summer, 9.92 ± 4.15 (cm) and 41.89 per cent during monsoon, 13.77 ± 4.69 (cm) and 34.05 per cent during winter (Table 3.13 and Fig. 3.8).

North Site

In the study January-December 2008 at north site the transparency ranged 5.50 ± 0.35 to 25.00 ± 0.11 (cm). The maximum value recorded 25.00 ± 0.11 (cm) and coefficient variation was 0.44 per cent was recorded in March and minimum value recorded 5.50 ± 0.35 (cm) and coefficient variation was 6.36 per cent was recorded in September. In the second year study January-December 2009 the transparency at north site ranged 4.50 ± 0.41 to 22 ± 0.19 (cm). The maximum value recorded 22 ± 0.19 (cm) and coefficient variation was 0.86 per cent was recorded in April; minimum value recorded 4.50 ± 0.41 (cm) and coefficient variation was 9.11 per cent was recorded in September.

During first year study January-December 2008 seasonal mean and coefficient variation values recorded 18.77 ± 4.59 (cm) and 24.44 per cent during summer, 8.25 ± 3.66 (cm) and 44.39 per cent during monsoon, 12.00 ± 2.67 (cm) and 22.30 per cent during winter (Fig. 3.7). In the second year study January-December 2009 seasonal mean and coefficient variation values recorded 18.80 ± 2.92 (cm) and 15.53 per cent during summer, 6.87 ± 2.95 (cm) and 42.97 per cent during monsoon and 11.25 ± 4.87 (cm) and 43.31 per cent during winter (Table 3.14 and Fig. 3.8).

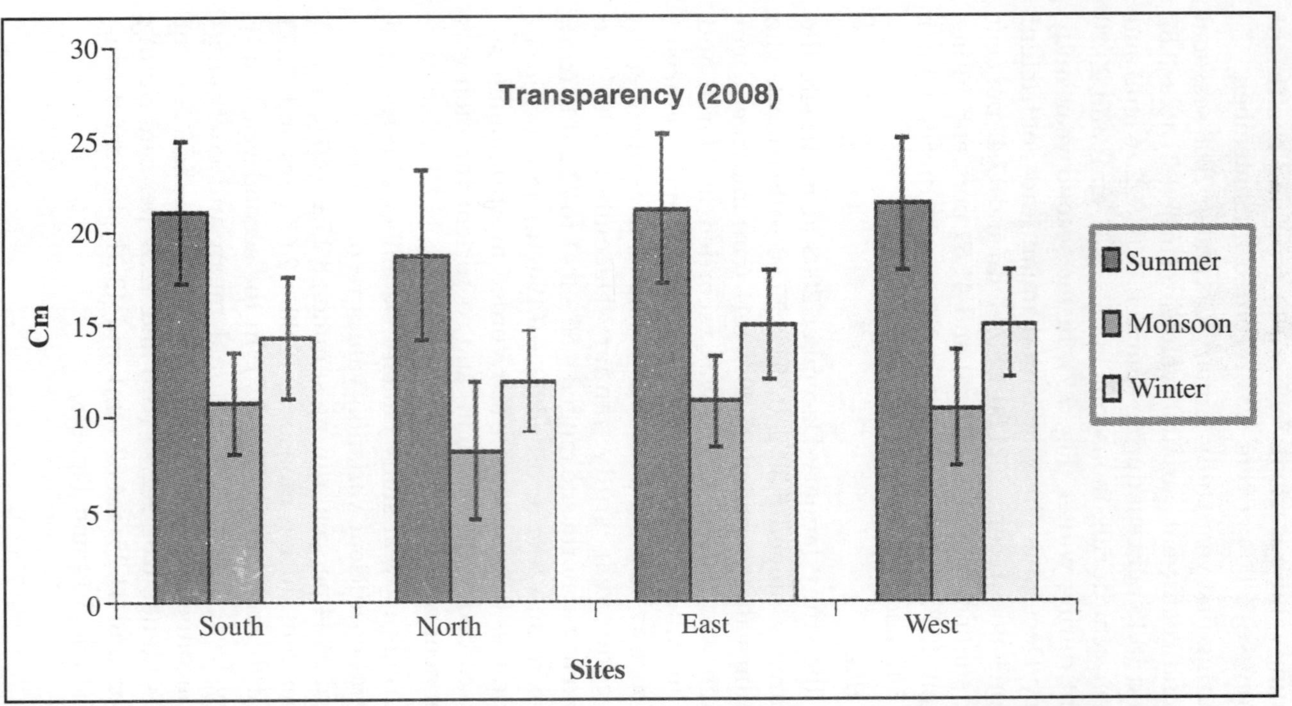

Fig. 3.7: Seasonal Variations in Transparency (cm) at Different Sites of Harsool-Savangi Dam January to December 2008

Table 3.13: Seasonal Variations in Transparency (cm) at South Site, Harsool-Savangi Dam

Season	Months Jan. 2008 - Dec. 2008	Monthly Mean Values	Monthly C.V. (%)	Seasonal Mean Values	Seasonal C.V. (%)	Months Jan. 2009 - Dec. 2009	Monthly Mean Values	Monthly C.V. (%)	Seasonal Mean Values	Seasonal C.V. (%)
	February	16±1.50	9.37			February	17±0.90	5.29		
	March	25±2.34	9.36			March	22.4±1.91	8.52		
Summer	April	22.7±1.29	5.68	21.10±3.82	18.13	April	26±1.57	6.03	21.5±3.74	17.42
	May	20.7±1.87	9.03			May	20.6±1.14	5.53		
	June	14±2.14	15.28			June	16±0.90	5.62		
	July	12.2±1.44	11.80			July	9.2±0.84	9.13		
Monsoon	August	9.1±0.51	5.60	10.82±2.76	25.53	August	7.5±0.12	1.60	9.92±4.15	41.89
	September	8±0.90	11.25			September	7±0.14	2.00		
	October	10±1.10	11.00			October	9±0.90	10.00		
	November	14±0.81	5.78			November	12±0.19	1.58		
Winter	December	15.1±0.99	6.55	14.27±3.31	23.20	December	14±0.21	1.50	13.77±4.69	34.05
	January	18±1.12	6.22			January	20.1±0.41	2.03		

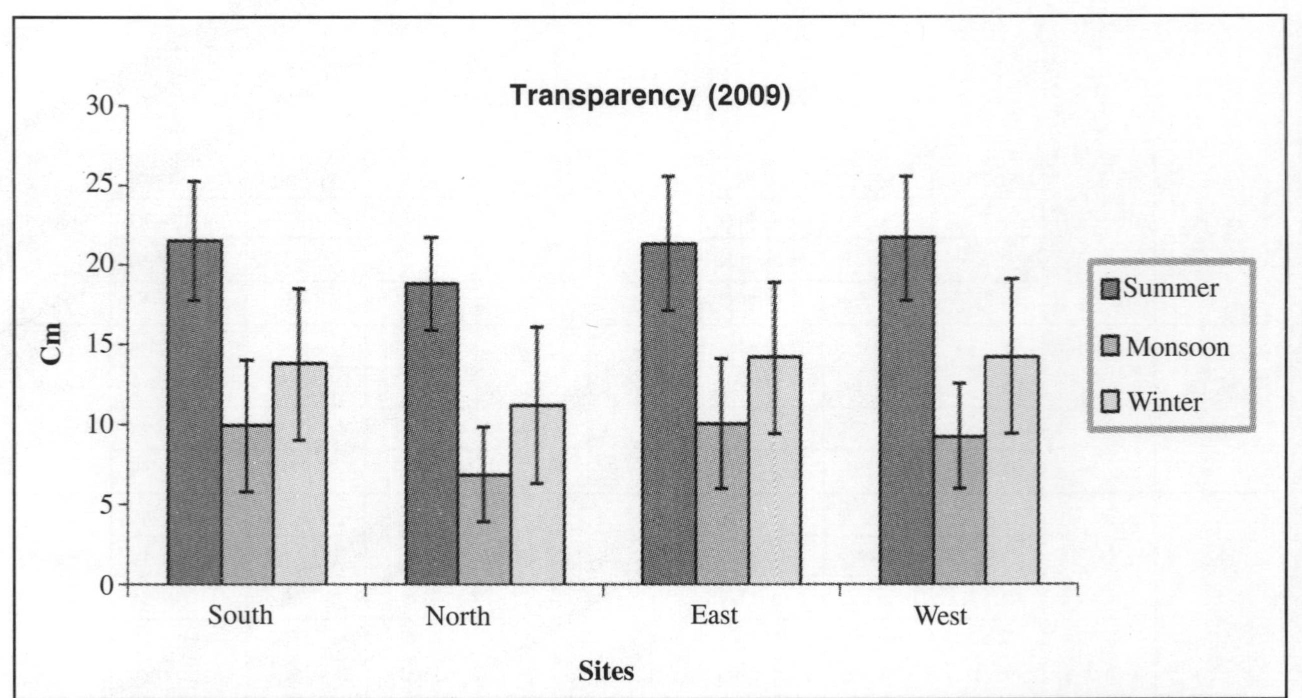

Fig. 3.8: Seasonal Variations in Transparency (cm) at Different Sites of Harsool-Savangi Dam January to December 2009

Table 3.14: Seasonal Variations in Transparency (cm) at North Site, Harsool-Savangi Dam

Season	Months Jan. 2008 - Dec. 2008	Monthly Mean Values	Monthly C.V. (%)	Seasonal Mean Values	Seasonal C.V. (%)	Months Jan. 2009 - Dec. 2009	Monthly Mean Values	Monthly C.V. (%)	Seasonal Mean Values	Seasonal C.V. (%)
	February	14±0.41	2.92			February	15±0.16	1.06		
	March	25±0.11	0.44			March	19.7±0.10	0.50		
Summer	April	18.6±0.19	1.02	18.77±4.59	24.44	April	22±0.19	0.86	18.80±2.92	15.53
	May	17.5±0.40	2.28			May	18.5±0.80	4.32		
	June	13.5±0.90	6.66			June	11±0.93	8.45		
	July	8±0.98	12.25			July	7±0.19	2.71		
Monsoon	August	6±0.80	13.33	08.25±3.66	44.39	August	5±0.88	17.60	06.87±2.95	42.97
	September	5.5±0.35	6.36			September	4.5±0.41	9.11		
	October	9±0.40	4.44	12.00±2.67		October	6.5±0.35	5.38	11.25±4.87	
	November	11.5±0.59	5.13			November	9.5±0.91	9.57		
Winter	December	12±0.19	1.58	12.00±2.67	22.30	December	11±0.99	9.00	11.25±4.87	43.31
	January	15.5±0.10	0.64			January	18±0.19	1.05		

East Site

In the first year study January-December 2008 at east site the transparency ranged 8.50 ± 0.15 to 26.00 ± 0.91 (cm). The maximum value recorded 26.00 ± 0.91 (cm) and coefficient variation was 3.50 per cent was recorded in March and minimum value recorded 8.50 ± 0.15 (cm) and coefficient variation was 1.76 per cent was recorded in September. During the second year January-December 2009 the transparency at east site ranged 7.10 ± 0.90 to 26.00 ± 0.14 (cm). The maximum value recorded 26.00 ± 0.14 (cm) and coefficient variation was 0.53 per cent was recorded in April; minimum value recorded 7.10 ± 0.90 (cm) and coefficient variation was 12.67 per cent was recorded in September.

During first year study January-December 2008 seasonal mean and coefficient variation values recorded 21.25 ± 4.01 (cm) and 18.87 per cent during summer, 10.87 ± 2.42 (cm) and 22.32 per cent during monsoon, 15.00 ± 2.94 (cm) and 19.62 per cent during winter (Fig. 3.7). In the second year study January-December 2009 seasonal mean and coefficient variation values recorded 21.32 ± 4.20 (cm) and 19.72 per cent during summer, 10.07 ± 4.07 (cm) and 40.49 per cent during monsoon and 14.20 ± 4.74 (cm) and 33.41 per cent during winter (Table 3.15 and Fig. 3.8).

West Site

In first year study January-December 2008 at west site the transparency ranged 8.00 ± 0.49 to 26.50 ± 0.10 (cm). The maximum value recorded 26.50 ± 0.10 (cm) and coefficient variation was 0.37 per cent was recorded in March and minimum value recorded 8.00 ± 0.49 (cm) and coefficient variation was 6.12 per cent was recorded in September. In the second year study January-December 2009 the transparency at west site ranged 7.00 ± 0.94 to 26.00 ± 0.14 (cm). The maximum value recorded 26.00 ± 0.14 (cm) and coefficient variation was 0.53 per cent was recorded in April; minimum value recorded 7.00 ± 0.94 (cm) and coefficient variation was 13.42 per cent was recorded in September.

Table 3.15: Seasonal Variations in Transparency (cm) at East Site, Harsool-Savangi Dam

Season	Months Jan. 2008 - Dec. 2008	Monthly Mean Values	Monthly C.V. (%)	Seasonal Mean Values	Seasonal C.V. (%)	Months Jan. 2009 - Dec. 2009	Monthly Mean Values	Monthly C.V. (%)	Seasonal Mean Values	Seasonal C.V. (%)
Summer	February	16.5±0.90	5.45	21.25±4.01	18.87	February	16±0.19	1.18	21.32±4.20	19.72
	March	26±0.91	3.50			March	22.8±0.41	1.79		
	April	22.5±0.70	3.11			April	26±0.14	0.53		
	May	20±0.41	2.05			May	20.5±0.11	0.53		
Monsoon	June	14±0.19	1.35	10.87±2.42	22.32	June	16±0.19	1.18	10.07±4.07	40.49
	July	11.5±1.10	9.56			July	9.5±0.10	1.05		
	August	9.5±0.99	10.42			August	7.7±0.21	2.72		
	September	8.5±0.15	1.76			September	7.1±0.90	12.67		
Winter	October	12±0.12	1.00	15.00±2.94	19.62	October	9.3±0.81	8.70	14.20±4.74	33.41
	November	15±0.20	1.33			November	12.3±0.75	6.09		
	December	14±0.41	2.92			December	14.7±0.50	3.40		
	January	19±0.19	1.00			January	20.5±0.65	3.17		

During the study January-December 2008 seasonal mean and coefficient variation values recorded 21.52 ± 3.57 (cm) and 16.62 per cent during summer, 10.50 ± 3.10 (cm) and 29.61 per cent during monsoon, 15.05 ± 2.92 (cm) and 19.42 per cent during winter (Fig. 3.7). In the second year study January-December 2009 seasonal mean and coefficient variation values recorded 21.67 ± 3.92 (cm) and 18.09 per cent during summer, 9.27 ± 3.28 (cm) and 35.38 per cent during monsoon and 14.27 ± 4.81 (cm) and 33.72 per cent during winter (Table 3.16 and Fig. 3.8).

In the present study January to December 2008 the maximum transparency was recorded in summer season at west site and minimum transparency was recorded in monsoon season at north site. In the second year study January-December 2009 the maximum transparency was recorded in summer season at south, east and west sites where as minimum transparency was recorded in monsoon season at north site (Tables 3.13, 3.14, 3.15 and 3.16).

During the study January 2008-December 2009 transparency indicating significant positive correlation with alkalinity, pH and fish and it indicating significant negative correlation with turbidity, electric conductivity, total solid, total dissolved solids, total suspended solids, biochemical oxygen demand, chemical oxygen demand, total hardness, nitrate and phosphate (Table 4.7 and 4.8).

In the present study, the transparency values were maximum during summer and minimum during monsoon. Low values of transparency in monsoon may be due to influx of rain water from catchment area, cloudiness, less penetration of light and high turbidity due to suspended inert particulate matter. However, high values of transparency in summer may be due to clear atmosphere and high light penetration. Particularly north site showed low values of transparency due to exclusive addition of sewage results increased turbidity, adversely affecting the transparency.

Table 3.16: Seasonal Variations in Transparency (cm) at West Site, Harsool-Savangi Dam

Season	Months Jan. 2008 - Dec. 2008	Monthly Mean Values	Monthly C.V. (%)	Seasonal Mean Values	Seasonal C.V. (%)	Months Jan. 2009 - Dec. 2009	Monthly Mean Values	Monthly C.V. (%)	Seasonal Mean Values	Seasonal C.V. (%)
	February	18±0.98	5.44			February	16.5±0.21	1.27		
	March	26.5±0.10	0.37			March	22.5±0.12	0.53		
Summer	April	21.1±0.16	0.75	21.52±3.57	16.62	April	26±0.14	0.53	21.67±3.92	18.09
	May	20.5±0.24	1.17			May	21.7±0.12	0.55		
	June	15±0.27	1.80			June	14±0.10	0.71		
	July	10±0.42	4.20			July	9±0.41	4.55		
Monsoon	August	9±0.34	3.77	10.50±3.10	29.61	August	7.1±0.90	12.67	9.27±3.28	35.38
	September	8±0.49	6.12			September	7±0.94	13.42		
	October	12±0.60	5.00			October	9.9±0.89	8.98		
	November	14.2±0.90	6.33			November	12±0.75	6.25		
Winter	December	15±0.91	6.06	15.05±2.92	19.42	December	14.2±0.19	1.33	14.27±4.81	33.72
	January	19±0.65	3.42			January	21±0.14	0.66		

pH

pH is defined as the intensity of the acidic or basic character of a solution at given temperature. pH is the negative logarithm of hydrogen ion concentration (pH = - log [H^+]). pH values from 0 to 7 are diminishingly acidic, whereas values of 7 to 14 are increasingly alkaline. At 25°C, pH 7.0 is neutral, where the activities of the hydrogen and hydroxyl ions are equal and it corresponds to 10-7 moles/L. The neutral point is temperature dependant and is pH 7.5 at 0°C and pH 6.5 at 60°C. The pH of natural water usually lies in the range of 4.4 to 8.5. pH has no direct adverse effects on health, however, a lower value below 4 will produce sour taste and higher value above 8.5 an alkaline taste. Higher values of pH have trend the scale formation in water heating apparatus and also reduce the germicidal potential of chloride. High pH induces the formation of trihalomethanes which are toxic. pH below 6.5 starts corrosion in pipes, thereby releasing toxic metals such as Zn, Pb, Cd and Cu, etc. in the water supplies, pH is an important factor in fixing alum does in drinking water treatment.

South Site

In the study January-December 2008 at south site the pH ranged 8.0 ± 0.95 to 8.6 ± 0.30. The maximum value recorded 8.6 ± 0.30 and coefficient variation was 3.48 per cent was recorded in May and minimum value recorded 8.0 ± 0.95 and coefficient variation was 11.87 per cent was recorded in January. In the second year study January-December 2009 the pH at south site ranged 8.0 ± 0.20 to 8.7 ± 0.11. The maximum value recorded 8.7 ± 0.11 and coefficient variation was 1.26 per cent was recorded in May; minimum value recorded 8.0 ± 0.20 and coefficient variation was 2.50 per cent was recorded in October.

During first year study January-December 2008 seasonal mean and coefficient variation values recorded 8.42 ± 0.17 and 2.02 per cent during summer, 8.20 ± 0.14 and 1.72 per cent during monsoon, 8.12 ± 0.15 and 1.84 per cent during winter (Fig. 3.9). In the second year study January-December 2009 seasonal mean and coefficient variation values recorded 8.47 ± 0.17 and 2.01 per cent during summer, 8.20 ± 0.18 and 2.22 per cent during monsoon and 8.10 ± 0.08 and 1.00 per cent during winter (Table 3.17 and Fig. 3.10).

North Site

In the study January-December 2008 at north site the pH ranged 7.8 ± 0.20 to 8.6 ± 0.21. The maximum value recorded 8.6 ± 0.21 and coefficient variation was 2.44 per cent was recorded in April and minimum value recorded 7.8 ± 0.20 and coefficient variation was 2.56 per cent was recorded in September. In the second year study January-December 2009 the pH at north site ranged 7.9 ± 0.13 to 8.5 ± 0.23. The maximum value recorded 8.5 ± 0.23 and coefficient variation was 2.70 per cent was recorded in April; minimum value recorded 7.9 ± 0.13 and coefficient variation was 1.64 per cent was recorded in September.

In the study January-December 2008 seasonal mean and coefficient variation values recorded 8.27 ± 0.25 and 3.02 per cent during summer, 8.12 ± 0.25 and 3.07 per cent during monsoon, 7.97 ± 0.09 and 1.20 per cent during winter (Fig. 3.9). In the second year study January-December 2009 seasonal mean and coefficient variation values recorded 8.42 ± 0.09 and 1.13 per cent during summer, 8.10 ± 0.18 and 2.25 per cent during monsoon and 8.10 ± 0.08 and 1.00 per cent during winter (Table 3.18 and Fig. 3.10).

East Site

During study January-December 2008 at east site the pH ranged 7.9 ± 0.80 to 8.6 ± 0.99. The maximum value recorded 8.6 ± 0.99 and coefficient variation was 11.51 per cent was recorded in April and minimum value recorded 7.9 ± 0.80 and coefficient variation was 10.00 per cent was recorded in January. In the second year study January-December 2009 the pH at east site ranged 8.0 ± 0.19 to 8.5 ± 0.50. The maximum value recorded 8.5 ± 0.50 and coefficient variation was 5.88 per cent was recorded in April; minimum value recorded 8.0 ± 0.19 and coefficient variation was 2.37 per cent was recorded in December.

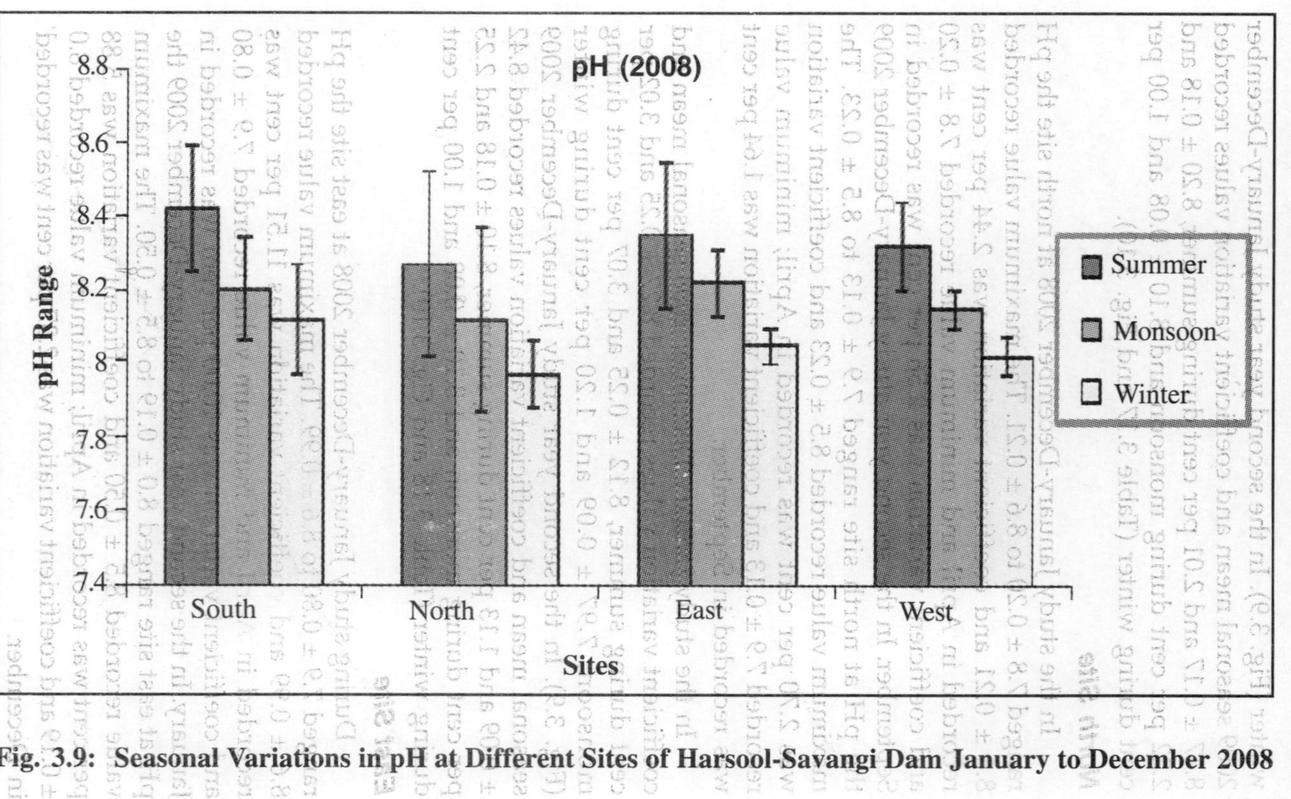

Fig. 3.9: Seasonal Variations in pH at Different Sites of Harsool-Savangi Dam January to December 2008

Table 3.17: Seasonal Variations in pH at South Site, Harsool-Savangi Dam

Season	Months Jan. 2008 - Dec. 2008	Monthly Mean Values	Monthly C.V. (%)	Seasonal Mean Values	Seasonal C.V. (%)	Months Jan. 2009 - Dec. 2009	Monthly Mean Values	Monthly C.V. (%)	Seasonal Mean Values	Seasonal C.V. (%)
	February	8.2±0.26	3.17			February	8.3±0.20	2.40		
	March	8.4±0.20	2.38			March	8.4±0.92	10.95		
Summer	April	8.5±0.19	2.23	8.42±0.17	2.02	April	8.5±0.81	9.52	8.47±0.17	2.01
	May	8.6±0.30	3.48			May	8.7±0.11	1.26		
	June	8.4±0.10	1.19			June	8.4±0.10	1.19		
	July	8.2±0.32	3.90			July	8.3±0.91	10.96		
Monsoon	August	8.1±0.82	10.12	8.20±0.14	1.72	August	8.1±0.20	2.50	8.20±0.18	2.22
	September	8.1±0.10	1.23			September	8.1±0.85	10.49		
Winter	October	8.2±0.90	10.97			October	8.0±0.20	2.50		
	November	8.3±0.40	4.81			November	8.1±0.80	9.87		
Winter	December	8.1±0.80	10.00	8.12±0.15	1.84	December	8.2±0.90	10.97	8.10±0.08	1.00
	January	8.0±0.95	11.87			January	8.1±0.40	4.93		

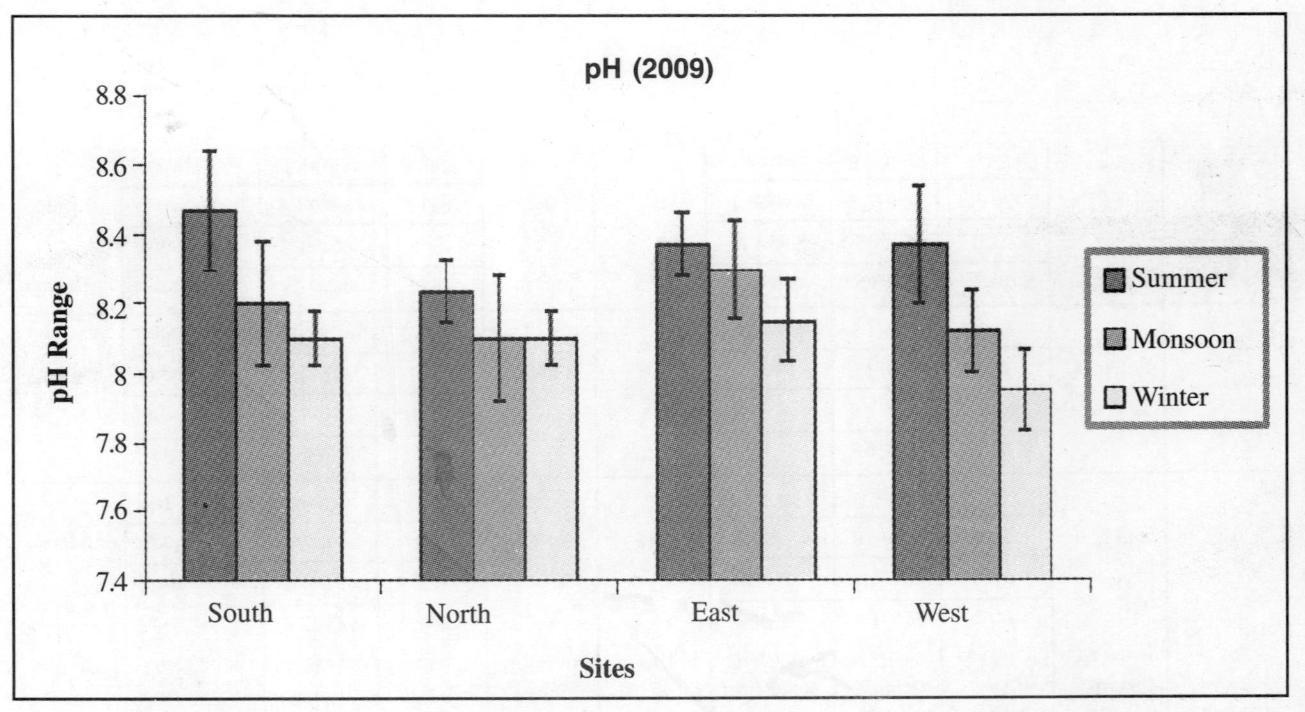

Fig. 3.10: Seasonal Variations in pH at Different Sites of Harsool-Savangi Dam January to December 2009

Table 3.18: Seasonal Variations in pH at North Site, Harsool-Savangi Dam

Season	Months Jan. 2008 - Dec. 2008	Monthly Mean Values	Monthly C.V. (%)	Seasonal Mean Values	Seasonal C.V. (%)	Months Jan. 2009 - Dec. 2009	Monthly Mean Values	Monthly C.V. (%)	Seasonal Mean Values	Seasonal C.V. (%)
	February	8.2±0.27	3.29			February	8.3±0.20	2.40		
	March	8.3±0.32	3.85			March	8.4±0.16	1.90		
Summer	April	8.6±0.21	2.44	8.27±0.25	3.02	April	8.5±0.23	2.70	8.42±0.09	1.13
	May	8.0±0.10	1.25			May	8.4±0.28	3.29		
	June	8.2±0.06	0.73			June	8.0±0.21	2.62		
	July	8.4±0.11	1.30			July	8.2±0.20	2.43		
Monsoon	August	8.1±0.19	2.34	8.12±0.25	3.07	August	8.3±0.19	2.28	8.10±0.18	2.25
	September	7.8±0.20	2.56			September	7.9±0.13	1.64		
	October	7.9±0.09	1.13			October	8.0±0.13	1.62		
	November	7.9±0.10	1.26			November	8.1±0.08	0.98		
Winter	December	8.0±0.07	0.87	7.97±0.09	1.20	December	8.2±0.15	1.82	8.10±0.08	1.00
	January	8.1±0.31	3.82			January	8.1±0.19	2.34		

In the study January-December 2008 seasonal mean and coefficient variation values recorded 8.35 ± 0.20 and 2.49 per cent during summer, 8.22 ± 0.09 and 1.16 per cent during monsoon, 8.05 ± 0.05 and 0.71 per cent during winter (Fig. 3.9). In the second year study January-December 2009 seasonal mean and coefficient variation values recorded 8.37 ± 0.09 and 1.14 per cent during summer, 8.30 ± 0.14 and 1.70 per cent during monsoon and 8.15 ± 0.12 and 1.58 per cent during winter (Table 3.19 and Fig. 3.10).

West Site

In the study January-December 2008 at west site the pH ranged 7.9 ± 0.42 to 8.5 ± 0.19. The maximum value recorded 8.5 ± 0.19 and coefficient variation was 2.23 per cent was recorded in May and minimum value recorded 7.9 ± 0.42 and coefficient variation was 5.25 per cent was recorded in December. In the second year study January-December 2009 the pH at west site ranged 7.8 ± 0.90 to 8.6 ± 0.21. The maximum value recorded 8.6 ± 0.21 and coefficient variation was 2.44 per cent was recorded in May; minimum value recorded 7.8 ± 0.90 and coefficient variation was 11.53 per cent was recorded in December.

During study January-December 2008 seasonal mean and coefficient variation values recorded 8.32 ± 0.12 and 1.51 per cent during summer, 8.15 ± 0.05 and 0.70 per cent during monsoon, 8.02 ± 0.05 and 0.62 per cent during winter (Fig. 3.9). In the second year study January-December 2009 seasonal mean and coefficient variation values recorded 8.37 ± 0.17 and 2.03 per cent during summer, 8.12 ± 0.12 and 1.54 per cent during monsoon and 7.95 ± 0.12 and 1.62 per cent during winter (Table 3.20 and Fig. 3.10).

In the present study January to December 2008 the maximum pH was recorded in summer season at south, north and east sites and minimum pH was recorded in monsoon season at north site. In the second year study January-December 2009 the maximum pH was recorded in summer season at south and north sites where as minimum pH was recorded in winter season at west site (Table 3.17, 3.18, 3.19 and 3.20).

Table 3.19: Seasonal Variations in pH at East Site, Harsool-Savangi Dam

Season	Months Jan. 2008 - Dec. 2008	Monthly Mean Values	Monthly C.V. (%)	Seasonal Mean Values	Seasonal C.V. (%)	Months Jan. 2009 - Dec. 2009	Monthly Mean Values	Monthly C.V. (%)	Seasonal Mean Values	Seasonal C.V. (%)
Summer	February	8.1±0.57	7.03	8.35±0.20	2.49	February	8.3±0.11	1.32	8.37±0.09	1.14
	March	8.3±0.18	2.16			March	8.4±0.10	1.19		
	April	8.6±0.99	11.51			April	8.5±0.50	5.88		
	May	8.4±0.20	2.38			May	8.3±0.42	5.06		
Monsoon	June	8.3±0.90	10.84	8.22±0.09	1.16	June	8.4±0.32	3.80	8.30±0.14	1.70
	July	8.2±0.85	10.36			July	8.3±0.19	2.28		
	August	8.1±0.80	9.87			August	8.4±0.60	7.14		
	September	8.3±0.88	10.60			September	8.1±0.69	8.51		
Winter	October	8.1±0.25	3.08	8.05±0.05	0.71	October	8.3±0.21	2.53	8.15±0.12	1.58
	November	8.0±0.13	1.62			November	8.2±0.13	1.58		
	December	8.1±0.20	2.46			December	8.0±0.19	2.37		
	January	7.9±0.80	10.00			January	8.1±0.24	2.96		

Table 3.20: Seasonal Variations in pH at West Site, Harsool-Savangi Dam

Season	Months Jan. 2008 - Dec. 2008	Monthly Mean Values	Monthly C.V. (%)	Seasonal Mean Values	Seasonal C.V. (%)	Months Jan. 2009 - Dec. 2009	Monthly Mean Values	Monthly C.V. (%)	Seasonal Mean Values	Seasonal C.V. (%)
	February	8.3±0.90	10.84			February	8.2±0.01	0.12		
	March	8.2±0.51	6.21			March	8.4±0.83	9.88		
Summer	April	8.3±0.10	1.20	8.32±0.12	1.51	April	8.3±0.35	4.21	8.37±0.17	2.03
	May	**8.5±0.19**	2.23			May	**8.6±0.21**	2.44		
	June	8.2±0.21	2.56			June	8.3±0.16	1.92		
	July	8.1±0.59	7.28			July	8.1±0.09	1.11		
Monsoon	August	8.1±0.12	1.48	8.15±0.05	0.70	August	8.1±0.11	1.35	8.12±0.12	1.54
	September	8.2±0.09	1.09			September	8.0±0.99	12.37		
	October	8.0±0.92	11.50			October	8.1±0.50	6.17		1.62
	November	8.1±0.55	6.79			November	7.9±0.12	1.51		
Winter	December	**7.9±0.42**	5.25	8.02±0.05	0.62	December	**7.8±0.90**	11.53	7.95±0.12	1.62
	January	8.0±0.60	7.50			January	8.0±0.65	8.12		

During the study January 2008-December 2009 pH indicating significant positive correlation with water temperature, transparency, alkalinity, sulphate, chloride and fish and it indicating significant negative correlation with electric conductivity, total solid, total dissolved solids, dissolved oxygen, biochemical oxygen demand, chemical oxygen demand, and phosphate (Table 4.7 and 4.8).

In the present study, the pH values were maximum during summer and minimum during monsoon.

In the present study, the pH range shows that the water of all the sampling sites of the dam was alkaline in nature in summer. High values of pH during summer might be low water levels and concentration of nutrients in water. The decreased pH values were due to dilution caused by the rainwater during monsoon.

Electrical Conductivity

Electrical conductivity is a numerical expression ability of an aqueous solution to carry electric current. This ability depends on the presence of ions, their total concentration, mobility, valence, relative concentrations and temperature measurement. Electrical conductivity measurements can be used to calculate total dissolved solids by multiplying electrical conductivity (in LS/cm) by an empirical factor, which vary 0.55 to 0.9, depending on the soluble components of the water and the temperature measurement.

Specific electrical conductivity is a numerical expression of its ability to carry an electric current. Further, it is an indicator of ionic composition and any alteration in its values reflects change in ionic concentration in a proportional way. The Electrical conductivity of water in the reservoir is a characteristic which is mainly associated with the dissolved material or solute concentration present in the reservoir water. Electrical conductivity and dissolved solids are directly proportional to each other mainly due to ionic composition of water. The factors such as rainfall and biodiversity cause changes in ionic composition and nature of bottom deposits influence the electrical conductivity (Anitha, 2002). Electrical conductivity is an important parameter to detect fish community and plays an important role in the released nutrients and consequently the productivity of aquatic ecosystem. It depends upon large amount of salts and silts carried by adjacent canals to agriculture sites. The chemical nature of solids dissolved in water mainly depends on the nature of bed rocks and soil developed from it. Physico-chemical factors which govern chemistry of water may also influence soil salinity especially in dry conditions (Holmes and Talsma, 1981).

South Site

During the study January-December 2008 at south site the electric conductivity ranged 200 ± 5.17 to 550 ± 16.59 (μmhos/cm). The maximum value recorded 550 ± 16.59 (μmhos/cm) and coefficient variation was 3.01 per cent was recorded in September and minimum value recorded 200 ± 5.17 (μmhos/cm) and coefficient variation was 2.58 per cent was recorded in February. In the second year January-December 2009 the electric conductivity at south site ranged 208 ± 7.10 to 567.90 ± 21.20 (μmhos/cm). The maximum value recorded 567.90 ± 21.20 (μmhos/cm) and coefficient variation was 3.73 per cent was recorded in September; minimum value recorded 208 ± 7.10 (μmhos/cm) and coefficient variation was 3.41 per cent was recorded in February.

During the study January-December 2008 seasonal mean and coefficient variation values recorded 239.75 ± 33.76 (μmhos/cm) and 14.08 per cent during summer, 492.50 ± 50.57 (μmhos/cm) and 10.27 per cent during monsoon, 400 ± 43.96 (μmhos/cm) and 10.99 per cent during winter (Fig. 3.11). In the second year study January-December 2009 seasonal mean and coefficient variation values recorded 281.05 ± 100.49 (μmhos/cm) and 35.75 per cent during summer, 520.60 ± 58.83 (μmhos/cm) and 11.30 per cent during monsoon and 435.55 ± 59.01 (μmhos/cm) and 13.54 per cent during winter (Table 3.21 and Fig. 3.12).

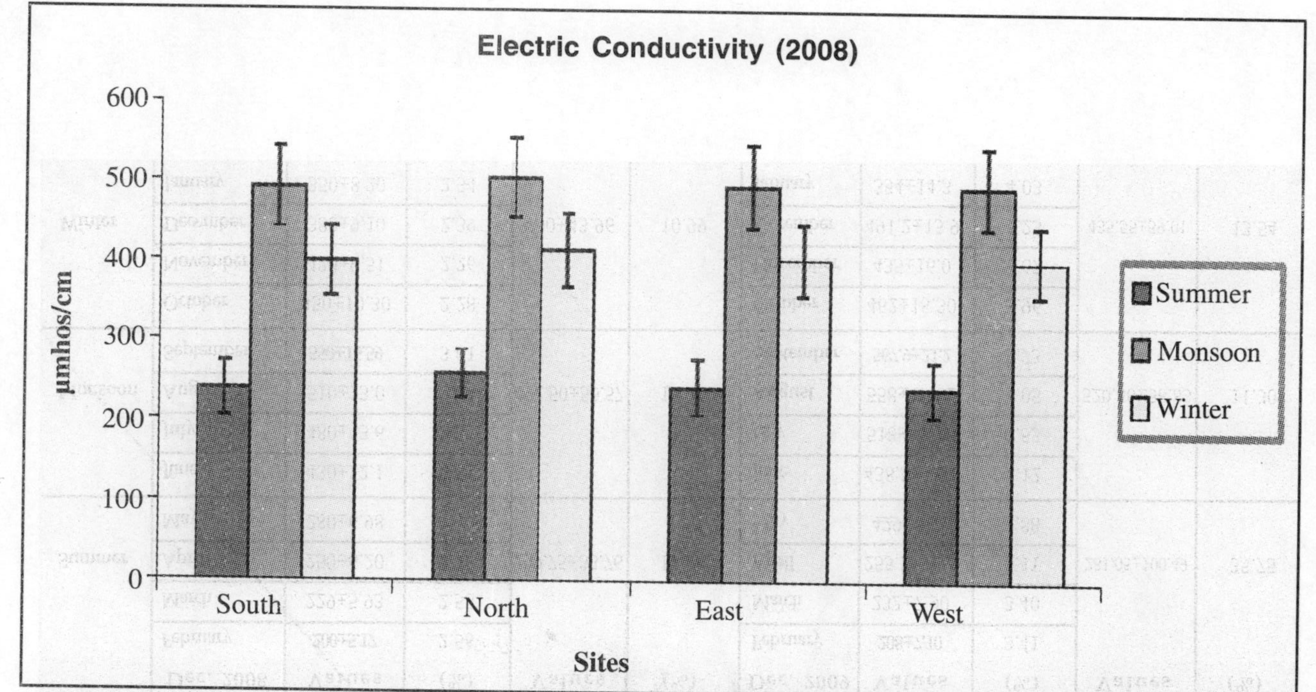

Fig. 3.11: Seasonal Variations in Electric Conductivity (µmhos/cm) at Different Sites of Harsool-Savangi Dam January to December 2008

Table 3.21: Seasonal Variations in Electric Conductivity (μmhos/cm) at South Site, Harsool-Savangi Dam

Season	Months Jan. 2008 - Dec. 2008	Monthly Mean Values	Monthly C.V. (%)	Seasonal Mean Values	Seasonal C.V. (%)	Months Jan. 2009 - Dec. 2009	Monthly Mean Values	Monthly C.V. (%)	Seasonal Mean Values	Seasonal C.V. (%)
Summer	February	200±5.17	2.58	239.75±33.76	14.08	February	208±7.10	3.41	281.05±100.49	35.75
	March	229±5.93	2.58			March	232±7.90	3.40		
	April	250±6.20	2.48			April	255.2±7.95	3.11		
	May	280±6.98	2.49			May	429±8.10	1.88		
Monsoon	June	430±12.1	2.81	492.50±50.57	10.27	June	438.5±18.1	4.12	520.60±58.83	11.30
	July	480±13.6	2.83			July	518±18.30	3.53		
	August	510±13.0	2.54			August	558±17.02	3.05		
	September	550±16.59	3.01			September	567.9±21.2	3.73		
Winter	October	450±10.30	2.28	400±43.96	10.99	October	462±18.30	3.96	435.55±59.01	13.54
	November	420±9.51	2.26			November	435±16.0	3.67		
	December	380±9.10	2.39			December	491.2±15.9	3.23		
	January	350±8.20	2.34			January	354±14.3	4.03		

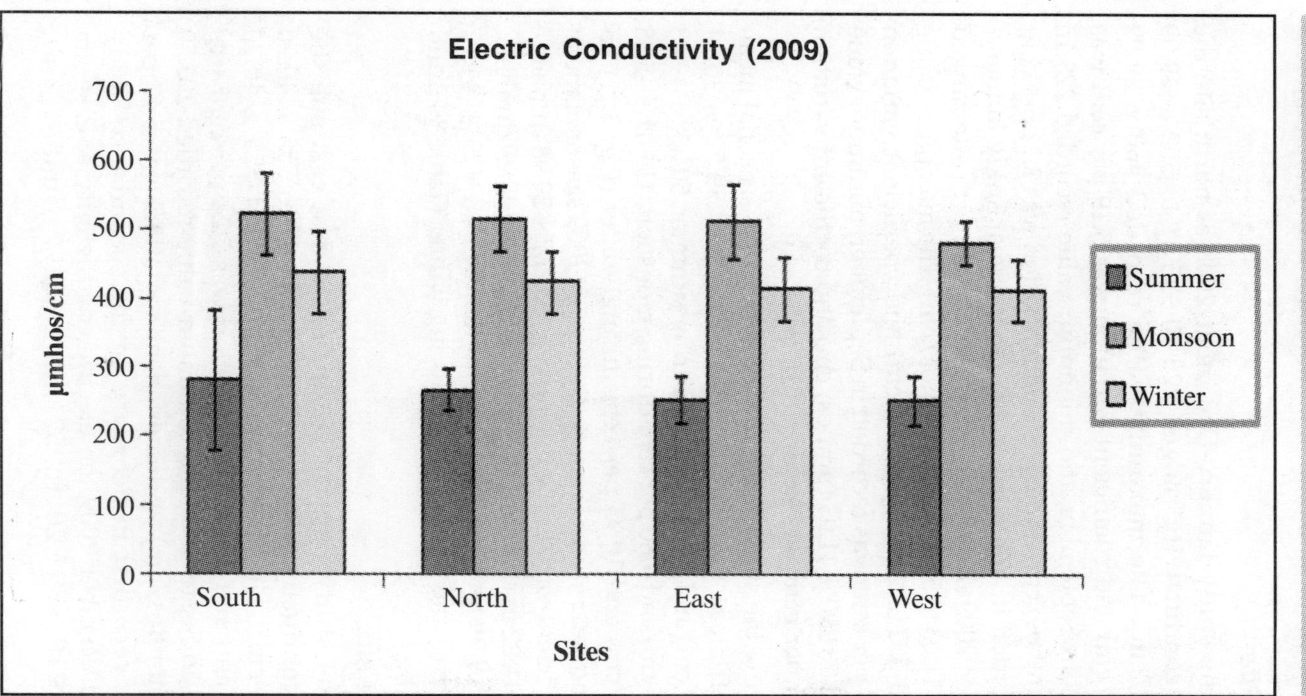

Fig. 3.12: Seasonal Variations in Electric Conductivity (µmhos/cm) at Different Sites of Harsool-Savangi Dam January to December 2009

North Site

In the study January-December 2008 at north site the electric conductivity ranged 225.10 ± 5.01 to 560 ± 29.09 (µmhos/cm). The maximum value recorded 560 ± 29.09 (µmhos/cm) and coefficient variation was 5.19 per cent was recorded in September and minimum value recorded 225.10 ± 5.01 (µmhos/cm) and coefficient variation was 2.22 per cent was recorded in February. In the second year study January-December 2009 the electric conductivity at north site ranged 231.90 ± 11.03 to 572 ± 26.00 (µmhos/cm). The maximum value recorded 572 ± 26.00 (µmhos/cm) and coefficient variation was 4.54 per cent was recorded in September; minimum value recorded 231.90 ± 11.03 (µmhos/cm) and coefficient variation was 4.75 per cent was recorded in February.

During the study January-December 2008 seasonal mean and coefficient variation values recorded 259.52 ± 30.21 (µmhos/cm) and 11.64 per cent during summer, 504.32 ± 49.43 (µmhos/cm) and 9.80 per cent during monsoon, 415.02 ± 45.38 (µmhos/cm) and 10.93 per cent during winter (Fig. 3.11). In the second year study January-December 2009 seasonal mean and coefficient variation values recorded 267 ± 29.98 (µmhos/cm) and 11.22 per cent during summer, 513.82 ± 48.29 (µmhos/cm) and 9.39 per cent during monsoon and 423 ± 44.77 (µmhos/cm) and 10.58 per cent during winter (Table 3.22 and Fig. 3.12).

3. East site

In the study January-December 2008 at east site the electric conductivity ranged 202.50 ± 11.09 to 555 ± 40.20 (µmhos/cm). The maximum value recorded 555 ± 40.20 (µmhos/cm) and coefficient variation was 7.24 per cent was recorded in September and minimum value recorded 202.50 ± 11.09 (µmhos/cm) and coefficient variation was 5.47 per cent was recorded in February. In the second year study January-December 2009 the electric conductivity at east site ranged 210 ± 13.20 to 571.50 ± 38.77 (µmhos/cm).

Table 3.22: Seasonal Variations in Electric Conductivity (µmhos/cm) at North Site, Harsool-Savangi Dam

Season	Months Jan. 2008 - Dec. 2008	Monthly Mean Values	Monthly C.V. (%)	Seasonal Mean Values	Seasonal C.V. (%)	Months Jan. 2009 - Dec. 2009	Monthly Mean Values	Monthly C.V. (%)	Seasonal Mean Values	Seasonal C.V. (%)
	February	225.1±5.01	2.22			February	231.9±11.03	4.75		
	March	248±6.53	2.63			March	256.1±13.19	5.15		
Summer	April	269±7.10	2.63	259.52±30.21	11.64	April	278±13.0	4.67	267±29.98	11.22
	May	296±6.0	2.02			May	302±15.10	5.00		
	June	442.3±22.3	5.04			June	457±31.07	6.79		
	July	494±24.50	4.95			July	499.3±29.0	5.80		
Monsoon	August	521±25.0	4.79	504.32±49.43	9.80	August	527±28.90	5.48	513.82±48.29	9.39
	September	560±29.09	5.19			September	572±26.0	4.54		
	October	465±20.1	4.32			October	474±21.20	4.47		
	November	438.1±21.0	4.79			November	445±23.70	5.32		
Winter	December	394±22.3	5.65	415.02±45.38	10.93	December	398±20.70	5.20	423±44.77	10.58
	January	363±23.8	6.55			January	375±19.0	5.06		

The maximum value recorded 571.50 ± 38.77 (µmhos/cm) and coefficient variation was 6.78 per cent was recorded in September; minimum value recorded 210 ± 13.20 (µmhos/cm) and coefficient variation was 6.28 per cent was recorded in February.

During the study January-December 2008 seasonal mean and coefficient variation values recorded 242.87 ± 34.16 (µmhos/cm) and 14.06 per cent during summer, 495.97 ± 51.06 (µmhos/cm) and 10.29 per cent during monsoon, 403.30 ± 45.08 (µmhos/cm) and 11.18 per cent during winter (Fig. 3.11). In the second year January-December 2009 seasonal mean and coefficient variation values recorded 252.70 ± 34.09 (µmhos/cm) and 13.49 per cent during summer, 509.65 ± 54.65 (µmhos/cm) and 10.72 per cent during monsoon and 412.42 ± 45.53 (µmhos/cm) and 11.04 per cent during winter (Table 3.23 and Fig. 3.12).

West Site

The study January-December 2008 at west site the electric conductivity ranged 201 ± 9.81 to 553 ± 22.90 (µmhos/cm). The maximum value recorded 553 ± 22.90 (µmhos/cm) and coefficient variation was 4.14 per cent was recorded in September and minimum value recorded 201 ± 9.81 (µmhos/cm) and coefficient variation was 4.88 per cent was recorded in February. In the second year study January-December 2009 the electric conductivity at west site ranged 209.50 ± 10.00 to 519 ± 21.90 (µmhos/cm). The maximum value recorded 519 ± 21.90 (µmhos/cm) and coefficient variation was 4.21 per cent was recorded in August; minimum value recorded 209.50 ± 10.00 (µmhos/cm) and coefficient variation was 4.77 per cent was recorded in February.

During the study January-December 2008 seasonal mean and coefficient variation values recorded 241.30 ± 34.08 (µmhos/cm) and 14.12 per cent during summer, 494.60 ± 50.67 (µmhos/cm) and 10.24 per cent during monsoon, 402.25 ± 44.48 (µmhos/cm) and 11.05 per cent during winter (Fig. 3.11). In the second year study January-December 2009 seasonal mean and coefficient variation values recorded 252.15 ± 35.07

Table 3.23: Seasonal Variations in Electric Conductivity (μmhos/cm) at East Site, Harsool-Savangi Dam

Season	Months Jan. 2008 - Dec. 2008	Monthly Mean Values	Monthly C.V. (%)	Seasonal Mean Values	Seasonal C.V. (%)	Months Jan. 2009 - Dec. 2009	Monthly Mean Values	Monthly C.V. (%)	Seasonal Mean Values	Seasonal C.V. (%)
Summer	February	202.5±11.09	5.47	242.87±34.16	14.06	February	210±13.20	6.28	252.70±34.09	13.49
	March	233±11.0	4.72			March	247.5±13.0	5.25		
	April	252±13.7	5.43			April	261±14.09	5.39		
	May	284±14.83	5.22			May	292.3±16.23	5.55		
Monsoon	June	433.9±31.3	7.21	495.97±51.06	10.29	June	442±34.01	7.69	509.65±54.65	10.72
	July	482±38.40	7.96			July	496.1±31.09	6.26		
	August	513±39.40	7.68			August	529±33.0	6.23		
	September	555±40.20	7.24			September	571.5±38.77	6.78		
Winter	October	452±29.0	6.41	403.3±45.08	11.18	October	465±31.0	6.66	412.42±45.53	11.04
	November	427.3±25.70	6.01			November	432±28.40	6.57		
	December	382.9±22.8	5.95			December	391.7±23.10	5.89		
	January	351±19.06	5.43			January	361±21.90	6.06		

(μmhos/cm) and 13.91 per cent during summer, 480.07 ± 32.61 (μmhos/cm) and 6.79 per cent during monsoon and 411.50 ± 45.82 (μmhos/cm) and 11.13 per cent during winter (Table 3.24 and Fig. 3.12).

In the present study January to December 2008 the maximum electric conductivity was recorded in monsoon season at north site and minimum electric conductivity was recorded in summer season at south site. In the second year study January-December 2009 the maximum electric conductivity was recorded in monsoon season at north site where as minimum electric conductivity was recorded in summer season at south site (Tables 3.21 and 3.22).

During the study January 2008-December 2009 electric conductivity indicating significant positive correlation with turbidity, total solid, total dissolved solids, total suspended solids, biochemical oxygen demand, chemical oxygen demand, total hardness, nitrate and phosphate and it indicating significant negative correlation with transparency, pH, alkalinity and fish (Table 4.7 and 4.8).

In the present study, the electrical conductivity recorded maximum during monsoon and minimum during summer. High value of electrical conductivity in monsoon could be due to inflow of high quantum of domestic sewage in rainy season and low values in summer might be due to higher temperature and stabilization of water due to sedimentation and increased concentration of slats because of discharged domestic sewage in the river join Harsool-Savangi Dam, Aurangabad [M.S].

Total Solids (TS)

The quality of water assessed with the presence of total solids in the sample water. The solid means the matter either filterable or unfilterable which remains as residue evaporation and subsequent drying at a defined temperature (APHA, 2005). In water total solids, total dissolved solids, total suspended solids are composed mainly of carbonates, bicarbonates, chlorides, sulphate, phosphates, nitrate, Ca, Mg, Na, K, Mn and organic matter and silts.

Table 3.24: Seasonal Variations in Electric Conductivity (µmhos/cm) at West Site, Harsool-Savangi Dam

Season	Months Jan. 2008 - Dec. 2008	Monthly Mean Values	Monthly C.V. (%)	Seasonal Mean Values	Seasonal C.V. (%)	Months Jan. 2009 - Dec. 2009	Monthly Mean Values	Monthly C.V. (%)	Seasonal Mean Values	Seasonal C.V. (%)
	February	201±9.81	4.88			February	209.5±10.0	4.77		
	March	231±8.10	3.50			March	243±10.50	4.32		
Summer	April	251.2±7.92	3.15	241.30±34.08	14.12	April	263.1±9.80	3.72	252.15±35.07	13.91
	May	282±7.01	2.48			May	293±8.11	2.76		
	June	433±18.20	4.20		10.24	June	442±24.50	5.54		
	July	480.5±19.0	3.95			July	490.3±24.10	4.91		
Monsoon	August	511.9±21.30	4.16	494.60±50.67	10.24	August	519±21.90	4.21	480.07±32.61	6.79
	September	553±22.9	4.14			September	469±20.0	4.26		
	October	451±16.0	3.54			October	462±18.0	3.89		11.13
	November	425±15.90	3.74			November	434±18.50	4.26		
Winter	December	382.1±14.50	3.79	402.25±44.48	11.05	December	392±19.0	4.84	411.50±45.82	11.13
	January	350.9±15.0	4.27			January	358±17.90	5.00		

South Site

During the study January-December 2008 at south site the total solids ranged 308 ± 2.95 to 461.20 ± 1.10 (mg/l). The maximum value recorded 461.20 ± 1.10 (mg/l) and coefficient variation was 0.23 per cent was recorded in September and minimum value recorded 308 ± 2.95 (mg/l) and coefficient variation was 0.95 per cent was recorded in April. In the second year study January-December 2009 the total solids at south site ranged 323.10 ± 2.10 to 484.40 ± 0.10 (mg/l). The maximum value recorded 484.40 ± 0.10 (mg/l) and coefficient variation was 0.02 per cent was recorded in September; minimum value recorded 323.10 ± 2.10 (mg/l) and coefficient variation was 0.64 per cent was recorded in April.

In the study January-December 2008 seasonal mean and coefficient variation values recorded 386.62 ± 52.51 (mg/l) and 13.58 per cent during summer, 442.42 ± 15.48 (mg/l) and 3.49 per cent during monsoon, 437.57 ± 11.95 (mg/l) and 2.73 per cent during winter (Fig. 3.13). In the second year study January-December 2009 seasonal mean and coefficient variation values recorded 398.10 ± 50.11 (mg/l) and 12.58 per cent during summer, 462.45 ± 16.05 (mg/l) and 3.47 and per cent during winter 451.52 ± 21.26 (mg/l) and 4.70 per cent during winter (Table 3.25 and Fig. 3.14).

North Site

In the study January-December 2008 at north site the total solids ranged 319.60 ± 19.10 to 473.50 ± 8.70 (mg/l). The maximum value recorded 473.50 ± 8.70 (mg/l) and coefficient variation was 1.83 per cent was recorded in September and minimum value recorded 319.60 ± 19.10 (mg/l) and coefficient variation was 5.97 per cent was recorded in April. In the second year study January-December 2009 the total solids at north site ranged 326.20 ± 3.10 to 482.40 ± 0.97 (mg/l). The maximum value recorded 482.40 ± 0.97 (mg/l) and coefficient variation was 0.20 per cent was recorded in September; minimum value recorded 326.20 ± 3.10 (mg/l) and coefficient variation was 0.95 per cent was recorded in April.

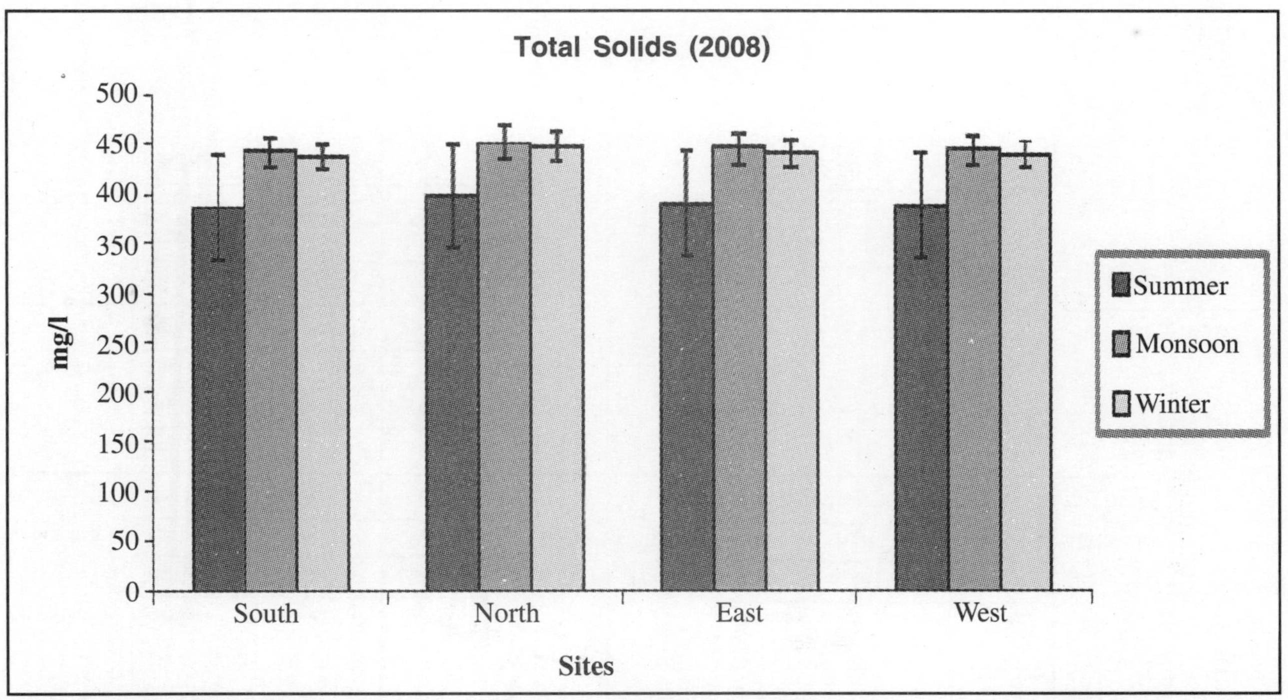

Fig. 3.13: Seasonal Variations in Total Solids (mg/l) at Different Sites of Harsool-Savangi Dam January to December 2008

Table 3.25: Seasonal Variations in Total Solids (mg/l) at South Site, Harsool-Savangi Dam

Season	Months Jan. 2008 - Dec. 2008	Monthly Mean Values	Monthly C.V. (%)	Seasonal Mean Values	Seasonal C.V. (%)	Months Jan. 2009 - Dec. 2009	Monthly Mean Values	Monthly C.V. (%)	Seasonal Mean Values	Seasonal C.V. (%)
Summer	February	417±2.19	0.52	386.62±52.51	13.58	February	418.6±2.10	0.50	398.10±50.11	12.58
	March	409.1±2.13	0.52			March	423.7±2.19	0.51		
	April	308±2.95	0.95			April	323.1±2.10	0.64		
	May	412.4±1.91	0.46			May	427±3.19	0.74		
Monsoon	June	428.1±1.31	0.30	442.42±15.48	3.49	June	448.2±1.09	0.24	462.45±16.05	3.47
	July	431.5±0.59	0.13			July	453.2±1.19	0.26		
	August	448.9±0.31	0.06			August	464±0.93	0.20		
	September	461.2±1.10	0.23			September	484.4±0.10	0.02		
Winter	October	452±2.50	0.55	437.57±11.95	2.73	October	479.4±2.0	0.41	451.52±21.26	4.70
	November	440.9±0.90	0.20			November	455±1.19	0.26		
	December	433.8±1.17	0.26			December	442±1.70	0.38		
	January	423.6±1.0	0.23			January	429.7±2.05	0.47		

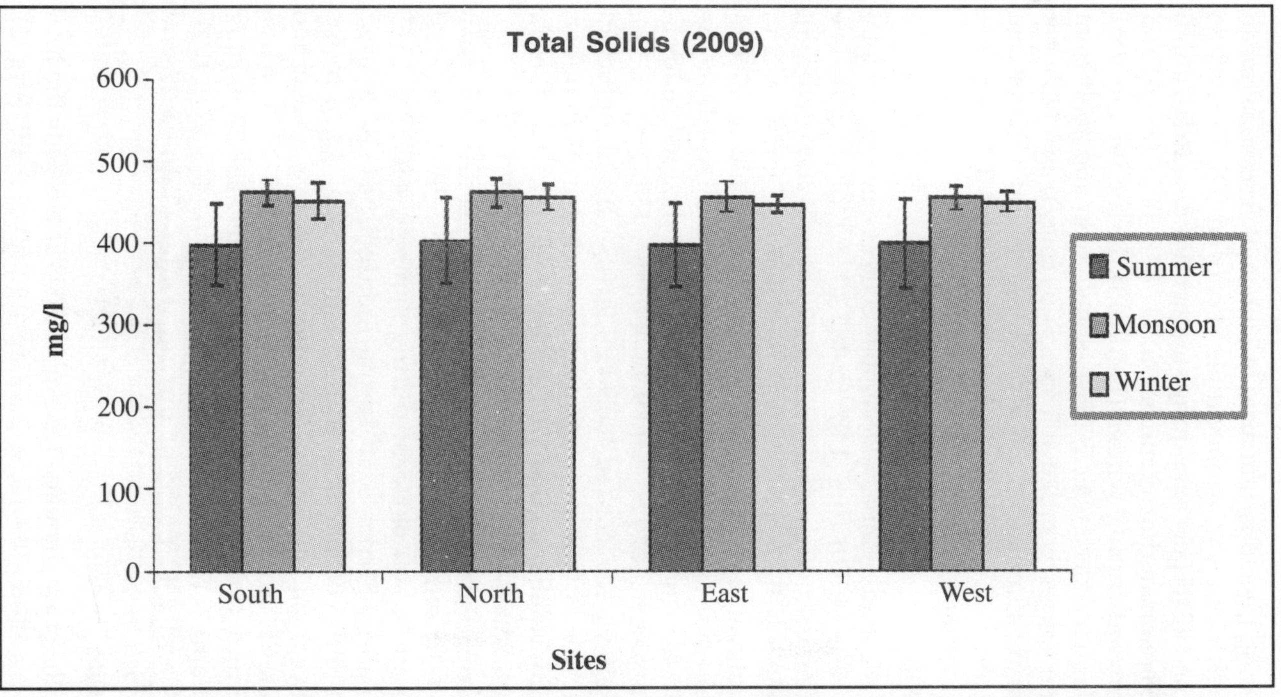

Fig. 3.14: Seasonal Variations in Total Solids (mg/l) at Different Sites of Harsool-Savangi Dam January to December 2009

During the study January-December 2008 seasonal mean and coefficient variation values recorded 397.35 ± 51.86 (mg/l) and 13.05 per cent during summer, 451.87 ± 16.50 (mg/l) and 3.65 per cent during monsoon, 447.82 ± 14.58 (mg/l) and 3.25 per cent during winter (Fig. 3.13). In the second year study January-December 2009 seasonal mean and coefficient variation values recorded 403.55 ± 51.65 (mg/l) and 12.79 per cent during summer, 462.30 ± 17.38 (mg/l) and 3.76 per cent during monsoon, 455.27 ± 15.60 (mg/l) and 3.42 per cent during winter (Table 3.26 and Fig. 3.14).

East Site

In the study January-December 2008 at east site the total solids ranged 310.10 ± 1.07 to 465.40 ± 1.29 (mg/l). The maximum value recorded 465.40 ± 1.29 (mg/l) and coefficient variation was 0.27 per cent was recorded in September and minimum value recorded 310.10 ± 1.07 (mg/l) and coefficient variation was 0.34 per cent was recorded in April. In the second year study January-December 2009 the total solids at east site ranged 320.50 ± 1.19 to 480.90 ± 1.90 (mg/l). The maximum value recorded 480.90 ± 1.90 (mg/l) and coefficient variation was 0.39 per cent was recorded in September; minimum value recorded 320.50 ± 1.19 (mg/l) and coefficient variation was 0.37 per cent was recorded in April.

During the study January-December 2008 seasonal mean and coefficient variation values recorded 389.95 ± 53.34 (mg/l) and 13.68 per cent during summer, 446.27 ± 15.69 (mg/l) and 3.51 per cent during monsoon, 441.82 ± 13.55 (mg/l) and 3.06 per cent during winter (Fig. 3.13). In the second year study January-December 2009 seasonal mean and coefficient variation values recorded 397.72 ± 51.56 (mg/l) and 12.56 per cent during summer, 456.20 ± 18.78 (mg/l) and 4.11 per cent during monsoon, 447.55 ± 10.87 (mg/l) and 2.42 per cent during winter (Table 3.27 and Fig. 3.14).

West Site

In the study January-December 2008 at west site the total solids ranged 309.10 ± 2.17 to 462.50 ± 1.00 (mg/l).

Table 3.26: Seasonal Variations in Total Solids (mg/l) at North Site, Harsool-Savangi Dam

Season	Months Jan. 2008 - Dec. 2008	Monthly Mean Values	Monthly C.V. (%)	Seasonal Mean Values	Seasonal C.V. (%)	Months Jan. 2009 - Dec. 2009	Monthly Mean Values	Monthly C.V. (%)	Seasonal Mean Values	Seasonal C.V. (%)
	February	425.7±2.10	0.49			February	428.8±4.21	0.98		
	March	421.4±7.50	1.77			March	426±2.35	0.55		
Summer	April	319.6±19.10	5.97	397.35±51.86	13.05	April	326.2±3.10	0.95	403.55±51.65	12.79
	May	422.7±8.50	2.01			May	433.2±2.19	0.50		
	June	435.9±2.55	0.58			June	442.9±2.30	0.51		
	July	442.8±3.0	0.67			July	454±1.19	0.26		
Monsoon	August	455.3±3.90	0.85	451.87±16.50	3.65	August	469.9±0.91	0.19	462.30±17.38	3.76
	September	473.5±8.70	1.83			September	482.4±0.97	0.20		
	October	463.7±4.30	0.92			October	470.9±1.27	0.26		
	November	453±1.90	0.41			November	462.6±1.29	0.27		
Winter	December	445.6±1.10	0.24	447.82±14.58	3.25	December	453±2.21	0.48	455.27±15.60	3.42
	January	429±7.13	1.66			January	434.6±2.0	0.46		

Table 3.27: Seasonal Variations in Total Solids (mg/l) at East Site, Harsool-Savangi Dam

Season	Months Jan. 2008 - Dec. 2008	Monthly Mean Values	Monthly C.V. (%)	Seasonal Mean Values	Seasonal C.V. (%)	Months Jan. 2009 - Dec. 2009	Monthly Mean Values	Monthly C.V. (%)	Seasonal Mean Values	Seasonal C.V. (%)
Summer	February	420.8±5.10	1.21	389.95±53.34	13.68	February	426.9±2.01	0.47	397.72±51.56	12.96
	March	412.3±1.19	0.28			March	419.9±2.17	0.51		
	April	**310.1±1.07**	0.34			April	**320.5±1.19**	0.37		
	May	416.6±2.10	0.50			May	423.6±1.71	0.40		
Monsoon	June	430.5±1.10	0.25	446.27±15.69	3.51	June	440±0.91	0.20	456.20±18.78	4.11
	July	436.9±2.0	0.45			July	443.3±0.57	0.12		
	August	452.3±1.90	0.42			August	460.6±1.10	0.23		
	September	**465.4±1.29**	0.27			September	**480.9±1.90**	0.39		
Winter	October	456.5±1.91	0.41	441.82±13.55	3.06	October	461.3±2.10	0.45	447.55±10.87	2.42
	November	447.8±0.50	0.11			November	450.9±2.0	0.44		
	December	438.1±0.19	0.04			December	441±1.97	0.44		
	January	424.9±5.10	1.20			January	437±3.05	0.69		

The maximum value recorded 462.50 ± 1.00 (mg/l) and coefficient variation was 0.21 per cent was recorded in September and minimum value recorded 309.10 ± 2.17 (mg/l) and coefficient variation was 0.70 per cent was recorded in April. In the second year study January-December 2009 the total solids at west site ranged 317.20 ± 1.07 to 474 ± 2.70 (mg/l). The maximum value recorded 474 ± 2.70 (mg/l) and coefficient variation was 0.56 per cent was recorded in September; minimum value recorded 317.20 ± 1.07 (mg/l) and coefficient variation was 0.33 per cent was recorded in April.

During the study January-December 2008 seasonal mean and coefficient variation values recorded 388.90 ± 53.31 (mg/l) and 13.70 per cent during summer, 444.47 ± 15.18 (mg/l) and 3.41 per cent during monsoon, 439.87 ± 12.95 (mg/l) and 2.94 per cent during winter (Fig. 3.13). In the second year study January-December 2009 seasonal mean and coefficient variation values recorded 398.82 ± 54.51 (mg/l) and 13.67 per cent during summer, 455.60 ± 14.38 (mg/l) and 3.15 per cent during monsoon, 450.20 ± 12.78 (mg/l) and 2.84 per cent during winter (Table 3.28 Fig. 3.14).

In the present study January to December 2008 the maximum total solids were recorded during monsoon season at north site and minimum total solids was recorded in summer season at south site. In the second year study January-December 2009 the maximum total solids were recorded during monsoon season at south site where as minimum total solids were recorded during summer season at west site (Tables 3.25, 3.26 and 3.28).

During the study January 2008-December 2009 total solids indicating significant positive correlation with turbidity, electric conductivity, total solid, total dissolved solids, total suspended solids, dissolved oxygen, biochemical oxygen demand, chemical oxygen demand, transparency, total hardness, nitrate and phosphate and it indicating significant negative correlation with water temperature, transparency, pH, alkalinity, chloride and fish (Table 4.7 and 4.8).

Table 3.28: Seasonal Variations in Total Solids (mg/l) at Eest Site, Harsool-Savangi Dam

Season	Months Jan. 2008 - Dec. 2008	Monthly Mean Values	Monthly C.V. (%)	Seasonal Mean Values	Seasonal C.V. (%)	Months Jan. 2009 - Dec. 2009	Monthly Mean Values	Monthly C.V. (%)	Seasonal Mean Values	Seasonal C.V. (%)
Summer	February	419.6±2.17	0.51	388.90±53.31	13.70	February	429.2±2.51	0.58	398.82±54.51	13.67
	March	411.2±2.19	0.53			March	421.4±2.33	0.55		
	April	309.1±2.17	0.70			April	317.2±1.07	0.33		
	May	415.7±1.91	0.45			May	427.5±1.71	0.40		
Monsoon	June	429.3±1.79	0.41	444.47±15.18	3.41	June	440.5±1.0	0.22	455.60±14.38	3.15
	July	434.9±0.93	0.21			July	449±2.50	0.55		
	August	451.2±0.12	0.02			August	458.9±1.10	0.23		
	September	462.5±1.0	0.21			September	474±2.70	0.56		
Winter	October	454.4±1.90	0.41	439.87±12.95	2.94	October	463.2±0.97	0.20	450.20±12.78	2.84
	November	445±1.19	0.26			November	457±0.50	0.10		
	December	436.1±0.95	0.21			December	446.6±0.17	0.03		
	January	424±3.01	0.70			January	434±3.19	0.73		

In the present study, the total solids were maximum during monsoon and minimum during summer. High values of total solids during monsoon due to siltation, deterioration, heavy precipitation and mixing run off rain water which carries mud, sand etc mixed in the dam water.

Total Dissolved Solids (TDS)

Total dissolved solids denote various types of minerals present in water. They do not contain any gas and colloids. In natural water dissolved solids are salts and variety of organic substances which readily dissolve in water and often impart a degree of hardness. The excessive total dissolved solids generally affect palatability. The total dissolved solids are indirectly proportional to temperature and directly proportional to levels of calcium and magnesium, phosphate and nitrate (Gonzalves and Joshi, 1946). Verma *et al*. (1978) observed that the excess amounts of dissolved solids resulted in to high osmotic pressure which caused imbalance of osmotic regulation and suffocation in the drain water.

South Site

During the study January-December 2008 at south site the total dissolved solids ranged 300 ± 11.32 to 449 ± 8.11 (mg/l). The maximum value recorded 449 ± 8.11 (mg/l) and coefficient variation was 1.80 per cent was recorded in September and minimum value recorded 300 ± 11.32 (mg/l) and coefficient variation was 3.77 per cent was recorded in April. In the second year study January-December 2009 the total dissolved solids at south site ranged 315 ± 12.81 to 472.30 ± 8.50 (mg/l). The maximum value recorded 472.30 ± 8.50 (mg/l) and coefficient variation was 1.79 per cent was recorded in September; minimum value recorded 315 ± 12.81 (mg/l) and coefficient variation was 4.06 per cent was recorded in April.

In the study January-December 2008 seasonal mean and coefficient variation values recorded 378.50 ± 52.43 (mg/l) and 13.85 per cent during summer, 431 ± 14.71 (mg/l) and 3.41 per cent during monsoon, 428.25 ± 10.99 (mg/l) and 2.56

per cent during winter (Fig. 3.15). In the second year study January-December 2009 seasonal mean and coefficient variation values recorded 389.75 ± 49.95 (mg/l) and 12.81 per cent during summer, 450.95 ± 15.42 (mg/l) and 3.42 and per cent during winter 440.75 ± 19.67 (mg/l) and 4.46 per cent during winter (Table 3.29 and Fig. 3.16).

North Site

In the study January-December 2008 at north site the total dissolved solids ranged 310.30 ± 9.25 to 460.50 ± 5.10 (mg/l). The maximum value recorded 460.50 ± 5.10 (mg/l) and coefficient variation was 1.10 per cent was recorded in September and minimum value recorded 310.30 ± 9.25 (mg/l) and coefficient variation was 2.98 per cent was recorded in April. In the second year study January-December 2009 the total dissolved solids at north site ranged 316 ± 6.71 to 469 ± 2.10 (mg/l). The maximum value recorded 469 ± 2.10 (mg/l) and coefficient variation was 0.44 per cent was recorded in September; minimum value recorded 316 ± 6.71 (mg/l) and coefficient variation was 2.12 per cent was recorded in April.

During the study January-December 2008 seasonal mean and coefficient variation values recorded 387.95 ± 51.80 (mg/l) and 13.35 per cent during summer, 439.87 ± 15.65 (mg/l) and 3.55 per cent during monsoon, 437.07 ± 13.07 (mg/l) and 2.99 per cent during winter (Fig. 3.15). In the second year study January-December 2009 seasonal mean and coefficient variation values recorded 393.37 ± 51.65 (mg/l) and 13.13 per cent during summer, 450 ± 16.30 (mg/l) and 3.62 per cent during monsoon, 444.02 ± 14.27 (mg/l) and 3.21 per cent during winter (Table 3.30 and Fig. 3.16).

East Site

In the study January-December 2008 at east site the total dissolved solids ranged 301.90 ± 14.01 to 453 ± 1.90 (mg/l). The maximum value recorded 453 ± 1.90 (mg/l) and coefficient variation was 0.41 per cent was recorded in September and minimum value recorded 301.90 ± 14.01 (mg/l) and coefficient variation was 4.64 per cent was recorded in April.

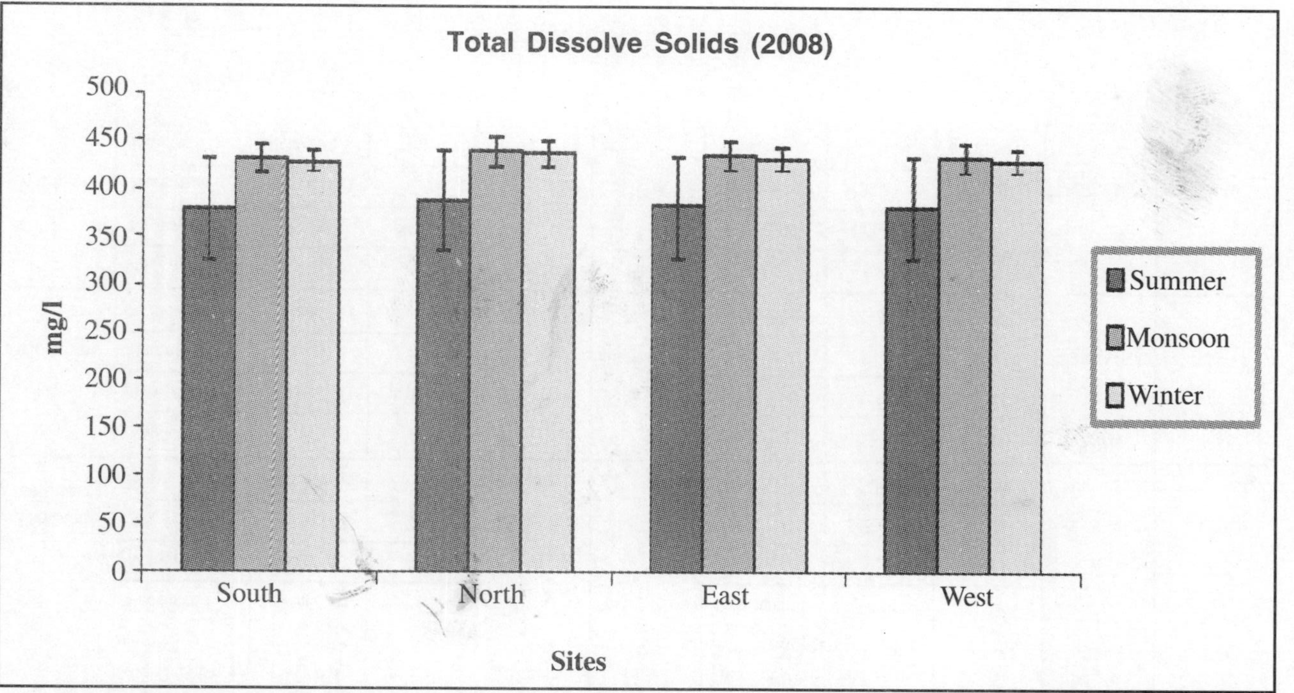

Fig. 3.15: Seasonal Variations in Total Dissolve Solids (mg/l) at Different Sites of Harsool-Savangi Dam January to December 2008

Table 3.29: Seasonal Variations in Total Dissolve Solids (mg/l) at South Site, Harsool-Savangi Dam

Season	Months Jan. 2008 - Dec. 2008	Monthly Mean Values	Monthly C.V. (%)	Seasonal Mean Values	Seasonal C.V. (%)	Months Jan. 2009 - Dec. 2009	Monthly Mean Values	Monthly C.V. (%)	Seasonal Mean Values	Seasonal C.V. (%)
Summer	February	409±3.09	0.75	378.50±52.43	13.85	February	410±4.85	1.18	389.75±49.95	12.81
	March	401±1.25	0.31			March	415.5±0.90	0.21		
	April	300±11.32	3.77			April	315±12.81	4.06		
	May	404±19.45	4.81			May	418.5±15.1	3.60		
Monsoon	June	418±5.03	1.20	431±14.71	3.41	June	438±6.65	1.51	450.95±15.42	3.42
	July	420±2.10	0.50			July	441.5±6.70	1.51		
	August	437±7.0	1.60			August	452±7.35	1.62		
	September	449±8.11	1.80			September	472.3±8.50	1.79		
Winter	October	441±4.40	0.99	428.25±10.99	2.56	October	467±3.70	0.79	440.75±19.67	4.46
	November	432±5.65	1.30			November	443±2.10	0.47		
	December	425±2.30	0.54			December	432±1.45	0.33		
	January	415±0.25	0.06			January	421±1.03	0.24		

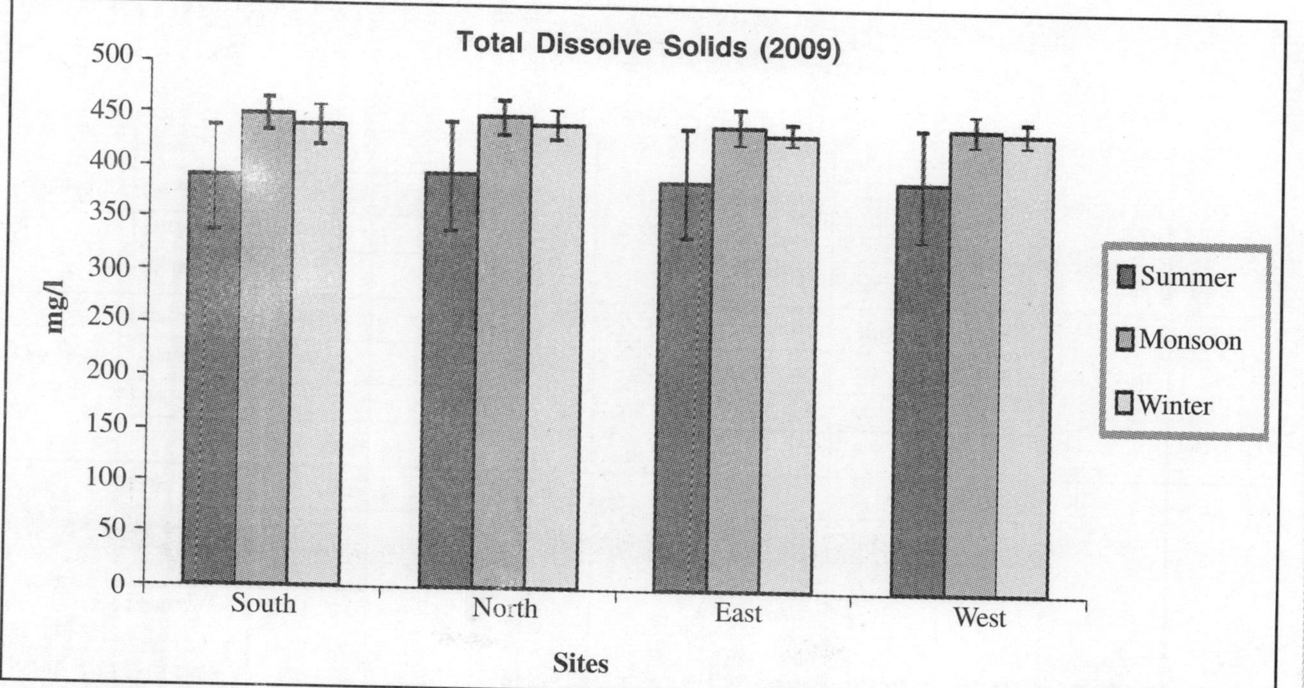

Fig. 3.16: Seasonal Variations in Total Dissolve Solids (mg/l) at Different Sites of Harsool-Savangi Dam January to December 2009

Table 3.30: Seasonal Variations in Total Dissolve Solids (mg/l) at North Site, Harsool-Savangi Dam

Season	Months Jan. 2008 - Dec. 2008	Monthly Mean Values	Monthly C.V. (%)	Seasonal Mean Values	Seasonal C.V. (%)	Months Jan. 2009 - Dec. 2009	Monthly Mean Values	Monthly C.V. (%)	Seasonal Mean Values	Seasonal C.V. (%)
Summer	February	416.5±2.80	0.67	387.95±51.80	13.35	February	419±1.19	0.28	393.37±51.65	13.13
	March	412±1.31	0.31			March	416±3.14	0.75		
	April	310.3±9.25	2.98			April	316±6.71	2.12		
	May	413±3.10	0.75			May	422.5±2.28	0.53		
Monsoon	June	425±2.35	0.55	439.87±15.65	3.55	June	432±4.08	0.94	450±16.30	3.62
	July	431±3.09	0.71			July	442±3.11	0.70		
	August	443±2.25	0.50			August	457±3.15	0.68		
	September	460.5±5.1	1.10			September	469±2.10	0.44		
Winter	October	451±2.35	0.52	437.07±13.07	2.99	October	458±5.10	1.11	444.02±14.27	3.21
	November	442±1.22	0.27			November	451.1±3.30	0.73		
	December	435.3±1.10	0.25			December	442±0.27	0.06		
	January	420±0.90	0.21			January	425±1.42	0.33		

In the second year study January-December 2009 the total dissolved solids at east site ranged 312 ± 25.10 to 467 ± 4.01 (mg/l). The maximum value recorded 467 ± 4.01 (mg/l) and coefficient variation was 0.85 per cent was recorded in September; minimum value recorded 312 ± 25.10 (mg/l) and coefficient variation was 8.00 per cent was recorded in April.

During the study January-December 2008 seasonal mean and coefficient variation values recorded 381.50 ± 53.16 (mg/l) and 13.93 per cent during summer, 434.55 ± 15.00 (mg/l) and 3.45 per cent during monsoon, 431.92 ± 12.44 (mg/l) and 2.88 per cent during winter (Fig. 3.15). In the second year study January-December 2009 seasonal mean and coefficient variation values recorded 389.05 ± 51.44 (mg/l) and 13.22 per cent during summer, 443.80 ± 17.39 (mg/l) and 3.92 per cent during monsoon, 436.87 ± 9.43 (mg/l) and 2.16 per cent during winter (Table 3.31 and Fig. 3.16).

West Site

During study January-December 2008 at west site the total dissolved solids ranged 301 ± 17.30 to 450.10 ± 2.12 (mg/l). The maximum value recorded 450.10 ± 2.12 (mg/l) and coefficient variation was 0.47 per cent was recorded in September and minimum value recorded 301 ± 17.30 (mg/l) and coefficient variation was 5.74 per cent was recorded in April. In the second year study January-December 2009 the total dissolved solids at west site ranged 309 ± 19.00 to 462 ± 2.05 (mg/l). The maximum value recorded 462 ± 2.05 (mg/l) and coefficient variation was 0.44 per cent was recorded in September; minimum value recorded 309 ± 19.00 (mg/l) and coefficient variation was 6.14 per cent was recorded in April.

In study January-December 2008 seasonal mean and coefficient variation values recorded 380.55 ± 53.13 (mg/l) and 13.96 per cent during summer, 432.80 ± 14.48 (mg/l) and 3.34 per cent during monsoon, 430.07 ± 11.89 (mg/l) and 2.76 per cent during winter (Fig. 3.15). In the second year study January-December 2009 seasonal mean and coefficient variation values recorded 389.70 ± 53.88 (mg/l) and 13.82 per cent during summer, 442.75 ± 14.59 (mg/l) and 3.29 per cent during monsoon, 439.70 ± 11.55 (mg/l) and 2.62 per cent during winter (Table 3.32 and Fig. 3.16).

Table 3.31: Seasonal Variations in Total Dissolve Solids (mg/l) at East Site, Harsool-Savangi Dam

Season	Months Jan. 2008 - Dec. 2008	Monthly Mean Values	Monthly C.V. (%)	Seasonal Mean Values	Seasonal C.V. (%)	Months Jan. 2009 - Dec. 2009	Monthly Mean Values	Monthly C.V. (%)	Seasonal Mean Values	Seasonal C.V. (%)
	February	412.1±3.71	0.90			February	418±4.31	1.03		
	March	404±4.19	1.03			March	411.2±7.25	1.76		
Summer	April	301.9±14.01	4.64	381.50±53.16	13.93	April	312±25.1	8.00	389.05±51.44	13.22
	May	408±6.87	1.68			May	415±11.5	2.77		
	June	420±3.15	0.75			June	429±3.09	0.72		
	July	425±2.17	0.51			July	432±5.12	1.18		
Monsoon	August	440.2±2.10	0.47	434.55±15.00	3.45	August	447.2±2.15	0.48	443.80±17.39	3.92
	September	453±1.90	0.41			September	467±4.01	0.85		
	October	445±0.52	0.11			October	449±2.20	0.48		
	November	437.6±0.27	0.06			November	439.5±1.57	0.35		
Winter	December	429.1±1.10	0.25	431.92±12.44	2.88	December	431±1.25	0.29	436.87±9.43	2.16
	January	416±2.50	0.60			January	428±0.30	0.07		

Table 3.32: Seasonal Variations in Total Dissolve Solids (mg/l) at West Site, Harsool-Savangi Dam

Season	Months Jan. 2008 - Dec. 2008	Monthly Mean Values	Monthly C.V. (%)	Seasonal Mean Values	Seasonal C.V. (%)	Months Jan. 2009 - Dec. 2009	Monthly Mean Values	Monthly C.V. (%)	Seasonal Mean Values	Seasonal C.V. (%)
	February	411±4.17	1.01			February	420.5±3.01	0.71		
	March	403±7.28	1.80			March	413±7.30	1.76		
Summer	April	301±17.3	5.74	380.55±53.13	13.96	April	309±19.0	6.14	389.70±53.88	13.82
	May	407.2±11.03	2.70			May	416.3±13.4	3.21		
Monsoon	June	418.9±3.17	0.75			June	428±5.50	1.28		
	July	423±5.81	1.37			July	436±4.32	0.99		
	August	439.2±3.01	0.68	432.80±14.48	3.34	August	445±2.11	0.47	442.75±14.59	3.29
	September	450.1±2.12	0.47			September	462±2.05	0.44		
Winter	October	443.1±1.03	0.23			October	451.3±2.0	0.44		
	November	435±1.0	0.22			November	446±3.15	0.70		
	December	427±2.4	0.56	430.07±11.89	2.76	December	436.5±0.19	0.04	439.70±11.55	2.62
	January	415.2±1.80	0.43			January	425±1.11	0.26		

In the present study January to December 2008 the maximum total dissolved solids were recorded during monsoon season at north site and minimum total dissolved solids was recorded in summer season at south site. In the second year study January-December 2009 the maximum total dissolved solids were recorded during monsoon season at south site where as minimum total dissolved solids were recorded during summer season at west site (Tables 3.29, 3.30 and 3.32).

During the study January 2008-December 2009 total dissolved solids indicating significant positive correlation with turbidity, electric conductivity, total solids, total suspended solids, dissolved oxygen, biochemical oxygen demand, chemical oxygen demand, total hardness, nitrate and phosphate and it indicating significant negative correlation with water temperature, transparency, pH, alkalinity, chloride and fish (Table 4.7 and 4.8).

In the present study, the total dissolved solids were maximum during monsoon and minimum during summer. High values of total dissolved solids during monsoon may be due to siltation, deterioration, heavy precipitation and mixing run off rain water which carries mud, sand etc mixed in the dam water.

Total Suspended Solids (TSS)

Considering environmental samples, the general idea is that "The more TSS in the water, it is more polluted". Total suspended solids concentrations and turbidity both indicate the amount of solids suspended in the water, whether mineral or organic. Total suspended solids can block fish gills, either killing them or reducing their growth rate. They also reduce light penetration. This reduces the ability of algae to produce food and oxygen. When the water slows down, when it enters a reservoir, a process called siltation. This causes the water to clear, but as the silt or sediment settles it may change the bottom. This silt may bottom-dwelling organisms, cover breeding areas and eggs. The National Academy of Sciences has recommended that the concentration of TSS should not reduce light penetration by more than 10 per cent.

South Site

The study January-December 2008 at south site the total suspended solids ranged 8 ± 0.10 to 12.20 ± 0.09 (mg/l). The maximum value recorded 12.20 ± 0.09 (mg/l) and coefficient variation was 0.73 per cent was recorded in September and minimum value recorded 8 ± 0.10 (mg/l) and coefficient variation was 1.25 per cent was recorded in April. During second year study January-December 2009 the total suspended solids at south site ranged 8.10 ± 0.25 to 12.40 ± 0.17 (mg/l). The maximum value recorded 12.40 ± 0.17 (mg/l) and coefficient variation was 1.37 per cent was recorded in October; minimum value recorded 8.10 ± 0.25 (mg/l) and coefficient variation was 3.08 per cent was recorded in April.

During study January-December 2008 seasonal mean and coefficient variation values recorded 8.25 ± 0.23 (mg/l) and 2.88 per cent during summer, 11.42 ± 0.92 (mg/l) and 8.12 per cent during monsoon, 9.57 ± 1.10 (mg/l) and 11.57 per cent during winter (Fig. 3.17). In the second year study January-December 2009 seasonal mean and coefficient variation values recorded 8.35 ± 0.23 (mg/l) and 2.85 per cent during summer, 11.50 ± 0.88 (mg/l) and 7.67 and per cent during winter 10.77 ± 1.73 (mg/l) and 16.11 per cent during winter (Table 3.33 and Fig. 3.18).

North Site

In the study January-December 2008 at north site the total suspended solids ranged 9 ± 0.55 to 13 ± 0.21 (mg/l). The maximum value recorded 13 ± 0.21 (mg/l) and coefficient variation was 1.61 per cent was recorded in September and minimum value recorded 9 ± 0.55 (mg/l) and coefficient variation was 6.11 per cent was recorded in January. In the second year study January-December 2009 the total suspended solids at north site ranged 9.60 ± 0.10 to 13.40 ± 0.23 (mg/l). The maximum value recorded 13.40 ± 0.23 (mg/l) and coefficient variation was 1.71 per cent was recorded in September; minimum value recorded 9.60 ± 0.10 (mg/l) and coefficient variation was 1.04 per cent was recorded in January.

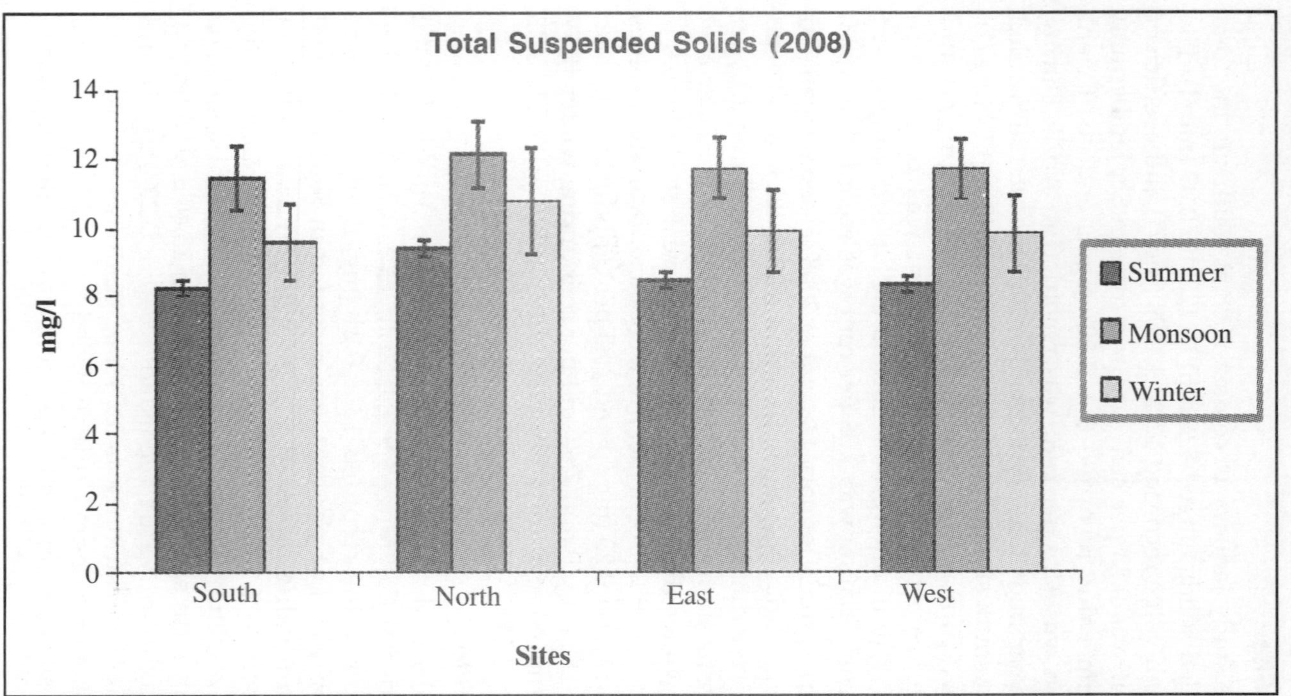

Fig. 3.17: Seasonal Variations in Total Suspended Solids (mg/l) at Different Sites of Harsool-Savangi Dam January to December 2008

Table 3.33: Seasonal Variations in Total Suspended Solids (mg/l) at South Site, Harsool-Savangi Dam

Season	Months Jan. 2008 - Dec. 2008	Monthly Mean Values	Monthly C.V. (%)	Seasonal Mean Values	Seasonal C.V. (%)	Months Jan. 2009 - Dec. 2009	Monthly Mean Values	Monthly C.V. (%)	Seasonal Mean Values	Seasonal C.V. (%)
	February	8.5±0.17	2.00			February	8.6±0.01	0.11		
	March	8.1±0.11	1.35			March	8.2±0.20	2.43		
Summer	April	8±0.10	1.25	8.25±0.23	2.88	April	8.1±0.25	3.08	8.35±0.23	2.85
	May	8.4±0.21	2.50			May	8.5±0.15	1.76		
	June	10.1±1.25	12.37			June	10.2±1.01	9.90		
	July	11.5±0.75	6.52			July	11.7±0.11	0.94		
Monsoon	August	11.9±0.25	2.10	11.42±0.92	8.12	August	12±0.23	1.91	11.5±0.88	7.67
	September	12.2±0.09	0.73			September	12.1±0.19	1.57		
	October	11±1.12	10.18			October	12.4±0.17	1.37		
	November	9.9±0.19	1.91			November	12±0.19	1.58		
Winter	December	8.8±0.27	3.06	9.57±1.10	11.57	December	10±0.13	1.30	10.77±1.73	16.11
	January	8.6±0.31	3.60			January	8.7±1.03	11.83		

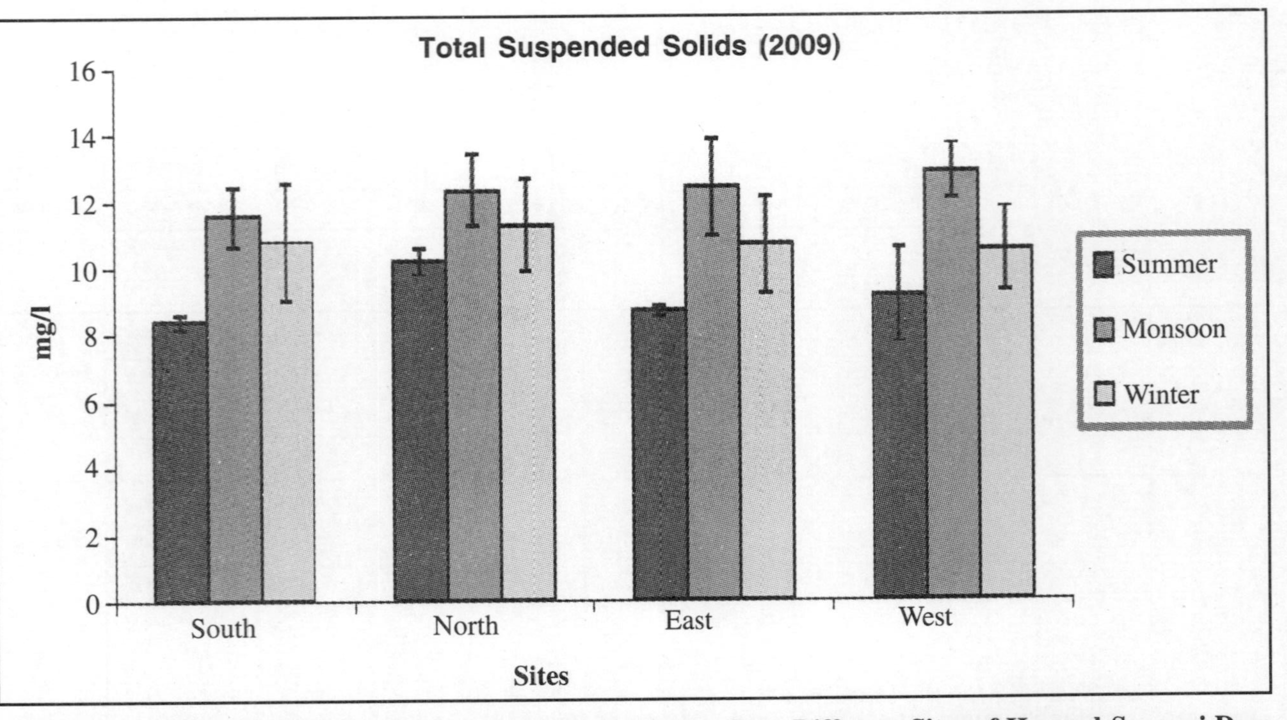

Fig. 3.18: Seasonal Variations in Total Suspended Solids (mg/l) at Different Sites of Harsool-Savangi Dam January to December 2009

During the study January-December 2008 seasonal mean and coefficient variation values recorded 9.40 ± 0.21 (mg/l) and 2.29 per cent during summer, 12.12 ± 0.97 (mg/l) and 8.00 per cent during monsoon, 10.75 ± 1.54 (mg/l) and 14.34 per cent during winter (Fig. 3.17). In the second year study January-December 2009 seasonal mean and coefficient variation values recorded 10.17 ± 0.38 (mg/l) and 3.79 per cent during summer, 12.30 ± 1.09 (mg/l) and 8.93 per cent during monsoon, 11.25 ± 1.36 (mg/l) and 12.11 per cent during winter (Table 3.34 and Fig. 3.18).

East Site

In study January-December 2008 at east site the total suspended solids ranged 8.20 ± 0.19 to 12.40 ± 0.03 (mg/l). The maximum value recorded 12.40 ± 0.03 (mg/l) and coefficient variation was 0.24 per cent was recorded in September and minimum value recorded 8.20 ± 0.19 (mg/l) and coefficient variation was 2.31 per cent was recorded in April. In the second year study January-December 2009 the total suspended solids at east site ranged 8.50 ± 0.19 to 13.90 ± 0.27 (mg/l). The maximum value recorded 13.90 ± 0.27 (mg/l) and coefficient variation was 1.94 per cent was recorded in September; minimum value recorded 8.50 ± 0.19 (mg/l) and coefficient variation was 2.23 per cent was recorded in April.

During the study January-December 2008 seasonal mean and coefficient variation values recorded 8.45 ± 0.23 (mg/l) and 2.81 per cent during summer, 11.72 ± 0.84 (mg/l) and 7.18 per cent during monsoon, 9.90 ± 1.21 (mg/l) and 12.31 per cent during winter (Fig. 3.17). In the second year study January-December 2009 seasonal mean and coefficient variation values recorded 8.67 ± 0.17 (mg/l) and 1.96 per cent during summer, 12.40 ± 1.46 (mg/l) and 11.79 and per cent during winter 10.67 ± 1.46 (mg/l) and 13.71 per cent during winter (Tables 3.35 and Fig. 3.18).

West Site

In study January-December 2008 at west site the total suspended solids ranged 8.10 ± 0.19 to 12.40 ± 0.24 (mg/l).

Table 3.34: Seasonal Variations in Total Suspended Solids (mg/l) at North Site, Harsool-Savangi Dam

Season	Months Jan. 2008 - Dec. 2008	Monthly Mean Values	Monthly C.V. (%)	Seasonal Mean Values	Seasonal C.V. (%)	Months Jan. 2009 - Dec. 2009	Monthly Mean Values	Monthly C.V. (%)	Seasonal Mean Values	Seasonal C.V. (%)
Summer	February	9.2±0.13	1.41	9.40±0.21	2.29	February	9.8±0.20	2.04	10.17±0.38	3.79
	March	9.4±0.15	1.59			March	10±0.19	1.90		
	April	9.3±0.11	1.18			April	10.2±0.10	0.98		
	May	9.7±0.07	0.72			May	10.7±0.15	1.40		
Monsoon	June	10.9±0.93	8.53	12.12±0.97	8.00	June	10.9±0.21	1.92	12.30±1.09	8.93
	July	11.8±0.87	7.37			July	12±0.17	1.41		
	August	12.8±0.91	7.10			August	12.9±0.25	1.93		
	September	13±0.21	1.61			September	13.4±0.23	1.71		
Winter	October	12.7±0.15	1.18	10.75±1.54	14.34	October	12.9±0.15	1.16	11.25±1.36	12.11
	November	11±0.50	4.54			November	11.5±0.10	0.86		
	December	10.3±0.19	1.84			December	11±0.29	2.63		
	January	9±0.55	6.11			January	9.6±0.10	1.04		

Table 3.35: Seasonal Variations in Total Suspended Solids (mg/l) at East Site, Harsool-Savangi Dam

Season	Months Jan. 2008 - Dec. 2008	Monthly Mean Values	Monthly C.V. (%)	Seasonal Mean Values	Seasonal C.V. (%)	Months Jan. 2009 - Dec. 2009	Monthly Mean Values	Monthly C.V. (%)	Seasonal Mean Values	Seasonal C.V. (%)
	February	8.7±0.17	1.95			February	8.9±0.01	0.11		
	March	8.3±0.10	1.20			March	8.7±0.11	1.26		
Summer	April	8.2±0.19	2.31	8.45±0.23	2.81	April	8.5±0.19	2.23	8.67±0.17	1.96
	May	8.6±0.13	1.51			May	8.6±0.13	1.51		
	June	10.5±1.15	10.95			June	11±0.19	1.72		
	July	11.9±0.07	0.58			July	11.3±0.23	2.03		
Monsoon	August	12.1±0.90	7.43	11.72±0.84	7.18	August	13.4±0.13	0.97	12.40±1.46	11.79
	September	12.4±0.03	0.24			September	13.9±0.27	1.94		
Winter	October	11.5±0.91	7.91	9.90±1.21	12.31	October	12.3±0.90	7.31		
	November	10.2±0.75	7.35			November	11.4±0.95	8.33		
Winter	December	9±0.23	2.55	9.90±1.21	12.31	December	10±0.70	7.00	10.67±1.46	13.71
	January	8.9±0.19	2.13			January	9±0.17	1.88		

The maximum value recorded 12.40 ± 0.24 (mg/l) and coefficient variation was 1.93 per cent was recorded in September and minimum value recorded 8.10 ± 0.19 (mg/l) and coefficient variation was 2.34 per cent was recorded in April. In the second year study January-December 2009 the total suspended solids at west site ranged 8.20 ± 0.17 to 13.90 ± 0.13 (mg/l). The maximum value recorded 13.90 ± 0.13 (mg/l) and coefficient variation was 0.93 per cent was recorded in August; minimum value recorded 8.20 ± 0.17 (mg/l) and coefficient variation was 2.07 per cent was recorded in April.

During the study January-December 2008 seasonal mean and coefficient variation values recorded 8.35 ± 0.23 (mg/l) and 2.85 per cent during summer, 11.67 ± 0.87 (mg/l) and 7.51 per cent during monsoon, 9.80 ± 1.12 (mg/l) and 11.45 per cent during winter (Fig. 3.17). In the second year study January-December 2009 seasonal mean and coefficient variation values recorded 9.12 ± 1.39 (mg/l) and 15.32 per cent during summer, 12.85 ± 0.81 (mg/l) and 6.30 per cent during monsoon, 10.50 ± 1.24 (mg/l) and 11.81 per cent during winter (Table 3.36 and Fig. 3.18).

In the present study January to December 2008 the maximum total suspended solids were recorded during monsoon season at north site and minimum total suspended solids were recorded during summer season at south site. In the second year study January-December 2009 the maximum total suspended solids were recorded during monsoon season at east and west sites where as minimum total suspended solids were recorded during summer season at south site (Tables 3.33, 3.34, 3.35 and 3.36).

During the study January 2008-December 2009 total suspended solids indicating significant positive correlation with turbidity, electric conductivity, total solids, total dissolved solids, biochemical oxygen demand, chemical oxygen demand, total hardness, nitrate and phosphate and it indicating significant negative correlation with transparency and fish (Tables 4.7 and 4.8).

Table 3.36: Seasonal Variations in Total Suspended Solids (mg/l) at West Site, Harsool-Savangi Dam

Season	Months Jan. 2008 - Dec. 2008	Monthly Mean Values	Monthly C.V. (%)	Seasonal Mean Values	Seasonal C.V. (%)	Months Jan. 2009 - Dec. 2009	Monthly Mean Values	Monthly C.V. (%)	Seasonal Mean Values	Seasonal C.V. (%)
	February	8.6±0.03	0.34			February	8.7±0.17	1.95		
	March	8.2±0.17	2.07			March	8.4±0.13	1.54		
Summer	April	8.1±0.19	2.34	8.35±0.23	2.85	April	8.2±0.17	2.07	9.12±1.39	15.32
	May	8.5±0.17	2.00			May	11.2±0.10	0.89		
	June	10.4±0.90	8.65	11.67±0.87	7.51	June	12.5±0.70	5.60		
	July	11.9±0.71	5.96			July	13±0.93	7.15		
Monsoon	August	12±0.20	1.66			August	13.9±0.13	0.93	12.85±0.81	6.30
	September	12.4±0.24	1.93			September	12±0.02	0.16		
	October	11.3±0.13	1.15	9.80±1.12	11.45	October	11.9±0.01	0.08		
	November	10±0.10	1.00			November	11±0.1	0.90		
Winter	December	9.1±0.19	2.08			December	10.1±0.2	1.98	10.50±1.24	11.81
	January	8.8±0.21	2.38			January	9±0.19	2.11		

In the present study, the TSS values were maximum during monsoon and minimum during summer. High values of total suspended solids during monsoon may be due to siltation, deterioration, heavy precipitation and mixing run off rain water which carried mud, sand etc mixed in the dam water.

Dissolved Oxygen (DO)

Dissolved oxygen is one of the most important abiotic factors influencing life of an aquatic ecosystem. Its depletion perhaps is the most critical manifestation of pollution and effects of low level of dissolved oxygen. The dissolved oxygen level in natural water depends on physical, chemical and biological activities of the water body. Concentration of dissolved oxygen decreases with increase in temperature. A healthy stream or lakes should have adequate dissolved oxygen. The oxygen rich water, bacteria and protozoan and microorganisms multiply rapidly and then become food for advanced aquatic animals. The presence of dissolved oxygen is essential to maintain variety of forms of biological life in water. Non-polluted surface waters naturally saturated with dissolved oxygen (Auti, 2002).

The factors, which are responsible for the status of dissolved oxygen in water, temperature, light and turbidity (Pawar and Mane, 2006). Turbidity affects the light penetration due to the presence of total suspended solids and thereby affecting the process of photosynthesis, which is responsible for the release the oxygen (Prasad *et al.* 1999). The determination of dissolved oxygen forms the basis of biochemical oxygen demand. Biochemical oxygen demand test is a procedure which involves the determination of oxygen consumed by living organism mainly bacteria while utilizing the organic matter present in the waste.

South Site

During the study January-December 2008 at south site the dissolve oxygen ranged 3.50 ± 0.05 to 5.30 ± 0.19 (mg/l).

The maximum value recorded 5.30 ± 0.19 (mg/l) and coefficient variation was 3.58 per cent was recorded in January and minimum value recorded 3.50 ± 0.05 (mg/l) and coefficient variation was 1.42 per cent was recorded in April. In the second year study January-December 2009 the dissolve oxygen at south site ranged 3.60 ± 0.10 to 5.20 ± 0.23 (mg/l). The maximum value recorded 5.20 ± 0.23 (mg/l) and coefficient variation was 4.42 per cent was recorded in November; minimum value recorded 3.60 ± 0.10 (mg/l) and coefficient variation was 2.77 per cent was recorded in April.

In study January-December 2008 seasonal mean and coefficient variation values recorded 3.85 ± 0.23 (mg/l) and 6.18 per cent during summer, 4.30 ± 0.18 (mg/l) and 4.24 per cent during monsoon, 5.07 ± 0.17 (mg/l) and 3.36 per cent during winter (Fig. 3.19). In the second year study January-December 2009 seasonal mean and coefficient variation values recorded 3.92 ± 0.23 (mg/l) and 6.02 per cent during summer, 4.35 ± 0.23 (mg/l) and 5.47, per cent during winter 5.05 ± 0.12 (mg/l) and 2.55 per cent during winter (Table 3 37 and Fig. 3.20).

North Site

During the study January-December 2008 at north site the dissolve oxygen ranged 4.30 ± 0.10 to 6.90 ± 0.21 (mg/l). The maximum value recorded 6.90 ± 0.21 (mg/l) and coefficient variation was 3.04 per cent was recorded in December and minimum value recorded 4.30 ± 0.10 (mg/l) and coefficient variation was 2.32 per cent was recorded in April. In the second year study January-December 2009 the dissolve oxygen at north site ranged 4.40 ± 0.07 to 7 ± 0.23 (mg/l). The maximum value recorded 7 ± 0.23 (mg/l) and coefficient variation was 3.28 per cent was recorded in November; minimum value recorded 4.40 ± 0.07 (mg/l) and coefficient variation was 1.59 per cent was recorded in April.

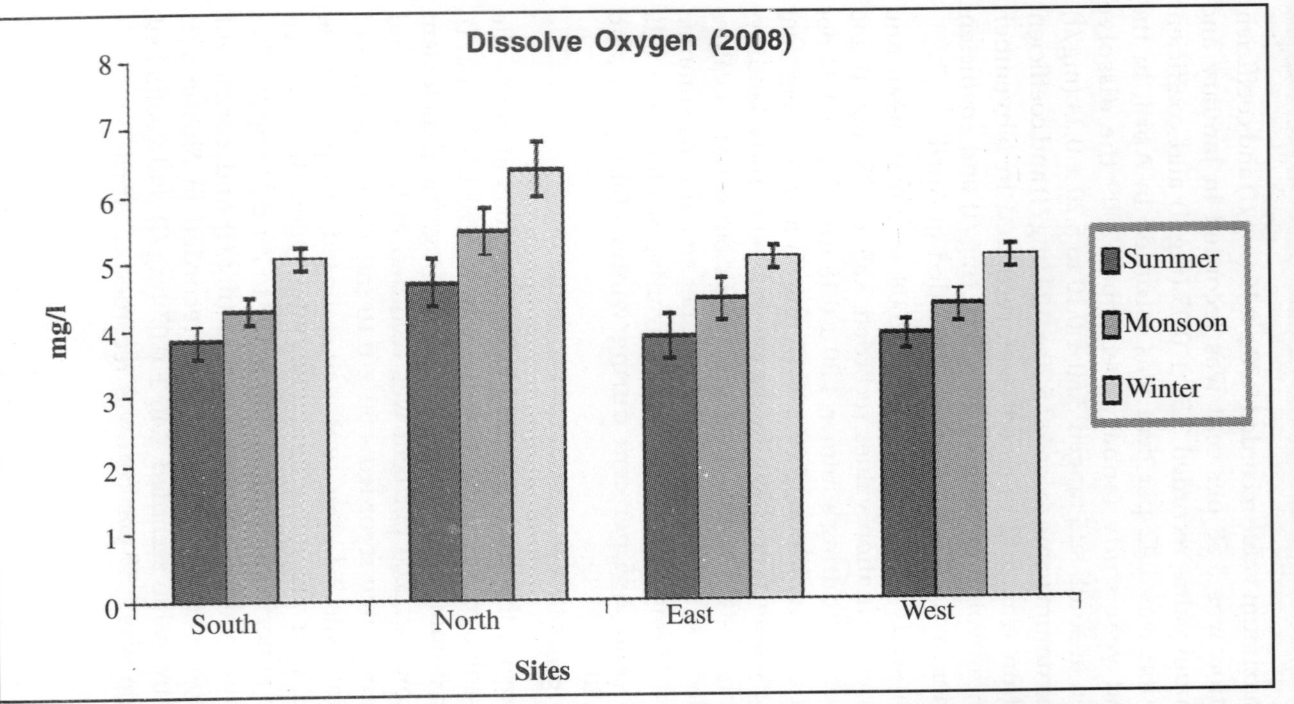

Fig. 3.19: Seasonal Variations in Dissolve Oxygen (mg/l) at Different Sites of Harsool-Savangi Dam January to December 2008

Table 3.37: Seasonal Variations in Dissolve Oxygen (mg/l) at South Site, Harsool-Savangi Dam

Season	Months Jan. 2008 - Dec. 2008	Monthly Mean Values	Monthly C.V. (%)	Seasonal Mean Values	Seasonal C.V. (%)	Months Jan. 2009 - Dec. 2009	Monthly Mean Values	Monthly C.V. (%)	Seasonal Mean Values	Seasonal C.V. (%)
Summer	February	4±0.10	2.50	3.85±0.23	6.18	February	4.1±0.19	4.63	3.92±0.23	6.02
	March	4±0.20	5.00			March	3.9±0.17	4.35		
	April	3.5±0.05	1.42			April	3.6±0.10	2.77		
	May	3.9±0.07	1.79			May	4.1±0.19	4.63		
Monsoon	June	4.1±0.19	4.63	4.30±0.18	4.24	June	4.2±0.03	0.71	4.35±0.23	5.47
	July	4.2±0.13	3.09			July	4.1±0.07	1.70		
	August	4.4±0.15	3.40			August	4.6±0.03	0.65		
	September	4.5±0.13	2.88			September	4.5±0.13	2.88		
Winter	October	4.9±0.23	4.69	5.07±0.17	3.36	October	4.9±0.31	6.32	5.05±0.12	2.55
	November	5±0.11	2.20			November	5.2±0.23	4.42		
	December	5.1±0.09	1.76			December	5.1±0.03	0.58		
	January	5.3±0.19	3.58			January	5.±0.10			

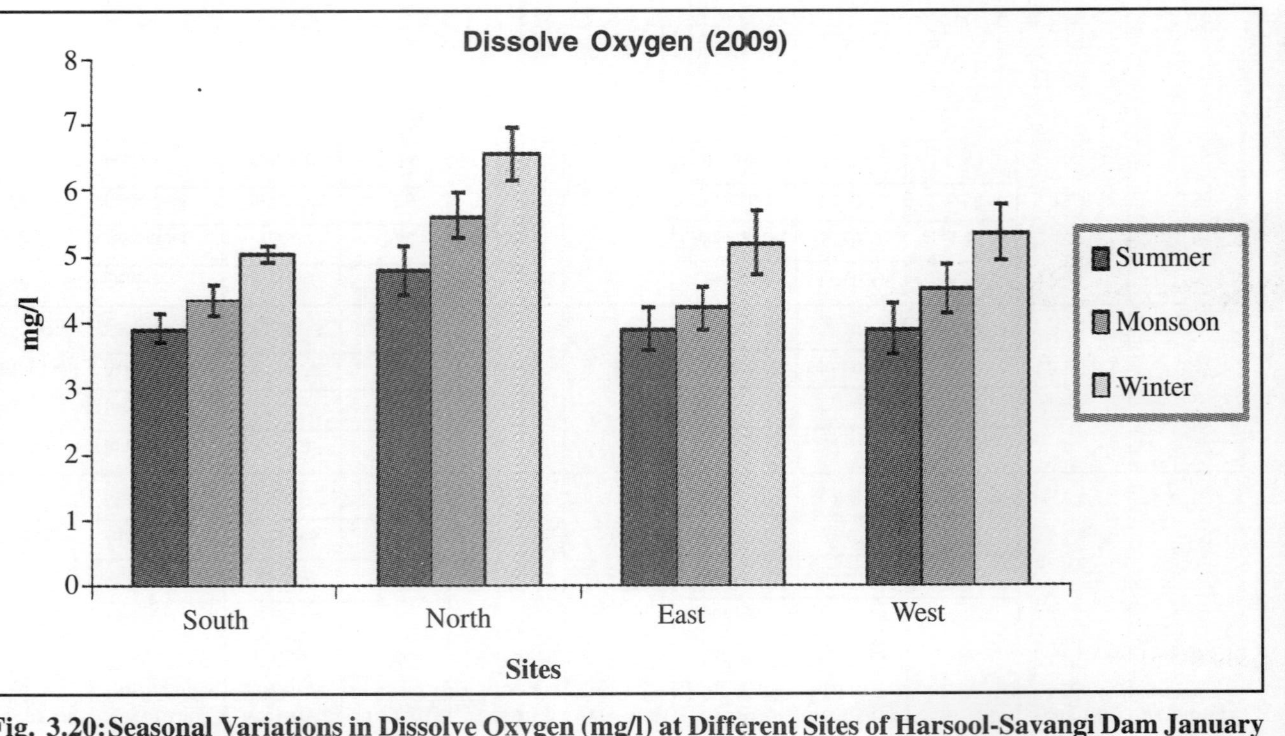

Fig. 3.20: Seasonal Variations in Dissolve Oxygen (mg/l) at Different Sites of Harsool-Savangi Dam January to December 2009

In the study January-December 2008 seasonal mean and coefficient variation values recorded 4.70 ± 0.35 (mg/l) and 7.57 per cent during summer, 5.47 ± 0.35 (mg/l) and 6.39 per cent during monsoon, 6.37 ± 0.41 (mg/l) and 6.45 per cent during winter (Fig. 3.19). In the second year study January-December 2009 seasonal mean and coefficient variation values recorded 4.80 ± 0.36 (mg/l) and 7.60 per cent during summer, 5.62 ± 0.35 (mg/l) and 6.22 per cent during monsoon, 6.57 ± 0.41 (mg/l) and 6.37 per cent during winter (Table 3.38 and Fig. 3.20).

East Site

The study January-December 2008 at east site the dissolve oxygen ranged 3.40 ± 0.17 to 5.30 ± 0.11 (mg/l). The maximum value recorded 5.30 ± 0.11 (mg/l) and coefficient variation was 2.07 per cent was recorded in December and minimum value recorded 3.40 ± 0.17 (mg/l) and coefficient variation was 5.00 per cent was recorded in April. In the second year study January-December 2009 the dissolve oxygen at east site ranged 3.60 ± 0.50 to 5.90 ± 0.05 (mg/l). The maximum value recorded 5.90 ± 0.05 (mg/l) and coefficient variation was 0.84 per cent was recorded in November; minimum value recorded 3.60 ± 0.50 (mg/l) and coefficient variation was 13.88 per cent was recorded in April.

During the study January-December 2008 seasonal mean and coefficient variation values recorded 3.90 ± 0.34 (mg/l) and 8.88 per cent during summer, 4.45 ± 0.31 (mg/l) and 6.98 per cent during monsoon, 5.07 ± 0.17 (mg/l) and 3.36 per cent during winter (Fig. 3.19). In the second year study January-December 2009 seasonal mean and coefficient variation values recorded 3.90 ± 0.31 (mg/l) and 8.10 per cent during summer, 4.22 ± 0.33 (mg/l) and 7.82 per cent during monsoon, 5.20 ± 0.48 (mg/l) and 9.28 per cent during winter (Table 3.39 and Fig. 3.20).

West Site

In the study January-December 2008 at west site the dissolve oxygen ranged 3.60 ± 0.09 to 5.30 ± 0.11 (mg/l).

Table 3.38: Seasonal Variations in Dissolve Oxygen (mg/l) at North Site, Harsool-Savangi Dam

Season	Months Jan. 2008 - Dec. 2008	Monthly Mean Values	Monthly C.V. (%)	Seasonal Mean Values	Seasonal C.V. (%)	Months Jan. 2009 - Dec. 2009	Monthly Mean Values	Monthly C.V. (%)	Seasonal Mean Values	Seasonal C.V. (%)
	February	5±0.01	0.20			February	5.2±0.19	3.65		
	March	4.5±0.19	4.22			March	4.6±0.10	2.17		
Summer	April	4.3±0.10	2.32	4.70±0.35	7.57	April	4.4±0.07	1.59	4.80±0.36	7.60
	May	5±0.13	2.60			May	5±0.09	1.80		
	June	5.3±0.19	3.58			June	5.2±0.15	2.88		
	July	5.1±0.17	3.33			July	5.5±0.19	3.45		
Monsoon	August	5.6±0.21	3.75	5.47±0.35	6.39	August	5.8±0.17	2.93	5.62±0.35	6.22
	September	5.9±0.13	2.20			September	6±0.21	3.50		
	October	6±0.10	1.66			October	6.6±0.27	4.09		
	November	6.5±0.09	1.38			November	7±0.23	3.28		
Winter	December	6.9±0.21	3.04	6.37±0.41	6.45	December	6.7±0.01	0.14	6.57±0.41	6.37
	January	6.1±0.19	3.11			January	6±0.50	8.33		

Fig. 3.39: Seasonal Variations in Dissolve Oxygen (mg/l) at East Site, Harsool-Savangi Dam

Season	Months Jan. 2008 - Dec. 2008	Monthly Mean Values	Monthly C.V. (%)	Seasonal Mean Values	Seasonal C.V. (%)	Months Jan. 2009 - Dec. 2009	Monthly Mean Values	Monthly C.V. (%)	Seasonal Mean Values	Seasonal C.V. (%)
	February	4±0.35	8.75			February	4.3±0.19	4.41		
	March	4±0.20	5.00			March	4±0.21	5.25		
Summer	April	3.4±0.17	5.00	3.90±0.34	8.88	April	3.6±0.5	13.88	3.90±0.31	8.10
	May	4.2±0.15	3.57			May	3.7±0.09	2.43		
	June	4.3±0.09	2.09			June	3.9±0.29	7.43		
	July	4.1±0.19	4.63			July	4±0.20	5.00		
Monsoon	August	4.6±0.10	2.17	4.45±0.31	6.98	August	4.4±0.11	2.50	4.22±0.33	7.82
	September	4.8±0.37	7.70			September	4.6±0.10	2.17		
	October	4.9±0.13	2.65			October	4.8±0.19	3.95		
	November	5±0.17	3.40			November	5.9±0.05	0.84		
Winter	December	5.3±0.11	2.07	5.07±0.17	3.36	December	5±0.17	3.40	5.20±0.48	9.28
	January	5.1±0.05	0.98			January	5.1±0.09	1.76		

The maximum value recorded 5.30 ± 0.11 (mg/l) and coefficient variation was 2.07 per cent was recorded in December and minimum value recorded 3.60 ± 0.09 (mg/l) and coefficient variation was 2.50 per cent was recorded in April. In the second year study January-December 2009 the dissolve oxygen at west site ranged 3.40 ± 0.17 to 5.90 ± 0.27 (mg/l). The maximum value recorded 5.90 ± 0.27 (mg/l) and coefficient variation was 4.57 per cent was recorded in December; minimum value recorded 3.40 ± 0.17 (mg/l) and coefficient variation was 5.00 per cent was recorded in April.

During the study January-December 2008 seasonal mean and coefficient variation values recorded 3.92 ± 0.23 (mg/l) and 6.02 per cent during summer, 4.35 ± 0.23 (mg/l) and 5.47 per cent during monsoon, 5.07 ± 0.17 (mg/l) and 3.36 per cent during winter (Fig. 3.19). In the second year study January-December 2009 seasonal mean and coefficient variation values recorded 3.90 ± 0.38 (mg/l) and 9.81 per cent during summer, 4.52 ± 0.38 (mg/l) and 8.53 per cent during monsoon, 5.37 ± 0.41 (mg/l) and 7.65 per cent during winter (Table 3.40 and Fig. 3.20).

In the present study January to December 2008 the maximum dissolve oxygen was recorded in winter season at north site and minimum dissolve oxygen was recorded in summer season at north site. In the second year study January-December 2009 the maximum dissolve oxygen was recorded in winter season at north site where as minimum dissolve oxygen was recorded in summer season at north site (Table 3.38).

During the study January 2008-December 2009 dissolved oxygen indicating significant positive correlation with total solid and total dissolved solids and it indicating significant negative correlation with water temperature, pH, alkalinity, sulphate and chloride (Tables 4.7 and 4.8).

In the present study, the maximum Dissolved Oxygen was recorded in the winter season and minimum during monsoon.

Table 3.40: Seasonal Variations in Dissolve Oxygen (mg/l) at West Site, Harsool-Savangi Dam

Season	Months Jan. 2008 - Dec. 2008	Monthly Mean Values	Monthly C.V. (%)	Seasonal Mean Values	Seasonal C.V. (%)	Months Jan. 2009 - Dec. 2009	Monthly Mean Values	Monthly C.V. (%)	Seasonal Mean Values	Seasonal C.V. (%)
Summer	February	4.1±0.13	3.17	3.92±0.23	6.02	February	4.2±0.19	4.52	3.90±0.38	9.81
	March	3.9±0.03	0.76			March	3.8±0.10	2.63		
	April	**3.6±0.09**	2.50			April	**3.4±0.17**	5.00		
	May	4.1±0.10	2.43			May	4.2±0.11	2.61		
Monsoon	June	4.2±0.50	11.90	4.35±0.23	5.47	June	4.3±0.10	2.32	4.52±0.38	8.53
	July	4.1±0.91	22.19			July	4.1±0.19	4.63		
	August	4.6±0.89	19.34			August	4.8±0.21	4.37		
	September	4.5±0.19	4.22			September	4.9±0.13	2.65		
Winter	October	4.9±0.90	18.36	5.07±0.17	3.36	October	5±0.21	4.20	5.37±0.41	7.65
	November	5±0.07	1.40			November	5.5±0.09	1.63		
	December	**5.3±0.11**	2.07			December	**5.9±0.27**	4.57		
	January	5.1±0.21	4.11			January	5.1±0.17	3.33		

High values of DO during winter could be due to increased photosynthesis by Phytoplankton (Devi, 2007) and during post-monsoon may be due to circulation of oxygen (Yadav *et al.*, 1987). A lower value during pre-monsoon was experienced probably due to decomposition of organic matter (Welch, 1952). Salaskar, (1998) also showed the inverse co-relation from temperature and dissolved oxygen. Shashikant and Raina, (1990) reported that the minimum and maximum in the concentration of dissolved oxygen in ponds are directly related with the maximum and minimum population of the phytoplanktons.

Biochemical Oxygen Demand (BOD)

BOD is an important parameter indicates the magnitude of water pollution by oxidizable organic matter. The main sources of organic pollution untreated domestic sewage, agricultural runoff, containing residual fertilizers and certain industrial effluents. The components of oxidizable matter include carbonaceous organic matter, nitrogenous compounds and chemically reducing compounds. In natural course the organic matters on oxidation enters into bio-geo-chemical cycles. However, when an aquatic ecosystem receives excessive organic pollution load due to low availability of dissolved oxygen, net biological oxygen demand generates. BOD thus can be defined as the quantity of dissolved oxygen in mg/l required under test condition (aerobic bacteria) for the organic matter for test sample (Khabade *et al.* 2002). Voznaya (1981) also found the high population of micro-organisms in Russian reservoirs during May and July. Organic material may exert demand for oxygen in a water body and oxidizable nitrogenous compound, which may react with dissolved molecular oxygen tensions in water.

South Site

During the study January-December 2008 at south site the biochemical oxygen demand ranged 3.40 ± 0.19 to 8.20 ± 0.09 (mg/l). The maximum value recorded 8.20 ± 0.09 (mg/l) and coefficient variation was 1.09 per cent was recorded in

September and minimum value recorded 3.40 ± 0.19 (mg/l) and coefficient variation was 5.58 per cent was recorded in May. In the second year study January-December 2009 the biochemical oxygen demand at south site ranged 4 ± 0.17 to 8.60 ± 0.20 (mg/l). The maximum value recorded 8.60 ± 0.20 (mg/l) and coefficient variation was 2.32 per cent was recorded in September; minimum value recorded 4 ± 0.17 (mg/l) and coefficient variation was 4.25 per cent was recorded in May.

In the study January-December 2008 seasonal mean and coefficient variation values recorded 4.05 ± 0.58 (mg/l) and 14.45 per cent during summer, 7.76 ± 0.46 (mg/l) and 6.02 per cent during monsoon, 5.87 ± 0.52 (mg/l) and 8.88 per cent during winter (Fig. 3.21). In the second year study January-December 2009 seasonal mean and coefficient variation values recorded 4.60 ± 0.64 (mg/l) and 14.08 per cent during summer, 8.07 ± 0.45 (mg/l) and 5.66 per cent during monsoon, 6.12 ± 1.05 (mg/l) and 17.29 per cent during winter (Table 3.41 and Fig. 3.22).

North Site

During the study January-December 2008 at north site the biochemical oxygen demand ranged 3.40 ± 0.19 to 7.90 ± 0.09 (mg/l). The maximum value recorded 7.90 ± 0.09 (mg/l) and coefficient variation was 1.13 per cent was recorded in September and minimum value recorded 3.40 ± 0.19 (mg/l) and coefficient variation was 5.58 per cent was recorded in May. In the second year study January-December 2009 the biochemical oxygen demand at north site ranged 3.90 ± 0.02 to 8.30 ± 0.17 (mg/l). The maximum value recorded 8.30 ± 0.17 (mg/l) and coefficient variation was 2.04 per cent was recorded in September; minimum value recorded 3.90 ± 0.02 (mg/l) and coefficient variation was 0.51 per cent was recorded in May.

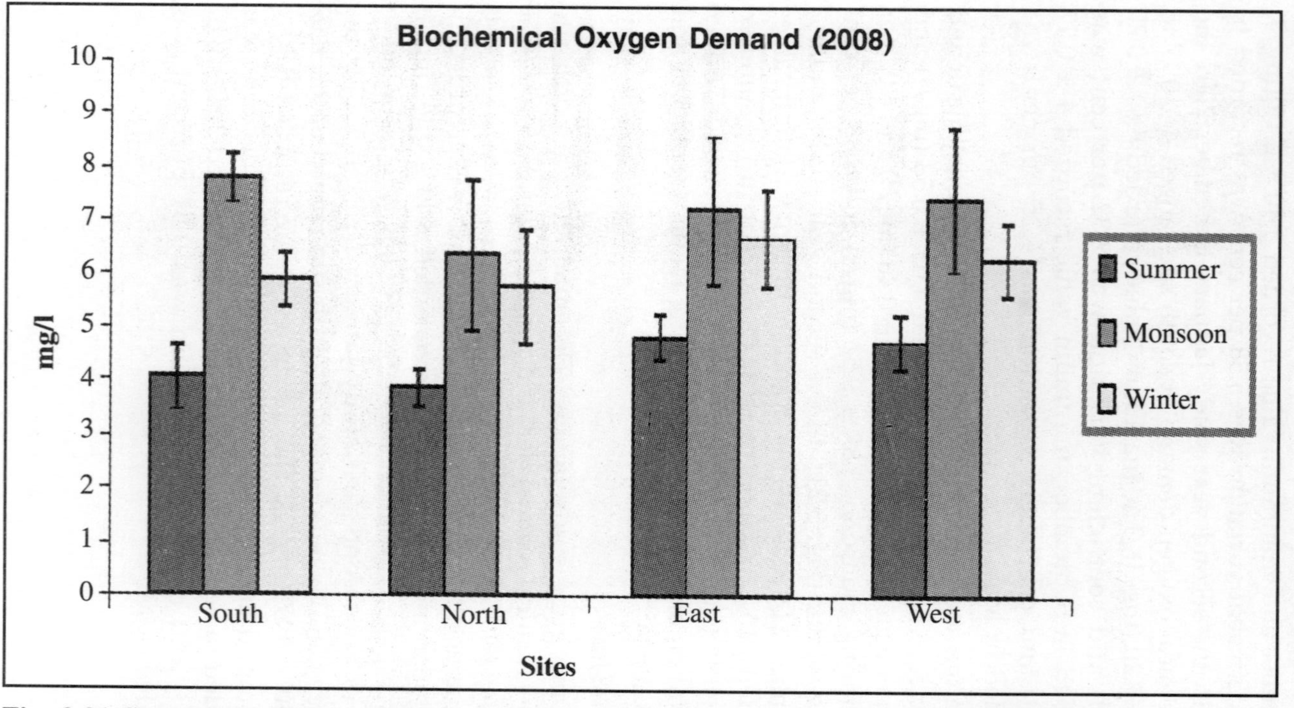

Fig. 3.21: Seasonal Variations in Biochemical Oxygen Demand (mg/l) at Different Sites of Harsool-Savangi Dam January to December 2008

Table 3.41: Seasonal Variations in Biochemical Oxygen Demand (mg/l) at South Site, Harsool-Savangi Dam

Season	Months Jan. 2008 - Dec. 2008	Monthly Mean Values	Monthly C.V. (%)	Seasonal Mean Values	Seasonal C.V. (%)	Months Jan. 2009 - Dec. 2009	Monthly Mean Values	Monthly C.V. (%)	Seasonal Mean Values	Seasonal C.V. (%)
Summer	February	4.69±0.18	3.83	4.05±0.58	14.45	February	5.3±0.12	2.26	4.60±0.64	14.08
	March	4.38±0.10	2.28			March	5±0.19	3.80		
	April	3.75±0.09	2.40			April	4.1±0.10	2.43		
	May	3.4±0.19	5.58			May	4±0.17	4.25		
Monsoon	June	7.1±0.11	1.54	7.76±0.46	6.02	June	7.5±0.11	1.466	8.07±0.45	5.66
	July	7.84±0.15	1.91			July	8±0.18	2.25		
	August	7.9±0.11	1.39			August	8.2±0.13	1.58		
	September	8.2±0.09	1.09			September	8.6±0.20	2.32		
Winter	October	6.6±0.18	2.72	5.87±0.52	8.88	October	7.5±0.09	1.20	6.12±1.05	17.29
	November	5.9±0.21	3.55			November	6.3±0.23	3.65		
	December	5.6±0.19	3.39			December	5±0.10	2.00		
	January	5.41±0.13	2.40			January	5.7±0.11	1.92		

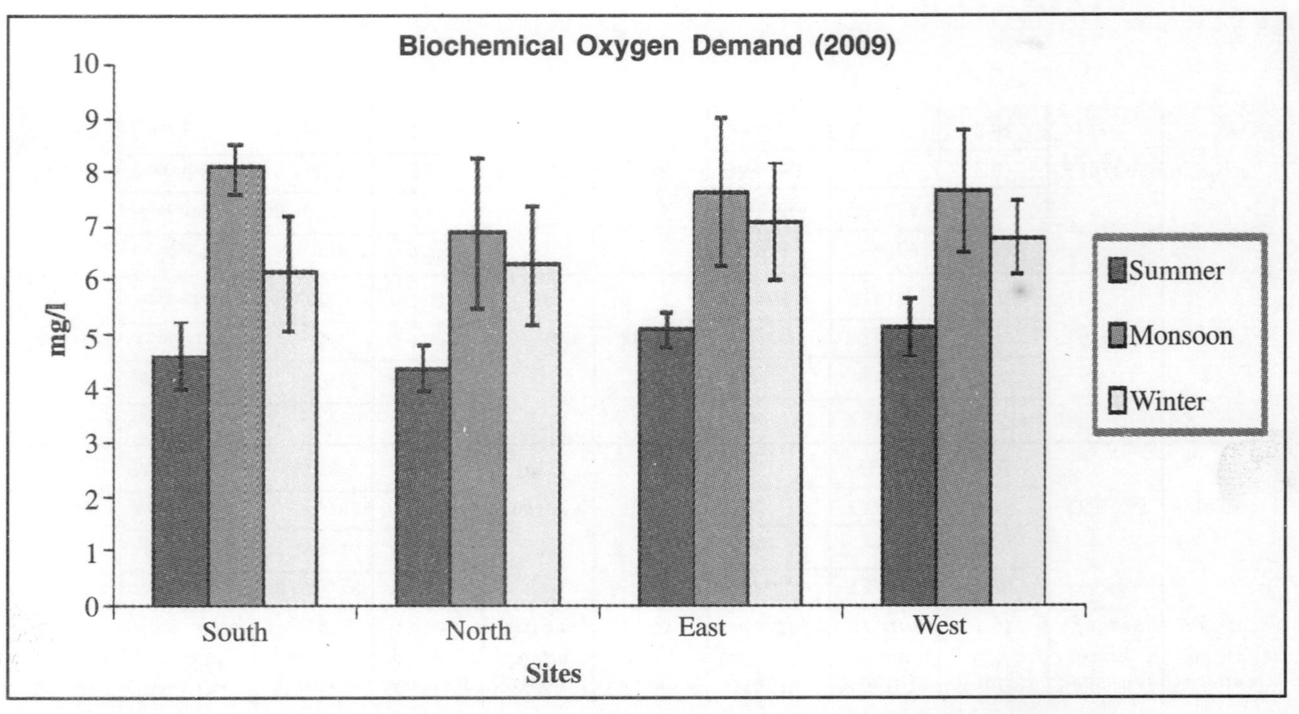

Fig 3.22: Seasonal Variations in Biochemical Oxygen Demand (mg/l) at Different Sites of Harsool-Savangi Dam January to December 2009

In the study January-December 2008 seasonal mean and coefficient variation values recorded 3.87 ± 0.35 (mg/l) and 9.27 per cent during summer, 6.35 ± 1.40 (mg/l) and 22.17 per cent during monsoon, 5.75 ± 1.08 (mg/l) and 18.91 per cent during winter (Fig. 3.21). In the second year study January-December 2009 seasonal mean and coefficient variation values recorded 4.37 ± 0.44 (mg/l) and 10.11 per cent during summer, 6.87 ± 1.39 (mg/l) and 20.27, per cent during winter 6.26 ± 1.09 (mg/l) and 17.50 per cent during winter (Table 3.42 and Fig. 3.22).

East Site

During the study January-December 2008 at east site the biochemical oxygen demand ranged 4.25 ± 0.19 to 8.75 ± 0.25 (mg/l). The maximum value recorded 8.75 ± 0.25 (mg/l) and coefficient variation was 2.85 per cent was recorded in September and minimum value recorded 4.25 ± 0.19 (mg/l) and coefficient variation was 4.47 per cent was recorded in May. In the second year study January-December 2009 the biochemical oxygen demand at east site ranged 4.70 ± 0.19 to 9.10 ± 0.11 (mg/l). The maximum value recorded 9.10 ± 0.11 (mg/l) and coefficient variation was 1.20 per cent was recorded in September; minimum value recorded 4.70 ± 0.19 (mg/l) and coefficient variation was 4.04 per cent was recorded in May.

In the study January-December 2008 seasonal mean and coefficient variation values recorded 4.82 ± 0.43 (mg/l) and 8.98 per cent during summer, 7.18 ± 1.37 (mg/l) and 19.20 per cent during monsoon, 6.66 ± 0.91 (mg/l) and 13.77 per cent during winter (Fig. 3.21). In the second year study January-December 2009 seasonal mean and coefficient variation values recorded 5.10 ± 0.31 (mg/l) and 6.20 per cent during summer, 7.62 ± 1.38 (mg/l) and 18.15 per cent during monsoon, 7.07 ± 1.09 (mg/l) and 15.41 per cent during winter (Table 3.43 and Fig. 3.22).

Table 3.42: Seasonal Variations in Biochemical Oxygen Demand (mg/l) at North Site, Harsool-Savangi Dam

Season	Months Jan. 2008 - Dec. 2008	Monthly Mean Values	Monthly C.V. (%)	Seasonal Mean Values	Seasonal C.V. (%)	Months Jan. 2009 - Dec. 2009	Monthly Mean Values	Monthly C.V. (%)	Seasonal Mean Values	Seasonal C.V. (%)
Summer	February	4.1±0.12	2.92	3.87±0.35	9.27	February	4.7±0.01	0.21	4.37±0.44	10.11
	March	4.2±0.10	2.38			March	4.8±0.09	1.87		
	April	3.8±0.17	4.47			April	4.1±0.19	4.63		
	May	3.4±0.19	5.58			May	3.9±0.02	0.51		
Monsoon	June	4.5±0.17	3.77	6.35±1.40	22.17	June	5±0.50	10.00	6.87±1.39	20.27
	July	6.3±0.19	3.01			July	6.8±0.90	13.23		
	August	6.7±0.12	1.79			August	7.4±1.01	13.64		
	September	7.9±0.09	1.13			September	8.3±0.17	2.04		
Winter	October	7.2±0.07	0.97	5.75±1.08	18.91	October	7.8±0.11	1.41	6.26±1.09	17.50
	November	5.8±0.21	3.62			November	6.2±0.19	3.06		
	December	5.4±0.19	3.51			December	5.8±0.21	3.62		
	January	4.6±0.11	2.39			January	5.25±0.03	0.57		

Table 3.43: Seasonal Variations in Biochemical Oxygen Demand (mg/l) at East Site, Harsool-Savangi Dam

Season	Months Jan. 2008 - Dec. 2008	Monthly Mean Values	Monthly C.V. (%)	Seasonal Mean Values	Seasonal C.V. (%)	Months Jan. 2009 - Dec. 2009	Monthly Mean Values	Monthly C.V. (%)	Seasonal Mean Values	Seasonal C.V. (%)
Summer	February	5.25±0.07	1.33	4.82±0.43	8.98	February	5.4±0.01	0.18	5.10±0.31	6.20
	March	5.04±0.09	1.78			March	5.3±0.05	0.94		
	April	4.75±0.11	2.31			April	5±0.07	1.40		
	May	4.25±0.19	4.47			May	4.7±0.19	4.04		
Monsoon	June	5.41±0.17	3.14	7.18±1.37	19.20	June	5.8±0.10	1.72	7.62±1.38	18.15
	July	7.08±0.18	2.54			July	7.5±0.17	2.26		
	August	7.5±0.20	2.66			August	8.1±0.20	2.46		
	September	8.75±0.25	2.85			September	9.1±0.11	1.20		
Winter	October	7.58±0.19	2.50	6.66±0.91	13.77	October	8±0.17	2.12	7.07±1.09	15.41
	November	7.25±0.01	0.13			November	7.9±0.21	2.65		
	December	6.25±0.03	0.48			December	6.7±0.09	1.34		
	January	5.58±0.19	3.40			January	5.7±0.10	1.75		

West Site

During the study January-December 2008 at west site the biochemical oxygen demand ranged 4.10 ± 0.07 to 8.80 ± 0.50 (mg/l). The maximum value recorded 8.80 ± 0.50 (mg/l) and coefficient variation was 5.68 per cent was recorded in September and minimum value recorded 4.10 ± 0.07 (mg/l) and coefficient variation was 1.70 per cent was recorded in May. In the second year study January-December 2009 the biochemical oxygen demand at west site ranged 4.50 ± 0.13 to 8.70 ± 0.05 (mg/l). The maximum value recorded 8.70 ± 0.05 (mg/l) and coefficient variation was 0.57 per cent was recorded in September; minimum value recorded 4.50 ± 0.13 (mg/l) and coefficient variation was 2.88 per cent was recorded in May.

In the study January-December 2008 seasonal mean and coefficient variation values recorded 4.73 ± 0.49 (mg/l) and 10.53 per cent during summer, 7.42 ± 1.34 (mg/l) and 18.08 per cent during monsoon, 6.29 ± 0.69 (mg/l) and 11.03 per cent during winter (Fig. 3.21). In the second year study January-December 2009 seasonal mean and coefficient variation values recorded 5.13 ± 0.52 (mg/l) and 40.87 per cent during summer, 7.65 ± 1.13 (mg/l) and 59.54 per cent during monsoon, 6.77 ± 0.68 (mg/l) and 40.44 per cent during winter (Table 3.44 and Fig. 3.22).

In the present study January to December 2008 the maximum biochemical oxygen demand was recorded in monsoon season at west site and minimum biochemical oxygen demand was recorded in summer season at south and north site. In the second year study January-December 2009 the maximum biochemical oxygen demand was recorded in monsoon season at east site where as minimum biochemical oxygen demand was recorded in summer season at north site (Tables 3.41, 3.42, 3.43 and 3.44).

Table 3.44: Seasonal Variations in Biochemical Oxygen Demand (mg/l) at West Site, Harsool-Savangi Dam

Season	Months Jan. 2008 - Dec. 2008	Monthly Mean Values	Monthly C.V. (%)	Seasonal Mean Values	Seasonal C.V. (%)	Months Jan. 2009 - Dec. 2009	Monthly Mean Values	Monthly C.V. (%)	Seasonal Mean Values	Seasonal C.V. (%)
	February	5.24±0.12	2.29			February	5.75±0.07	1.21		
	March	5±0.10	2.00			March	5.3±0.09	1.69		
Summer	April	4.6±0.19	4.13	4.73±0.49	10.53	April	5±0.11	2.20	5.13±0.52	40.87
	May	4.1±0.07	1.70			May	4.5±0.13	2.88		
	June	5.8±0.01	0.17			June	6.2±0.19	3.06		
	July	6.9±0.18	2.60			July	7.3±0.20	2.73		
Monsoon	August	8.2±0.20	2.43	7.42±1.34	18.08	August	8.4±0.10	1.19	7.65±1.13	59.54
	September	8.8±0.50	5.68			September	8.7±0.05	0.57		
	October	7±0.90	12.85			October	7.6±0.09	1.18		
	November	6.7±0.12	1.79			November	7±0.13	1.85		
Winter	December	6±0.18	3.00	6.29±0.69	11.03	December	6.5±0.17	2.61	6.77±0.68	40.44
	January	5.46±0.10	1.83			January	6±0.19	3.16		

In the study January 2008-December 2009 biochemical oxygen demand indicating significant positive correlation with turbidity, electric conductivity, total solid, total dissolved solids, total suspended solids, chemical oxygen demand, total hardness, nitrate and phosphate and it indicating significant negative correlation with transparency, pH, alkalinity and fish (Tables 4.7 and 4.8).

In the present study, the BOD values were maximum during monsoon and minimum during summer. Higher values of BOD in monsoon, as compared to those in winter and summer might be because of the presence of pollutants mixed with rain water.

Chemical Oxygen Demand (COD)

COD is the measure of oxygen required for oxidizing the organic compounds present in water by means of chemical reactions involving oxidizing substances such as potassium chromate and potassium permanganate. The estimation of COD is of great importance for water having unfavorable conditions for the growth of microbes, such as the presence of toxic chemicals. The chemical oxygen demand test determines the oxygen required for chemical oxidation of organic matter with the help of strong chemical oxidant. The COD is a test, which is measured in terms of quantity of oxygen-required for oxidation of organic matter to produce carbon dioxide and water. It is a fact that all organic compounds with few exception, can be oxidized for the action of strong oxidizing agents under acidic condition, COD test is useful in pinpointing toxic condition and presence of biological resistant substances. High organic pollution indicates high value of COD.

South Site

During the study January-December 2008 at south site the chemical oxygen demand ranged 8.40 ± 0.07 to 20.50 ± 0.90 (mg/l). The maximum value recorded 20.50 ± 0.90 (mg/l) and coefficient variation was 4.39 per cent was recorded in September and minimum value recorded 8.40 ± 0.07 (mg/l) and coefficient variation was 0.83 per cent was recorded in May. In the second year study January-December 2009 the chemical oxygen demand at south site ranged 9.60 ± 0.19 to 20.80 ± 0.21 (mg/l). The maximum value recorded 20.80 ± 0.21 (mg/l) and coefficient variation was 1.00 per cent was recorded in September; minimum value recorded 9.60 ± 0.19 (mg/l) and coefficient variation was 1.97 per cent was recorded in May.

In the study January-December 2008 seasonal mean and coefficient variation values recorded 9.97 ± 1.50 (mg/l) and 15.10 per cent during summer, 18.65 ± 1.47 (mg/l) and 7.93 per cent during monsoon, 14.22 ± 1.32 (mg/l) and 9.33 per cent during winter (Fig. 3.23). In the second year study January-December 2009 seasonal mean and coefficient variation values recorded 11.17 ± 1.65 (mg/l) and 14.83 per cent during summer, 19.50 ± 1.17 (mg/l) and 6.02 per cent during monsoon, 14.82 ± 2.60 (mg/l) and 17.57 per cent during winter (Table 3.45 and Fig. 3.24).

North Site

During the study January-December 2008 at north site the chemical oxygen demand ranged 8.20 ± 0.12 to 19 ± 1.19 (mg/l). The maximum value recorded 19 ± 1.19 (mg/l) and coefficient variation was 6.26 per cent was recorded in September and minimum value recorded 8.20 ± 0.12 (mg/l) and coefficient variation was 1.46 per cent was recorded in May. In the second year study January-December 2009 the chemical oxygen demand at north site ranged 9.40 ± 0.07 to 20.10 ± 0.90 (mg/l). The maximum value recorded 20.10 ± 0.90 (mg/l) and coefficient variation was 4.47 per cent was recorded in September; minimum value recorded 9.40 ± 0.07 (mg/l) and coefficient variation was 0.74 per cent was recorded in May.

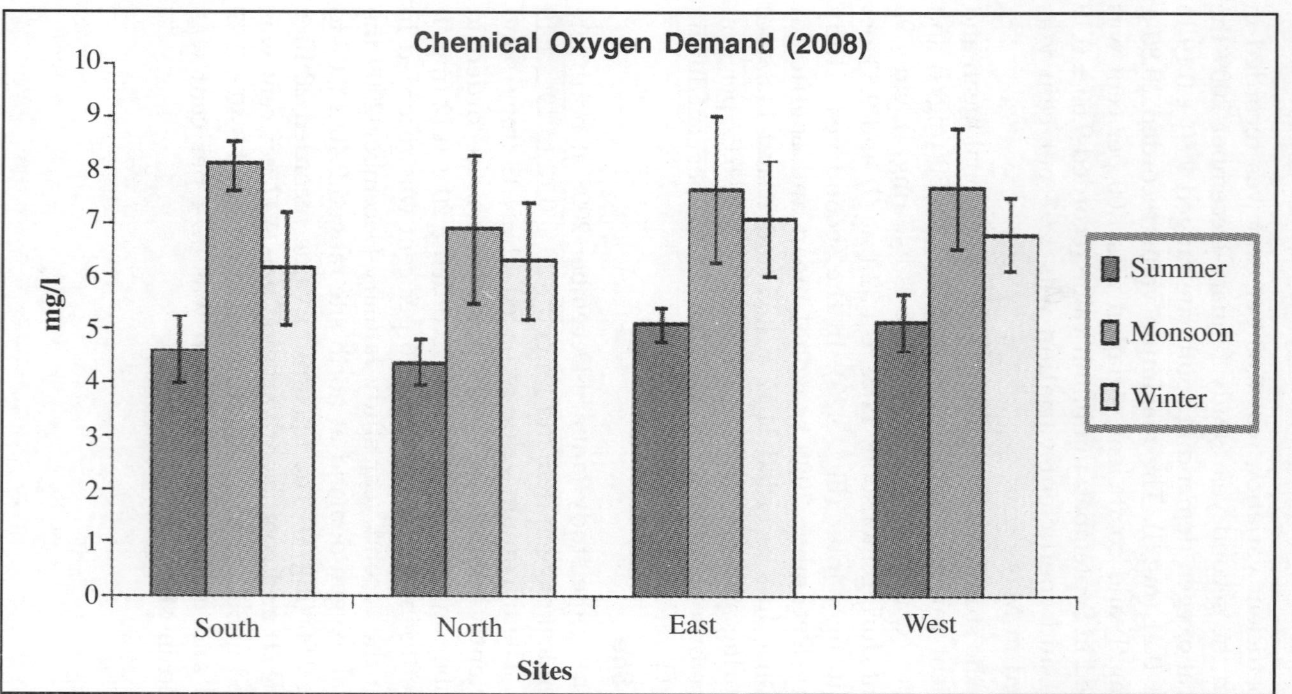

Fig. 3.23: Seasonal Variations in Chemical Oxygen Demand (mg/l) at Different Sites of Harsool-Savangi Dam January to December 2008

Table 3.45: Seasonal Variations in Chemical Oxygen Demand (mg/l) at South Site, Harsool-Savangi Dam

Season	Months Jan. 2008 - Dec. 2008	Monthly Mean Values	Monthly C.V. (%)	Seasonal Mean Values	Seasonal C.V. (%)	Months Jan. 2009 - Dec. 2009	Monthly Mean Values	Monthly C.V. (%)	Seasonal Mean Values	Seasonal C.V. (%)
Summer	February	11.5±0.09	0.78	9.97±1.50	15.10	February	13.1±0.07	0.53	11.17±1.65	14.83
	March	11±0.19	1.72			March	12±0.50	4.16		
	April	9±0.11	1.22			April	10±0.11	1.10		
	May	8.4±0.07	0.83			May	9.6±0.19	1.97		
Monsoon	June	17±1.29	7.58	18.65±1.47	7.93	June	18±0.13	0.72	19.50±1.17	6.02
	July	18.1±0.20	1.10			July	19.3±0.09	0.46		
	August	19±0.27	1.42			August	19.9±0.01	0.05		
	September	20.5±0.90	4.39			September	20.8±0.21	1.00		
Winter	October	16±1.10	6.87	14.22±1.32	9.33	October	18.2±0.15	0.82	14.82±2.60	17.57
	November	14.2±2.09	14.71			November	15.2±0.17	1.11		
	December	13.9±0.90	6.47			December	12±0.10	0.83		
	January	12.8±0.29	2.26			January	13.9±0.09	0.64		

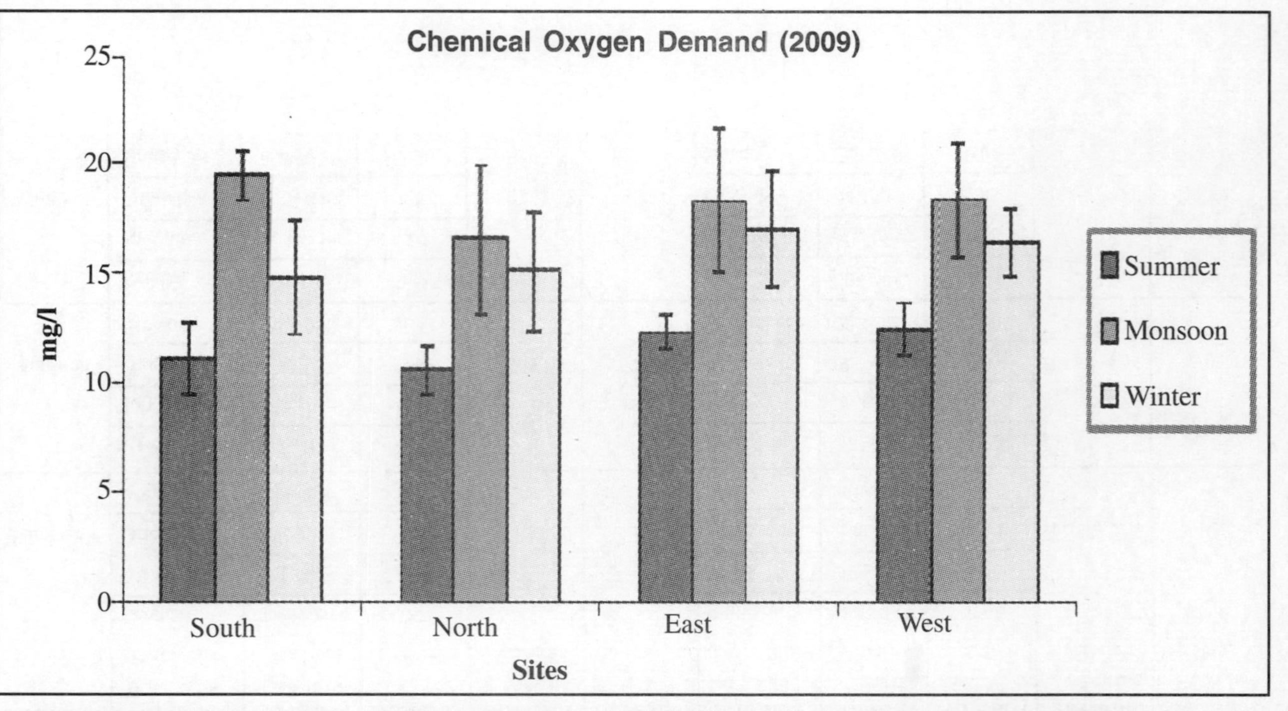

Fig. 3.24: Seasonal Variations in Chemical Oxygen Demand (mg/l) at Different Sites of Harsool-Savangi Dam January to December 2009

In the study January-December 2008 seasonal mean and coefficient variation values recorded 9.40 ± 0.87 (mg/l) and 9.31 per cent during summer, 15.35 ± 3.30 (mg/l) and 21.54 per cent during monsoon, 13.95 ± 2.65 (mg/l) and 19.00 per cent during winter (Fig. 3.23). In the second year study January-December 2009 seasonal mean and coefficient variation values recorded 10.60 ± 1.08 (mg/l) and 10.18 per cent during summer, 16.57 ± 3.41 (mg/l) and 20.57 per cent during monsoon, 15.12 ± 2.70 (mg/l) and 17.86 per cent during winter (Table 3.46 and Fig. 3.24).

East Site

During the study January-December 2008 at east site the chemical oxygen demand ranged 10.20 ± 0.27 to 21 ± 0.57 (mg/l). The maximum value recorded 21 ± 0.57 (mg/l) and coefficient variation was 2.71 per cent was recorded in September and minimum value recorded 10.20 ± 0.27 (mg/l) and coefficient variation was 2.64 per cent was recorded in May. In the second year study January-December 2009 the chemical oxygen demand at east site ranged 11.40 ± 0.97 to 22 ± 1.19 (mg/l). The maximum value recorded 22 ± 1.19 (mg/l) and coefficient variation was 5.40 per cent was recorded in September; minimum value recorded 11.40 ± 0.97 (mg/l) and coefficient variation was 8.50 per cent was recorded in May.

In the study January-December 2008 seasonal mean and coefficient variation values recorded 11.57 ± 1.04 (mg/l) and 8.98 per cent during summer, 17.37 ± 3.30 (mg/l) and 18.99 per cent during monsoon, 16 ± 2.20 (mg/l) and 13.76 per cent during winter (Fig. 3.23). In the second year study January-December 2009 seasonal mean and coefficient variation values recorded 12.35 ± 0.75 (mg/l) and 6.07 per cent during summer, 18.37 ± 3.35 (mg/l) and 18.23 per cent during monsoon, 17.05 ± 2.64 (mg/l) and 15.51 per cent during winter (Table 3.47 and Fig. 3.24).

Table 3.46: Seasonal Variations in Chemical Oxygen Demand (mg/l) at North Site, Harsool-Savangi Dam

Season	Months Jan. 2008 - Dec. 2008	Monthly Mean Values	Monthly C.V. (%)	Seasonal Mean Values	Seasonal C.V. (%)	Months Jan. 2009 - Dec. 2009	Monthly Mean Values	Monthly C.V. (%)	Seasonal Mean Values	Seasonal C.V. (%)
Summer	February	10±0.01	0.10	9.40±0.87	9.31	February	11.3±0.90	7.96	10.60±1.08	10.18
	March	10.1±0.05	0.49			March	11.7±0.09	0.76		
	April	9.3±0.10	1.07			April	10±1.10	11.00		
	May	8.2±0.12	1.46			May	9.4±0.07	0.74		
Monsoon	June	11±0.50	4.54	15.35±3.30	21.54	June	12±1.19	9.91	16.57±3.41	20.57
	July	15.3±0.90	5.88			July	16.4±2.27	13.84		
	August	16.1±1.01	6.27			August	17.8±0.50	2.80		
	September	19±1.19	6.26			September	20.1±0.90	4.47		
Winter	October	17.5±1.07	6.11	13.95±2.65	19.00	October	18.9±1.21	6.40	15.12±2.70	17.86
	November	14.1±2.0	14.18			November	15±3.51	23.40		
	December	13±0.8	6.15			December	14±1.37	9.78		
	January	11.2±1.02	9.10			January	12.6±0.99	7.85		

Table 3.47: Seasonal Variations in Chemical Oxygen Demand (mg/l) at East Site, Harsool-Savangi Dam

Season	Months Jan. 2008 - Dec. 2008	Monthly Mean Values	Monthly C.V. (%)	Seasonal Mean Values	Seasonal C.V. (%)	Months Jan. 2009 - Dec. 2009	Monthly Mean Values	Monthly C.V. (%)	Seasonal Mean Values	Seasonal C.V. (%)
	February	12.6±0.50	3.96			February	13±0.01	0.07		
	March	12.1±0.09	0.74			March	12.9±0.07	0.54		
Summer	April	11.4±0.19	1.66	11.57±1.04	8.98	April	12.1±0.8	6.61	12.35±0.75	6.07
	May	10.2±0.27	2.64			May	11.4±0.97	8.50		
	June	13±2.0	15.38			June	14±1.27	9.07		
	July	17.5±2.19	12.51			July	18±2.09	11.61		
Monsoon	August	18±0.20	1.11	17.37±3.30	18.99	August	19.5±0.83	4.25	18.37±3.35	18.23
	September	21±0.57	2.71			September	22±1.19	5.40		
	October	18.2±1.90	10.43			October	19.4±1.37	7.06		
	November	17.4±0.93	5.34			November	19±0.90	4.73		
Winter	December	15±1.87	12.46	16.00±2.20	13.76	December	16±1.71	10.68	17.05±2.64	15.51
	January	13.4±1.75	13.05			January	13.8±1.51	10.94		

West Site

During the study January-December 2008 at west site the chemical oxygen demand ranged 10 ± 0.75 to 20.60 ± 1.10 (mg/l). The maximum value recorded 20.60 ± 1.10 (mg/l) and coefficient variation was 5.33 per cent was recorded in September and minimum value recorded 10 ± 0.75 (mg/l) and coefficient variation was 7.50 per cent was recorded in May. In the second year study January-December 2009 the chemical oxygen demand at west site ranged 11 ± 1.20 to 21 ± 1.09 (mg/l). The maximum value recorded 21 ± 1.09 (mg/l) and coefficient variation was 5.19 per cent was recorded in September; minimum value recorded 11 ± 1.20 (mg/l) and coefficient variation was 10.90 per cent was recorded in May.

In the study January-December 2008 seasonal mean and coefficient variation values recorded 11.35 ± 1.03 (mg/l) and 9.11 per cent during summer, 17.80 ± 3.40 (mg/l) and 17.13 per cent during monsoon, 15.22 ± 1.76 (mg/l) and 11.59 per cent during winter (Fig. 3.23). In the second year study January-December 2009 seasonal mean and coefficient variation values recorded 12.47 ± 1.18 (mg/l) and 9.47 per cent during summer, 18.42 ± 2.63 (mg/l) and 14.30 per cent during monsoon, 16.42 ± 1.58 (mg/l) and 9.66 per cent during winter (Table 3.48 and Fig. 3.24).

In the present study January to December 2008 the maximum chemical oxygen demand was recorded in monsoon season at east site and minimum chemical oxygen demand was recorded in summer season at north site. In the second year study January-December 2009 the maximum chemical oxygen demand was recorded in monsoon season at east site where as minimum chemical oxygen demand was recorded in summer season at north site (Tables 3.46 and 3.47).

During the study January 2008-December 2009 chemical oxygen demand indicating significant positive correlation with turbidity, electric conductivity, total solid, total dissolved solids, total suspended solids, biochemical oxygen demand, total hardness, nitrate and phosphate and it indicating significant negative correlation with transparency, pH, alkalinity and fish (Tables 4.7 and 4.8).

Table 3.48: Seasonal Variations in Chemical Oxygen Demand (mg/l) at West Site, Harsool-Savangi Dam

Season	Months Jan. 2008 - Dec. 2008	Monthly Mean Values	Monthly C.V. (%)	Seasonal Mean Values	Seasonal C.V. (%)	Months Jan. 2009 - Dec. 2009	Monthly Mean Values	Monthly C.V. (%)	Seasonal Mean Values	Seasonal C.V. (%)
Summer	February	12.3±0.09	0.73	11.35±1.03	9.11	February	13.8±0.10	0.72	12.47±1.18	9.47
	March	12±0.10	0.83			March	12.9±0.09	0.69		
	April	11.1±0.90	8.10			April	12.2±0.70	5.73		
	May	10±0.75	7.50			May	11±1.20	10.90		
Monsoon	June	14±1.71	12.21	17.80±3.04	17.13	June	15.1±1.19	7.88	18.42±2.63	14.30
	July	16.7±1.29	7.72			July	17.6±2.19	12.44		
	August	19.9±2.0	10.05			August	20±2.05	10.25		
	September	20.6±1.10	5.33			September	21±1.09	5.19		
Winter	October	17±1.0	5.88	15.22±1.76	11.59	October	18.3±1.99	10.87	16.42±1.58	9.66
	November	16.3±0.90	5.52			November	17±0.90	5.29		
	December	14.5±0.17	1.17			December	15.8±1.99	12.59		
	January	13.1±0.07	0.53			January	14.6±0.74	5.06		

In the present study, the COD was maximum during monsoon and minimum during summer. Maximum values of COD in monsoon may due to mixing of runoff water due to which carries mud, dead and decaying biomass on the other hand minimum COD in summer was probably due to settlement of organic matter.

Alkalinity

Alkalinity of surface water is primarily a function of carbonate, hydroxide content and also includes the contributions from borates, phosphates, silicates and other bases. Alkalinity is a measure amount of strong acid needed to lower the pH of a sample to 8.3, which gives free alkalinity (phenolphthalein alkalinity) and to a pH 4.5 gives total alkalinity. Total alkalinity is the sum of hydroxides, carbonates and bicarbonates.Total Alkalinity is a measure of capacity of water to neutralize a strong acid. Alkaline water increases productivity and supports the diversity of aquatic life. The total alkalinity of the water is high may be due to the carbonates and bicarbonates. The alkalinity is harmful for irrigation, which leads to the soil damage, crop yield and imparts bitter taste to the water. Alkalinity is generally imparted by the salts of carbonates, bicarbonates, phosphates, nitrate, borates and silicates etc. together with hydroxyl ion concentration in Free State. However, most of water rich in carbonates and bicarbonates with low concentration of other alkalinity imparting ion (Trivedy and Goel, 1984). Water having 40 mg/l or more level of total alkalinity is considered to be more productive than waters of lower alkalinity (Moyle, 1946). It is measured as buffering capacity of water. The range of total alkalinity in India was between 40 mg/l to over 1000 m/l (Jhingran, 1977).

South Site

During the study January-December 2008 at south site the alkalinity ranged 161 ± 2.30 to 219 ± 8.00 (mg/l). The maximum value recorded 219 ± 8.00 (mg/l) and coefficient variation was 3.65 per cent was recorded in May and minimum value recorded 161 ± 2.30 (mg/l) and coefficient variation was 1.42 per cent was recorded in January. In the second year study January-December 2009 the alkalinity at south site ranged 168 ± 0.60 to 221 ± 7.20 (mg/l). The maximum value recorded 221 ± 7.20 (mg/l) and coefficient variation was 3.25 per cent was recorded in May; minimum value recorded 168 ± 0.60 (mg/l) and coefficient variation was 0.35 per cent was recorded in January.

In the study January-December 2008 seasonal mean and coefficient variation values recorded 200.25 ± 16 .68 (mg/l) and 8.33 per cent during summer, 180.50 ± 8.66 (mg/l) and 4.79 per cent during monsoon, 165.75 ± 3.59 (mg/l) and 2.16 per cent during winter (Fig. 3.25). In the second year study January-December 2009 seasonal mean and coefficient variation values recorded 201.75 ± 16.66 (mg/l) and 8.25 per cent during summer, 185.25 ± 8.42 (mg/l) and 4.54 and per cent during winter 169.75 ± 1.70 (mg/l) and 1.00 per cent during winter (Table 3.49 and Fig. 3.26).

North Site

During the study January-December 2008 at north site the alkalinity ranged 190 ± 0.11 to 237.50 ± 1.01 (mg/l). The maximum value recorded 237.50 ± 1.01 (mg/l) and coefficient variation was 0.42 per cent was recorded in May and minimum value recorded 190 ± 0.11 (mg/l) and coefficient variation was 0.05 per cent was recorded in September. In the second year study January-December 2009 the alkalinity at north site ranged 171.90 ± 0.40 to 240 ± 1.30 (mg/l). The maximum value recorded 240 ± 1.30 (mg/l) and coefficient variation was 0.54 per cent was recorded in May; minimum value recorded 171.90 ± 0.40 (mg/l) and coefficient variation was 0.23 per cent was recorded in January.

In the study January-December 2008 seasonal mean and coefficient variation values recorded 223 ± 10.55 (mg/l) and 4.73 per cent during summer, 194.47 ± 4.21 (mg/l) and 2.16 per cent during monsoon, 200.17 ± 7.18 (mg/l) and 3.58 per cent during winter (Fig. 3.25). In the second year study January-December 2009 seasonal mean and coefficient variation values recorded 218.50 ± 19.67 (mg/l) and 9.00 per cent during summer, 221.75 ± 11.86 (mg/l) and 5.35 and per cent during winter 184.50 ± 10.16 (mg/l) and 5.51 per cent during winter (Table 3.50 and Fig. 3.26).

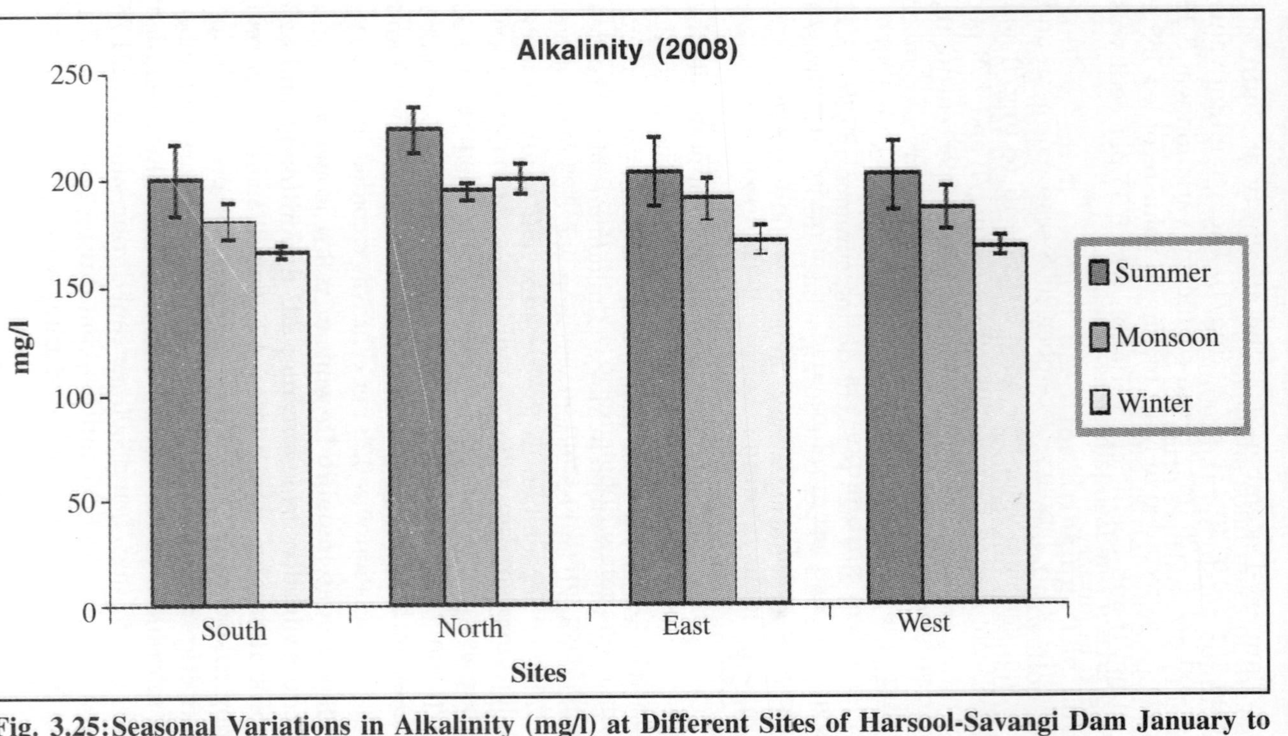

Fig. 3.25: Seasonal Variations in Alkalinity (mg/l) at Different Sites of Harsool-Savangi Dam January to December 2008

Table 3.49: Seasonal Variations in Alkalinity (mg/l) at South Site, Harsool-Savangi Dam

Season	Months Jan. 2008 - Dec. 2008	Monthly Mean Values	Monthly C.V. (%)	Seasonal Mean Values	Seasonal C.V. (%)	Months Jan. 2009 - Dec. 2009	Monthly Mean Values	Monthly C.V. (%)	Seasonal Mean Values	Seasonal C.V. (%)
	February	180±4.91	2.72			February	182±3.20	1.75		
	March	195±5.09	2.61			March	196±8.01	4.08		
Summer	April	207±7.03	3.39	200.25±16.68	8.33	April	208±3.91	1.87	201.75±16.66	8.25
	May	219±8.0	3.65			May	221±7.20	3.25		
	June	191±9.10	4.76			June	195±8.0	4.10		
	July	182±4.50	2.47			July	189±2.10	1.11		
Monsoon	August	179±2.24	1.25	180.50±8.66	4.79	August	181±1.80	0.99	185.25±8.42	4.54
	September	170±0.90	0.52			September	176±3.0	1.70		
	October	169±0.50	0.29			October	172±4.60	2.67		
	November	165±0.95	0.57			November	169±1.10	0.65		
Winter	December	168±1.01	0.60	165.75±3.59	2.16	December	170±0.9	0.52	169.75±1.70	1.00
	January	161±2.30	1.42			January	168±0.6	0.35		

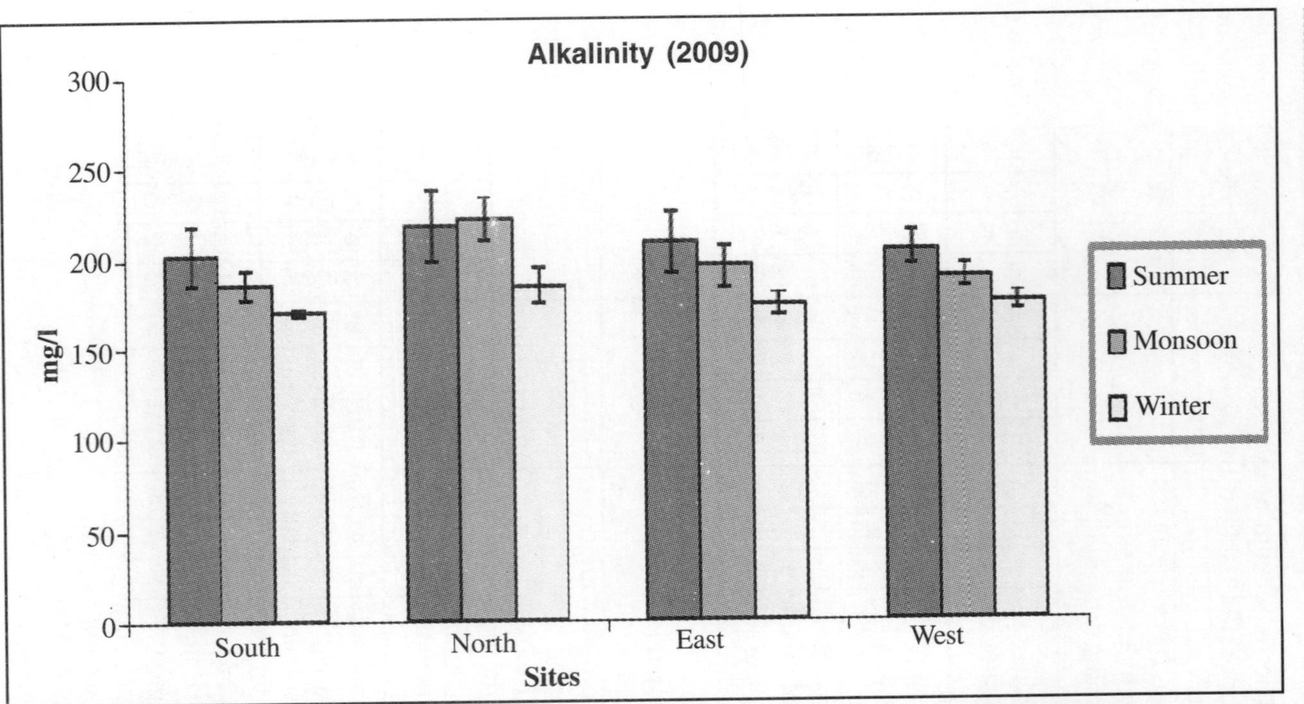

Fig. 3.26: Seasonal Variations in Alkalinity (mg/l) at Different Sites of Harsool-Savangi Dam January to December 2009

Table 3.50: Seasonal Variations in Alkalinity (mg/l) at North Site, Harsool-Savangi Dam

Season	Months Jan. 2008 - Dec. 2008	Monthly Mean Values	Monthly C.V. (%)	Seasonal Mean Values	Seasonal C.V. (%)	Months Jan. 2009 - Dec. 2009	Monthly Mean Values	Monthly C.V. (%)	Seasonal Mean Values	Seasonal C.V. (%)
Summer	February	214±0.23	0.10	223±10.55	4.73	February	195±0.80	0.41	218.50±19.67	9.00
	March	216.5±0.81	0.37			March	211±1.09	0.51		
	April	224±0.92	0.41			April	228±1.02	0.44		
	May	237.5±1.01	0.42			May	240±1.30	0.54		
Monsoon	June	200±1.20	0.60	194.47±4.21	2.16	June	219.5±1.90	0.86	221.75±11.86	5.35
	July	195±0.30	0.15			July	238±2.0	0.84		
	August	192.9±0.31	0.16			August	220±1.83	0.83		
	September	190±0.11	0.05			September	209.5±0.93	0.44		
Winter	October	192±0.34	0.17	200.17±7.18	3.58	October	196±0.84	0.42	184.50±10.16	5.51
	November	198±0.39	0.19			November	188.1±1.03	0.54		
	December	201.5±0.34	0.16			December	182±0.90	0.49		
	January	209.2±0.4	0.19			January	171.9±0.40	0.23		

East Site

During the study January-December 2008 at east site the alkalinity ranged 162 ± 0.15 to 221 ± 2.30 (mg/l). The maximum value recorded 221 ± 2.30 (mg/l) and coefficient variation was 1.04 per cent was recorded in May and minimum value recorded 162 ± 0.15 (mg/l) and coefficient variation was 0.09 per cent was recorded in January. In the second year study January-December 2009 the alkalinity at east site ranged 165 ± 0.20 to 227 ± 2.00 (mg/l). The maximum value recorded 227 ± 2.00 (mg/l) and coefficient variation was 0.88 per cent was recorded in May; minimum value recorded 165 ± 0.20 (mg/l) and coefficient variation was 0.12 per cent was recorded in January.

In the study January-December 2008 seasonal mean and coefficient variation values recorded 203.72 ± 16.31 (mg/l) and 8.01 per cent during summer, 190.47 ± 10.15 (mg/l) and 5.33 per cent during monsoon, 171.27 ± 6.81 (mg/l) and 3.97 per cent during winter (Fig. 3.25). In the second year study January-December 2009 seasonal mean and coefficient variation values recorded 208.12 ± 17.04 (mg/l) and 8.18 per cent during summer, 194.87 ± 11.42 (mg/l) and 5.86 per cent during monsoon, 173.87 ± 6.22 (mg/l) and 3.57 per cent during winter (Table 3.51 and Fig. 3.26).

West Site

During the study January-December 2008 at west site the alkalinity ranged 161.90 ± 1.01 to 219.90 ± 2.00 (mg/l). The maximum value recorded 219.90 ± 2.00 (mg/l) and coefficient variation was 0.90 per cent was recorded in May and minimum value recorded 161.90 ± 1.01 (mg/l) and coefficient variation was 0.62 per cent was recorded in January. In the second year study January-December 2009 the alkalinity at west site ranged 169.5 ± 1.20 to 216 ± 4.92 (mg/l). The maximum value recorded 216 ± 4.92 (mg/l) and coefficient variation was 2.27 per cent was recorded in April; minimum value recorded 169.5 ± 1.20 (mg/l) and coefficient variation was 0.70 per cent was recorded in November.

Table 3.51: Seasonal Variations in Alkalinity (mg/l) at East Site, Harsool-Savangi Dam

Season	Months Jan. 2008 - Dec. 2008	Monthly Mean Values	Monthly C.V. (%)	Seasonal Mean Values	Seasonal C.V. (%)	Months Jan. 2009 - Dec. 2009	Monthly Mean Values	Monthly C.V. (%)	Seasonal Mean Values	Seasonal C.V. (%)
Summer	February	182.9±1.23	0.67	203.72±16.31	8.01	February	187±2.01	1.07	208.12±17.04	8.18
	March	200±1.04	0.52			March	203.5±2.80	1.37		
	April	211±1.90	0.90			April	215±2.09	0.97		
	May	221±2.30	1.04			May	227±2.0	0.88		
Monsoon	June	204.3±2.11	1.03	190.47±10.15	5.33	June	209.3±1.90	0.90	194.87±11.42	5.86
	July	190±2.35	1.23			July	197±0.61	0.30		
	August	187.6±1.12	0.59			August	191.2±0.75	0.39		
	September	180±0.90	0.50			September	182±0.12	0.06		
Winter	October	178±0.82	0.46	171.27±6.81	3.97	October	179.5±0.11	0.06	173.87±6.22	3.57
	November	171±0.50	0.29			November	176±0.10	0.05		
	December	174.1±0.10	0.05			December	175±0.10	0.05		
	January	162±0.15	0.09			January	165±0.20	0.12		

In the study January-December 2008 seasonal mean and coefficient variation values recorded 202 ± 16.26 (mg/l) and 8.05 per cent during summer, 185.87 ± 10.05 (mg/l) and 5.40 per cent during monsoon, 168.27 ± 4.41 (mg/l) and 2.62 per cent during winter (Fig. 3.25). In the second year study January-December 2009 seasonal mean and coefficient variation values recorded 204.42 ± 9.53 (mg/l) and 4.66 per cent during summer, 189.25 ± 6.31 (mg/l) and 3.33 per cent during monsoon, 174.97 ± 5.07 (mg/l) and 2.90 per cent during winter (Table 3.52 and Fig. 3.26).

In the present study January to December 2008 the maximum alkalinity was recorded in summer season at north site and minimum alkalinity was recorded in winter season at south site. In the second year study January-December 2009 the maximum alkalinity was recorded in summer season at north site where as minimum alkalinity was recorded in winter season at east site (Tables 3.49, 3.50 and 3.51).

During the study January 2008-December 2009 alkalinity indicating significant positive correlation with water temperature, transparency, pH, sulphate, chloride and fish and it indicating significant negative correlation with electric conductivity, total solid, total dissolved solids, dissolved oxygen, biochemical oxygen demand, chemical oxygen demand and phosphate (Tables 4.7 and 4.8).

In the present study, the alkalinity was maximum during summer and minimum during monsoon. This may be increase the rate of organic decomposition which CO_2 is liberated and reacts with water to form HCO_3, in that way increasing the total alkalinity in summer. The increased alkalinity during summer and winter is due to the concentration of nutrients in water. Alkalinity decrease was due to dilution caused by the rainwater during monsoon.

Total Hardness

Hardness is due to concentration of alkaline earth metals. Ca^{++} and Mg^{++} ions are the principal cations imparting hardness, it prevents leather forming. Ca^{++} and Mg^{++} are the most abundant elements in natural surface and ground water

Table 3.52: Seasonal Variations in Alkalinity (mg/l) at West Site, Harsool-Savangi Dam

Season	Months Jan. 2008 - Dec. 2008	Monthly Mean Values	Monthly C.V. (%)	Seasonal Mean Values	Seasonal C.V. (%)	Months Jan. 2009 - Dec. 2009	Monthly Mean Values	Monthly C.V. (%)	Seasonal Mean Values	Seasonal C.V. (%)
Summer	February	182±0.70	0.38	202±16.26	8.05	February	193.5±1.20	0.62	204.42±9.53	4.66
	March	197.1±0.33	0.16			March	201±3.10	1.54		
	April	209±2.17	1.03			April	**216±4.92**	2.27		
	May	**219.9±2.0**	0.90			May	207.2±5.08	2.45		
Monsoon	June	199±1.90	0.95	185.87±10.05	5.40	June	196.1±1.20	0.61	189.25±6.31	3.33
	July	187.3±0.30	0.16			July	191±0.90	0.47		
	August	182±0.21	0.11			August	189±0.95	0.50		
	September	175.2±0.10	0.05			September	180.9±1.01	0.55		
Winter	October	171.9±0.12	0.06	168.27±4.41	2.62	October	178±0.70	0.39	174.97±5.07	2.90
	November	169±0.30	0.17			November	**169.5±1.20**	0.70		
	December	170.3±0.31	0.18			December	180.4±2.0	1.10		
	January	**161.9±1.01**	0.62			January	172±2.90	1.68		

and exist mainly as carbonates, bicarbonates and carbon dioxide constituted major source of inorganic carbon for producers in an aquatic ecosystem. They also act as buffers regulating the pH of the medium. The bicarbonate alkalinity is considered more important which influences the density of bottom fauna. The ecological significance of major cations i.e. calcium and magnesium in the biotic dynamics of aquatic fauna and flora is a well-established fact. Hardly a group of fresh water animal exists in which the distribution of some species has not been related to calcium concentration in the environment. Magnesium is essential for flora in chlorophyll biosynthesis and enzymatic transformations, particularly the phosphorylation in algae, fungi and bacteria (Wetzel, 1975).

South Site

In the study January-December 2008 at south site the total hardness ranged 350 ± 2.41 to 550 ± 7.50 (mg/l). The maximum value recorded 550 ± 7.50 (mg/l) and coefficient variation was 1.36 per cent was recorded in September and minimum value recorded 350 ± 2.41 (mg/l) and coefficient variation was 0.68 per cent was recorded in February. In the second year study January-December 2009 the total hardness at south site ranged 353 ± 3.09 to 558 ± 0.50 (mg/l). The maximum value recorded 558 ± 0.50 (mg/l) and coefficient variation was 0.08 per cent was recorded in September; minimum value recorded 353 ± 3.09 (mg/l) and coefficient variation was 0.87 per cent was recorded in February.

During the study January-December 2008 seasonal mean and coefficient variation values recorded 386.25 ± 38.69 (mg/l) and 10.01 per cent during summer, 526 + 17.14 (mg/l) and 3.25 per cent during monsoon, 426.75 ± 42.05 (mg/l) and 9.85 per cent during winter (Fig. 3.27). In the second year study January-December 2009 seasonal mean and coefficient variation values recorded 388.75 ± 37.84 (mg/l) and 9.73 per cent during summer, 530.75 ± 19.05 (mg/l) and 3.58 per cent during monsoon, 434.75 ± 44.06 (mg/l) and 10.13 per cent during winter (Table 3.53 and Fig. 3.28).

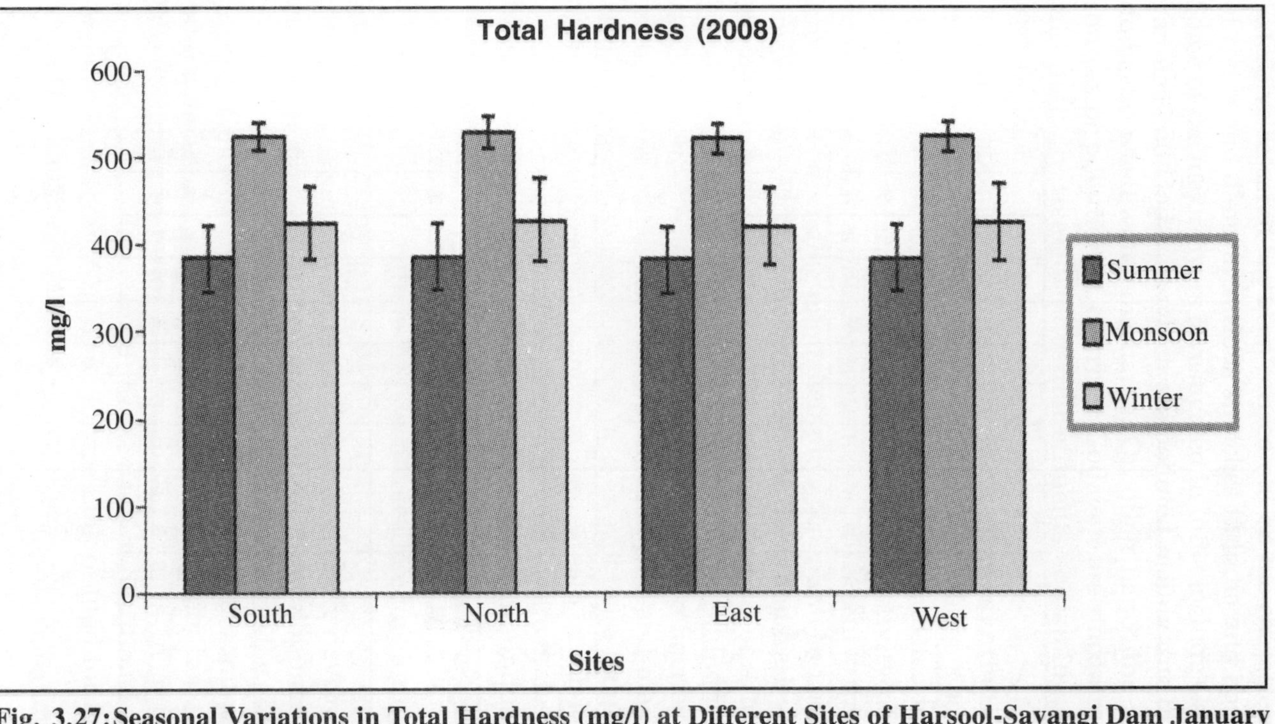

Fig. 3.27: Seasonal Variations in Total Hardness (mg/l) at Different Sites of Harsool-Savangi Dam January to December 2008

Table 3.53: Seasonal Variations in Total Hardness (mg/l) at South Site, Harsool-Savangi Dam

Season	Months Jan. 2008 - Dec. 2008	Monthly Mean Values	Monthly C.V. (%)	Seasonal Mean Values	Seasonal C.V. (%)	Months Jan. 2009 - Dec. 2009	Monthly Mean Values	Monthly C.V. (%)	Seasonal Mean Values	Seasonal C.V. (%)
	February	350±2.41	0.68			February	353±3.09	0.87		
	March	361±1.19	0.32			March	365±3.99	1.09		
Summer	April	399±1.35	0.33	386.25±38.69	10.01	April	400±2.21	0.55	388.75±37.84	9.73
	May	435±2.09	0.48			May	437±2.70	0.61		
	June	510±1.5	0.29			June	515±2.51	0.48		
	July	519±3.69	0.71			July	521±1.19	0.22		
Monsoon	August	525±3.27	0.62	526±17.14	3.25	August	529±1.23	0.23	530.75±19.05	3.58
	September	550±7.50	1.36			September	558±0.50	0.08		
	October	480±2.11	0.43			October	489±1.91	0.39		
	November	435±0.56	0.12			November	441±3.10	0.70		
Winter	December	412±1.17	0.28	426.75±42.05	9.85	December	427±4.25	0.99	434.75±44.06	10.13
	January	380±0.91	0.23			January	382±4.11	1.07		

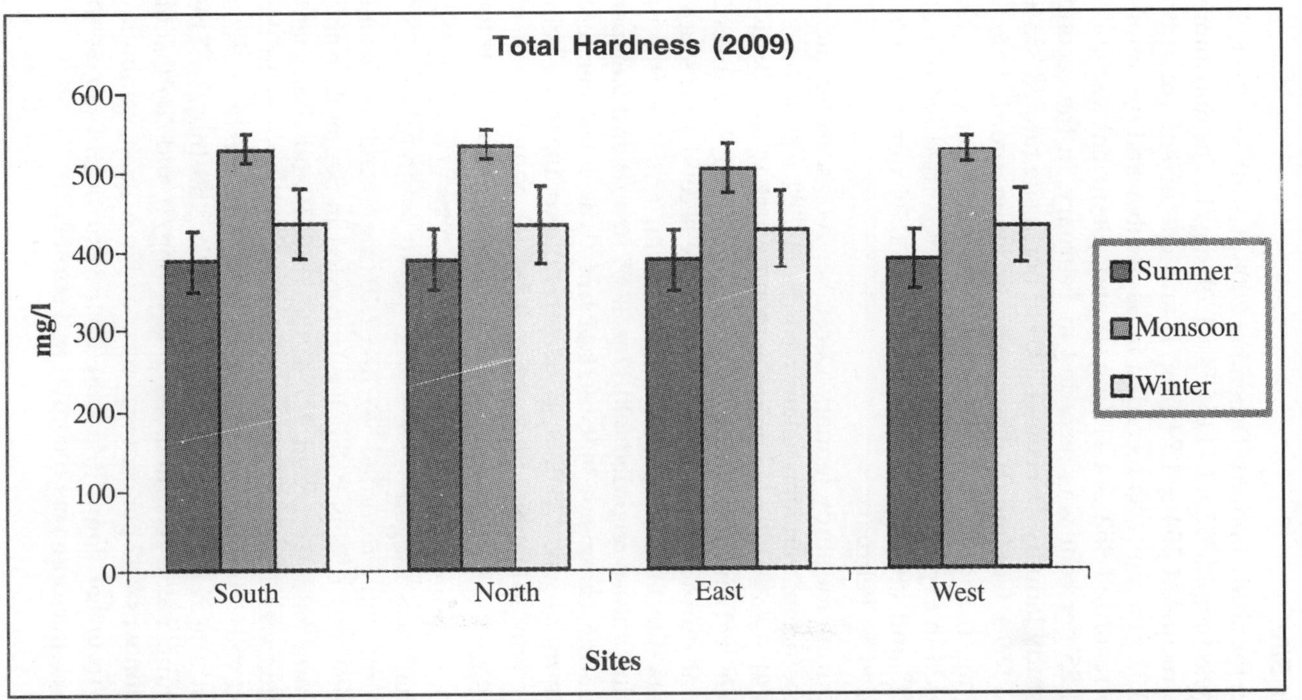

Fig. 3.28: Seasonal Variations in Total Hardness (mg/l) at Different Sites of Harsool-Savangi Dam January to December 2009

North Site

In the study January-December 2008 at north site the total hardness ranged 352 ± 4.41 to 554 ± 1.79 (mg/l). The maximum value recorded 554 ± 1.79 (mg/l) and coefficient variation was 0.32 per cent was recorded in September and minimum value recorded 352 ± 4.41 (mg/l) and coefficient variation was 1.25 per cent was recorded in February. In the second year study January-December 2009 at north site ranged 355 ± 1.21 to 559 ± 1.19 (mg/l). The maximum value recorded 559 ± 1.19 (mg/l) and coefficient variation was 0.21 per cent was recorded in September; minimum value recorded 355 ± 1.21 (mg/l) and coefficient variation was 0.34 per cent was recorded in February.

During the study January-December 2008 seasonal mean and coefficient variation values recorded 387.92 ± 38.46 (mg/l) and 9.91 per cent during summer, 530.32 ± 18.17 (mg/l) and 3.42 per cent during monsoon, 429.65 ± 47.35 (mg/l) and 11.02 per cent during winter (Fig. 3.27). In the second year study January-December 2009 seasonal mean and coefficient variation values recorded 390.37 ± 37.85 (mg/l) and 9.69 per cent during summer, 534.95 ± 18.42 (mg/l) and 3.44 per cent during monsoon, 433.07 ± 47.63 (mg/l) and 10.99 per cent during winter (Table 3.54 and Fig. 3.28).

East Site

During the study January-December 2008 at east site the total hardness ranged 347 ± 5.51 to 547.10 ± 2.10 (mg/l). The maximum value recorded 547.10 ± 2.10 (mg/l) and coefficient variation was 0.38 per cent was recorded in September and minimum value recorded 347 ± 5.51 (mg/l) and coefficient variation was 1.58 per cent was recorded in February. In the second year study January-December 2009 the total hardness at east site ranged 354 ± 2.41 to 531 ± 2.50 (mg/l). The maximum value recorded 531 ± 2.50 (mg/l) and coefficient variation was 0.47 per cent was recorded in August; minimum value recorded 354 ± 2.41 (mg/l) and coefficient variation was 0.68 per cent was recorded in February.

Table 3.54: Seasonal Variations in Total Hardness (mg/l) at North Site, Harsool-Savangi Dam

Season	Months Jan. 2008 - Dec. 2008	Monthly Mean Values	Monthly C.V. (%)	Seasonal Mean Values	Seasonal C.V. (%)	Months Jan. 2009 - Dec. 2009	Monthly Mean Values	Monthly C.V. (%)	Seasonal Mean Values	Seasonal C.V. (%)
Summer	February	352±4.41	1.25	387.92±38.46	9.91	February	355±1.21	0.34	390.37±37.85	9.69
	March	363.5±4.21	1.15			March	366.5±1.10	0.30		
	April	399±3.90	0.97			April	401±2.21	0.55		
	May	437.2±1.19	0.27			May	439±3.24	0.73		
Monsoon	June	512±1.10	0.21	530.32±18.17	3.42	June	516.3±3.49	0.67	534.95±18.42	3.44
	July	521.3±2.25	0.43			July	526±0.70	0.13		
	August	534±0.90	0.16			August	538.5±0.50	0.09		
	September	554±1.79	0.32			September	559±1.19	0.21		
Winter	October	492.5±3.19	0.64	429.65±47.35	11.02	October	496±2.12	0.42	433.07±47.63	10.99
	November	435±3.77	0.86			November	438±1.75	0.39		
	December	410.1±1.09	0.26			December	415.3±2.10	0.50		
	January	381±0.91	0.23			January	383±0.19	0.04		

In the study January-December 2008 seasonal mean and coefficient variation values recorded 383.52 ± 38.24 (mg/l) and 9.97 per cent during summer, 522.52 ± 17.98 (mg/l) and 3.44 per cent during monsoon, 421.57 ± 44.20 (mg/l) and 10.48 per cent during winter (Fig. 3.27). In the second year study January-December 2009 seasonal mean and coefficient variation values recorded 389.30 ± 38.09 (mg/l) and 9.78 per cent during summer, 504 ± 31.96 (mg/l) and 6.34 per cent during monsoon, 426.75 ± 47.65 (mg/l) and 11.16 per cent during winter (Table 3.55 and Fig. 3.28).

West Site

During the study January-December 2008 at west site the total hardness ranged 349.90 ± 5.90 to 549.30 ± 1.27 (mg/l). The maximum value recorded 549.30 ± 1.27 (mg/l) and coefficient variation was 0.23 per cent was recorded in September and minimum value recorded 349.90 ± 5.90 (mg/l) and coefficient variation was 1.68 per cent was recorded in February. In the second year study January-December 2009 the total hardness at west site ranged 355 ± 2.19 to 550 ± 1.62 (mg/l). The maximum value recorded 550 ± 1.62 (mg/l) and coefficient variation was 0.29 per cent was recorded in September; minimum value recorded 355 ± 2.19 (mg/l) and coefficient variation was 0.61 per cent was recorded in February.

In the study January-December 2008 seasonal mean and coefficient variation values recorded 385.52 ± 38.43 (mg/l) and 9.96 per cent during summer, 524.82 ± 17.73 (mg/l) and 3.37 per cent during monsoon, 425.80 ± 43.45 (mg/l) and 10.20 per cent during winter (Fig. 3.27). In the second year study January-December 2009 seasonal mean and coefficient variation values recorded 390.62 ± 37.21 (mg/l) and 9.52 per cent during summer, 528.75 ± 15.98 (mg/l) and 3.02 per cent during monsoon, 431.25 ± 45.90 (mg/l) and 10.64 per cent during winter (Table 3.56 and Fig. 3.28).

Table 3.55: Seasonal Variations in Total Hardness (mg/l) at East Site, Harsool-Savangi Dam

Season	Months Jan. 2008 - Dec. 2008	Monthly Mean Values	Monthly C.V. (%)	Seasonal Mean Values	Seasonal C.V. (%)	Months Jan. 2009 - Dec. 2009	Monthly Mean Values	Monthly C.V. (%)	Seasonal Mean Values	Seasonal C.V. (%)
Summer	February	347±5.51	1.58	383.52±38.24	9.97	February	354±2.41	0.68	389.30±38.09	9.78
	March	359±4.49	1.25			March	366±3.09	0.84		
	April	396.9±1.19	0.29			April	398±2.14	0.53		
	May	431.2±0.90	0.20			May	439.2±3.25	0.73		
Monsoon	June	506±1.32	0.26	522.52±17.98	3.44	June	509±3.17	0.62	504±31.96	6.34
	July	513±1.12	0.21			July	518±2.19	0.42		
	August	524±1.97	0.37			August	531±2.50	0.47		
	September	547.1±2.10	0.38			September	458±1.90	0.41		
Winter	October	480±2.09	0.43	421.57±44.20	10.48	October	491±1.35	0.27	426.75±47.65	11.16
	November	429±2.19	0.51			November	432±2.0	0.46		
	December	399.3±2.53	0.63			December	403±1.10	0.27		
	January	378±3.75	0.99			January	381±0.50	0.13		

Table 3.56: Seasonal Variations in Total Hardness (mg/l) at West Site, Harsool-Savangi Dam

Season	Months Jan. 2008 - Dec. 2008	Monthly Mean Values	Monthly C.V. (%)	Seasonal Mean Values	Seasonal C.V. (%)	Months Jan. 2009 - Dec. 2009	Monthly Mean Values	Monthly C.V. (%)	Seasonal Mean Values	Seasonal C.V. (%)
Summer	February	349.9±5.90	1.68	385.52±38.43	9.96	February	355±2.19	0.61	390.62±37.21	9.52
	March	360±4.21	1.16			March	369±1.29	0.34		
	April	398.2±2.70	0.67			April	399.5±2.1	0.52		
	May	434±2.19	0.50			May	439±0.70	0.15		
Monsoon	June	508±1.10	0.21	524.82±17.73	3.37	June	512±2.19	0.42	528.75±15.98	3.02
	July	517±1.19	0.23			July	523±2.12	0.40		
	August	525±0.90	0.17			August	530±1.97	0.37		
	September	549.3±1.27	0.23			September	550±1.62	0.29		
Winter	October	482±3.17	0.65	425.80±43.45	10.20	October	489±1.50	0.30	431.25±45.90	10.64
	November	433±2.91	0.67			November	441±0.90	0.20		
	December	409±0.50	0.12			December	415±0.19	0.04		
	January	379.2±0.10	0.02			January	380±0.91	0.23		

In the present study January to December 2008 the maximum total hardness was recorded in monsoon season at north site and minimum total hardness was recorded in summer season at east site. In the second year study January-December 2009 the maximum total hardness was recorded in monsoon season at north site where as minimum total hardness was recorded in summer season at south site (Tables 3.53, 3.54 and 3.55).

During the study January 2008-December 2009 total hardness indicating significant positive correlation with turbidity, electric conductivity, total solid, total dissolved solids, total suspended solids, biochemical oxygen demand, chemical oxygen demand, nitrate and phosphate and it indicating significant negative correlation with transparency and fish (Tables 4.7 and 4.8).

In the present study, the maximum hardness was recorded in monsoon and minimum in summer season. Hardness is mainly due to calcium and magnesium, the major cation present in natural waters as calcium and magnesium, its main source being leaching of rocks in the catchments. Maximum total hardness was recorded during the monsoon may be leaching of rocks in catchments area. Its concentration restricts water use, while it is an important component in the exoskeleton of arthropods and shells in molluscs (Piska, 2000).

Sulphate

Sulphate present in fertilizers contributes water pollution and increase sulphate concentration in water body. They also come from runoff water, which contains relatively large quantities of organic and mineral sulphur compounds. Water containing magnesium sulphate levels about 1000 mg/l acts as a purgative in human adults, lower concentrations may still affect new users and children (Joshi and Sakhre, 2003).

Sulphates are found in appreciable quantities in all the natural waters, particularly high dry and semi dry regions where natural waters, in general have high salt content. Sulphate is important constituent producing water with calcium and magnesium. High amounts of sulphate impart bitter taste to water. Sulphur exists in a number of oxidation states, from the most oxidized sulphate to the most reduced sulphide.

The biological reduction of sulphur can take place in both aerobic and anaerobic conditions. Under the aerobic conditions reduction of sulphate is an assimilatory process where as under the aerobic conditions a specialized group of anaerobic bacteria, the sulphate reducing bacteria use sulphates as the terminal electron acceptors and form hydrogen sulphide, as a result of the dissimulator reduction of sulphate. The sulphate reducing bacteria are also terminal oxidizers of organic matter in a sulphate rich environment (Lovley and Klug, 1983). The supply of sulphate ions in surface water under natural conditions are due to the reactions of water with sulphate containing rock and with the biochemical and partly chemical oxidation of sulphides and other compounds of sulphur. The most stable from of sulphur in water at 25 °C and atmospheric pressure are SO_4, H_2SO_4, free sulphur and HS-H_2S (Singh, 1984).

South Site

In the study January-December 2008 at south site the sulphate ranged 10 ± 1.10 to 18.50 ± 1.13 (mg/l). The maximum value recorded 18.50 ± 1.13 (mg/l) and coefficient variation was 6.10 per cent was recorded in May and minimum value recorded 10 ± 1.10 (mg/l) and coefficient variation was 11.00 per cent was recorded in January. In the second year study January-December 2009 the sulphate at south site ranged 11 ± 0.90 to 18.90 ± 0.23 (mg/l). The maximum value recorded 18.90 ± 0.23 (mg/l) and coefficient variation was 1.21 per cent was recorded in May; minimum value recorded 11 ± 0.90 (mg/l) and coefficient variation was 8.18 per cent was recorded in January.

During the study January-December 2008 seasonal mean and coefficient variation values recorded 17.15 ± 0.96 (mg/l) and 5.64 per cent during summer, 15.77 ± 1.03 (mg/l) and 6.57 per cent during monsoon, 12.30 ± 1.73 (mg/l) and 14.14 per cent during winter (Fig. 3.29). In the second year study January-December 2009 seasonal mean and coefficient variation values recorded 18.20 ± 0.54 (mg/l) and 3.00 per cent during summer, 15.42 ± 0.49 (mg/l) and 3.23 per cent during monsoon, 12.77 ± 1.27 (mg/l) and 9.95 per cent during winter (Table 3.57 and Fig. 3.30).

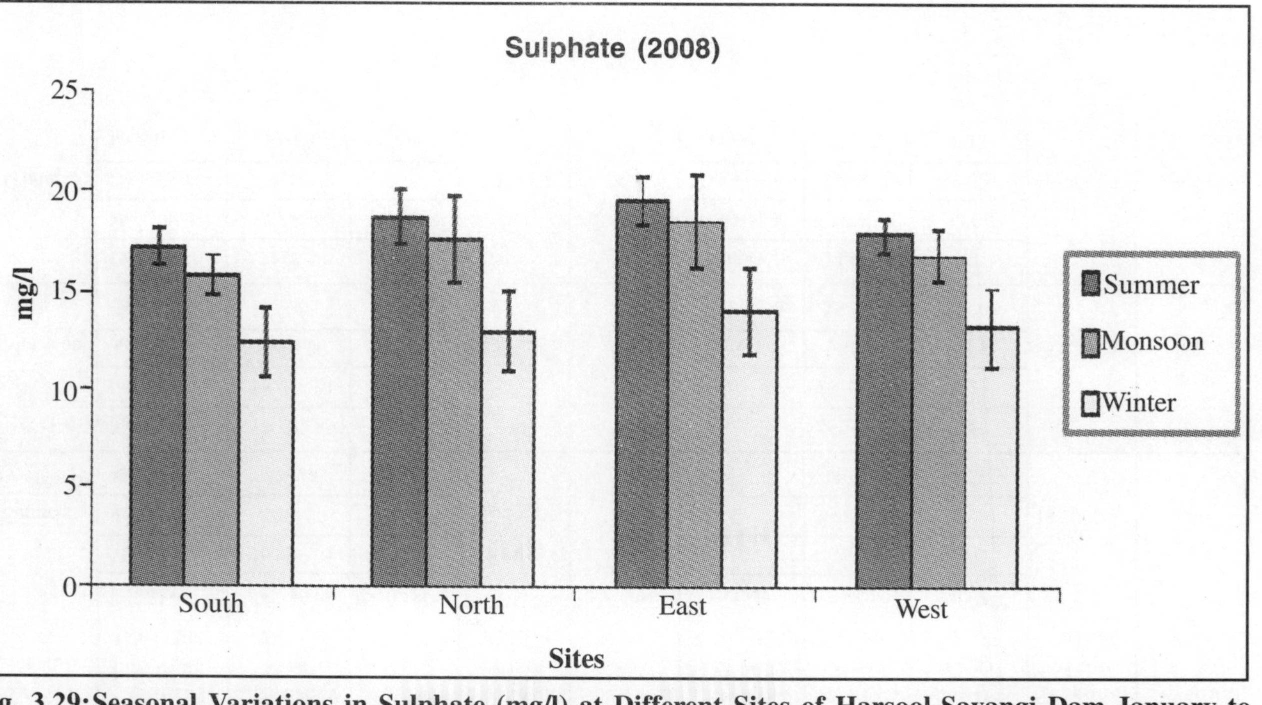

Fig. 3.29: Seasonal Variations in Sulphate (mg/l) at Different Sites of Harsool-Savangi Dam January to December 2008

Table 3.57: Seasonal Variations in Sulphate (mg/l) at South Site, Harsool-Savangi Dam

Season	Months Jan. 2008 - Dec. 2008	Monthly Mean Values	Monthly C.V. (%)	Seasonal Mean Values	Seasonal C.V. (%)	Months Jan. 2009 - Dec. 2009	Monthly Mean Values	Monthly C.V. (%)	Seasonal Mean Values	Seasonal C.V. (%)
	February	16.2±0.03	0.18			February	17.6±0.09	0.51		
	March	16.9±0.05	0.29			March	18±0.10	0.55		
Summer	April	17±0.90	5.29	17.15±0.96	5.64	April	18.3±0.40	2.18	18.20±0.54	3.00
	May	18.5±1.13	6.10			May	18.9±0.23	1.21		
	June	17.1±0.83	4.85			June	16.1±1.01	6.27		
	July	16.1±0.91	5.65			July	15.5±0.51	3.29		
Monsoon	August	15±0.20	1.33	15.77±1.03	6.57	August	15.1±0.01	0.06	15.42±0.49	3.23
	September	14.9±0.09	0.60			September	15±0.03	0.20		
	October	14±0.30	2.14			October	14±0.57	4.07		
	November	13.2±0.40	3.03			November	13.2±1.50	11.36		
Winter	December	12±0.45	3.75	12.30±1.73	14.14	December	12.9±1.19	9.22	12.77±1.27	9.95
	January	10±1.10	11.00			January	11±0.90	8.18		

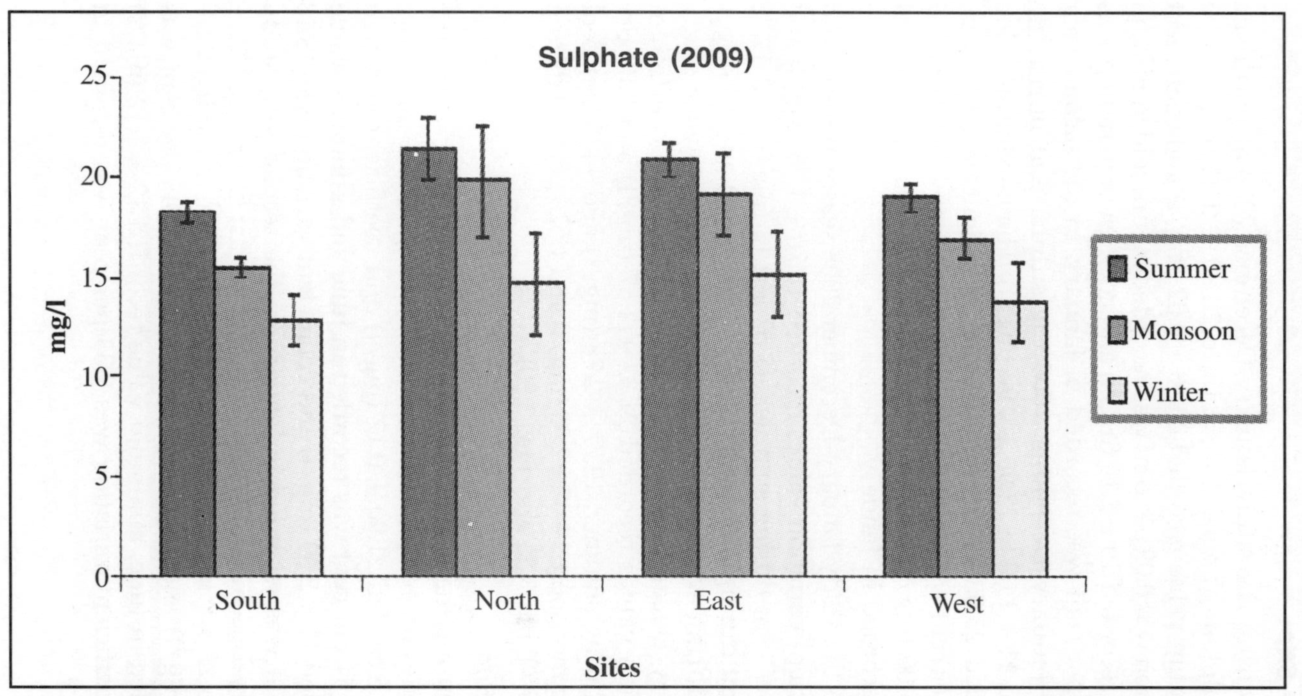

Fig. 3.30: Seasonal Variations in Sulphate (mg/l) at Different Sites of Harsool-Savangi Dam January to December 2009

North Site

During the study January-December 2008 at north site the sulphate ranged 10 ± 2.15 to 20.80 ± 0.02 (mg/l). The maximum value recorded 20.80 ± 0.02 (mg/l) and coefficient variation was 0.09 per cent was recorded in June and minimum value recorded 10 ± 2.15 (mg/l) and coefficient variation was 21.50 per cent was recorded in January. In the second year study January-December 2009 the sulphate at north site ranged 11 ± 1.00 to 23.90 ± 0.90 (mg/l). The maximum value recorded 23.90 ± 0.90 (mg/l) and coefficient variation was 3.76 per cent was recorded in June; minimum value recorded 11 ± 1.00 (mg/l) and coefficient variation was 9.09 per cent was recorded in January.

In the study January-December 2008 seasonal mean and coefficient variation values recorded 18.70 ± 1.38 (mg/l) and 7.42 per cent during summer, 17.57 ± 2.18 (mg/l) and 12.45 per cent during monsoon, 12.90 ± 2.03 (mg/l) and 15.77 per cent during winter (Fig. 3.29). In the second year study January-December 2009 seasonal mean and coefficient variation values recorded 21.32 ± 1.57 (mg/l) and 7.39 per cent during summer, 19.77 ± 2.78 (mg/l) and 14.07 per cent during monsoon, 14.67 ± 2.53 (mg/l) and 17.26 per cent during winter (Table 3.58 and Fig. 3.30).

East Site

During the study January-December 2008 at east site the sulphate ranged 11 ± 2.00 to 21.90 ± 0.12 (mg/l). The maximum value recorded 21.90 ± 0.12 (mg/l) and coefficient variation was 0.54 per cent was recorded in June and minimum value recorded 11 ± 2.00 (mg/l) and coefficient variation was 18.18 per cent was recorded in January. In the second year study January-December 2009 the sulphate at east site ranged 12 ± 1.12 to 22 ± 0.10 (mg/l). The maximum value recorded 22 ± 0.10 (mg/l) and coefficient variation was 0.45 per cent was recorded in June; minimum value recorded 12 ± 1.12 (mg/l) and coefficient variation was 9.33 per cent was recorded in January.

Table 3.58: Seasonal Variations in Sulphate (mg/l) at North Site, Harsool-Savangi Dam

Season	Months Jan. 2008 - Dec. 2008	Monthly Mean Values	Monthly C.V. (%)	Seasonal Mean Values	Seasonal C.V. (%)	Months Jan. 2009 - Dec. 2009	Monthly Mean Values	Monthly C.V. (%)	Seasonal Mean Values	Seasonal C.V. (%)
Summer	February	17.3±0.37	2.13	18.7±1.38	7.42	February	19.3±0.90	4.66	21.32±1.57	7.39
	March	18±0.42	2.33			March	21±1.03	4.90		
	April	19±0.50	2.63			April	22±1.10	5.00		
	May	20.5±0.75	3.65			May	23±1.09	4.73		
Monsoon	June	20.8±0.02	0.09	17.57±2.18	12.45	June	23.9±0.9	3.76	19.77±2.78	14.07
	July	17±0.58	3.41			July	19±2.10	11.05		
	August	16.5±0.50	3.03			August	18.2±1.90	10.43		
	September	16±1.19	7.43			September	18±0.87	4.83		
Winter	October	14.5±1.10	7.58	12.90±2.03	15.77	October	16.5±1.85	11.21	14.67±2.53	17.26
	November	14.1±1.0	7.09			November	16.2±1.20	7.40		
	December	13±1.90	14.61			December	15±1.19	7.93		
	January	10±2.15	21.50			January	11±1.0	9.09		

In the study January-December 2008 seasonal mean and coefficient variation values recorded 19.52 ± 1.25 (mg/l) and 6.41 per cent during summer, 18.52 ± 2.38 (mg/l) and 12.85 per cent during monsoon, 14 ± 2.16 (mg/l) and 15.43 per cent during winter (Fig. 3.29). In the second year study January-December 2009 seasonal mean and coefficient variation values recorded 20.87 ± 0.88 (mg/l) and 4.21 per cent during summer, 19.12 ± 2.04 (mg/l) and 10.67 and per cent during winter 15.12 ± 2.17 (mg/l) and 14.37 per cent during winter (Table 3.59 and Fig. 3.30).

West Site

During the study January-December 2008 at west site the sulphate ranged 10.40 ± 2.19 to 18.90 ± 0.09 (mg/l). The maximum value recorded 18.90 ± 0.09 (mg/l) and coefficient variation was 0.47 per cent was recorded in May and minimum value recorded 10.40 ± 2.19 (mg/l) and coefficient variation was 21.05 per cent was recorded in January. In the second year study January-December 2009 the sulphate at west site ranged 11 ± 0.50 to 19.80 ± 0.31 (mg/l). The maximum value recorded 19.80 ± 0.31 (mg/l) and coefficient variation was 1.56 per cent was recorded in May; minimum value recorded 11 ± 0.50 (mg/l) and coefficient variation was 4.54 per cent was recorded in January.

In the study January-December 2008 seasonal mean and coefficient variation values recorded 17.85 ± 0.86 (mg/l) and 4.85 per cent during summer, 16.80 ± 1.24 (mg/l) and 7.38 per cent during monsoon, 13.12 ± 1.99 (mg/l) and 15.17 per cent during winter (Fig. 3.29). In the second year study January-December 2009 seasonal mean and coefficient variation values recorded 18.95 ± 0.69 (mg/l) and 3.66 per cent during summer, 16.90 ± 1.02 (mg/l) and 6.05 per cent during monsoon, 13.77 ± 1.91 (mg/l) and 13.93 per cent during winter (Table 3.60 and Fig. 3.30).

Table 3.59: Seasonal Variations in Sulphate (mg/l) at East Site, Harsool-Savangi Dam

Season	Months Jan. 2008 - Dec. 2008	Monthly Mean Values	Monthly C.V. (%)	Seasonal Mean Values	Seasonal C.V. (%)	Months Jan. 2009 - Dec. 2009	Monthly Mean Values	Monthly C.V. (%)	Seasonal Mean Values	Seasonal C.V. (%)
Summer	February	18.1±0.90	4.97	19.52±1.25	6.41	February	20±0.30	1.50	20.87±0.88	4.21
	March	19±1.10	5.78			March	20.3±0.45	2.21		
	April	20±0.97	4.85			April	21.3±1.03	4.83		
	May	21±1.31	6.23			May	21.9±0.09	0.41		
Monsoon	June	21.9±0.12	0.54	18.52±2.38	12.85	June	22±0.10	0.45	19.12±2.04	10.67
	July	18±1.51	8.38			July	19.1±0.23	1.20		
	August	17.9±0.77	4.30			August	18±0.98	5.44		
	September	16.3±0.50	3.06			September	17.4±0.17	0.97		
Winter	October	16±0.73	4.56	14.00±2.16	15.43	October	17±0.02	0.11	15.12±2.17	14.37
	November	15±1.0	6.66			November	16±0.10	0.62		
	December	14±1.29	9.21			December	15.5±0.15	0.96		
	January	11±2.0	18.18			January	12±1.12	9.33		

Table 3.60: Seasonal Variations in Sulphate (mg/l) at West Site, Harsool-Savangi Dam

Season	Months Jan. 2008 - Dec. 2008	Monthly Mean Values	Monthly C.V. (%)	Seasonal Mean Values	Seasonal C.V. (%)	Months Jan. 2009 - Dec. 2009	Monthly Mean Values	Monthly C.V. (%)	Seasonal Mean Values	Seasonal C.V. (%)
Summer	February	17±0.02	0.11	17.85±0.86	4.85	February	18.1±0.80	4.41	18.95±0.69	3.66
	March	17.3±0.05	0.28			March	18.9±0.10	0.52		
	April	18.2±0.30	1.64			April	19±0.40	2.10		
	May	18.9±0.09	0.47			May	19.8±0.31	1.56		
Monsoon	June	18.3±0.12	0.65	16.80±1.24	7.38	June	18.3±0.47	2.56	16.90±1.02	6.05
	July	17.2±0.25	1.45			July	17±0.16	0.94		
	August	16.3±0.19	1.16			August	16.3±0.13	0.79		
	September	15.4±0.90	5.84			September	16±0.12	0.75		
Winter	October	15±0.30	2.00	13.12±1.99	15.17	October	14.9±0.19	1.27	13.77±1.91	13.93
	November	14.1±0.19	1.34			November	15.2±0.90	5.92		
	December	13±1.10	8.46			December	14±1.10	7.85		
	January	10.4±2.19	21.05			January	11±0.50	4.54		

In the present study January to December 2008 the maximum sulphate was recorded in monsoon season at east site and minimum sulphate was recorded in winter season at south and north site. In the second year study January-December 2009 the maximum sulphate was recorded in monsoon season at north site where as minimum sulphate was recorded in winter season at south, north and west site (Tables 3.57, 3.58, 3.59 and 3.60).

During the study January 2008-December 2009 sulphate indicating significant positive correlation with water temperature, pH, alkalinity and chloride and it indicating significant negative correlation with dissolved oxygen and fish (Tables 4.7 and 4.8).

In the present study, the maximum Sulphate was recorded at the site north which may be due to pollution from organic matter.

In the present study, the Sulphate was maximum during monsoon and minimum during winter. Maximum Sulphate concentration during monsoon may be dilution and utilization of sulphate by aquatic plants. However, the low sulphate concentration was noted during winter may be due to biodegradation and low water level.

Chloride

Chloride anion is generally present in natural waters. Chloride as chloride anions (Cl^-) are major anions in wastewater. The chloride concentration is higher in organic wastes and its higher level in natural water is definite indication of pollution from domestic sewage. A number of workers have reported that chloride in lake water was due to domestic sewage. The ecological significance of chloride lies in its potential to regulate salinity of water and exert consequent osmotic stress on biotic communities. An increase in chloride concentration in lakes, rivers and dams is due to the discharge of municipal and industrial wastes reported by Kant and Raina (1990).

Chlorides are high concentration indicators of large amount of organic matter in the water due to eutrophication.

Verma and Dalela, (1975) pointed out that presence of high amount of chloride influences the amount of dissolved oxygen, which may adversely affect the number of aquatic organisms. Chloride content, which was high during the present study, may be due to anthropogenic activities in addition with the progression of a trophy and edging of the dam. The rising concentration depends upon dumping of effluents from of municipal as well as industrial activities, as well as prevailing human activities.

South Site

In the study January-December 2008 at south site the Chloride ranged 20.30 ± 1.27 to 33 ± 1.97 (mg/l). The maximum value recorded 33 ± 1.97 (mg/l) and coefficient variation was 5.96 per cent was recorded in May and minimum value recorded 20.30 ± 1.27 (mg/l) and coefficient variation was 6.25 per cent was recorded in January. In the second year study January-December 2009 the Chloride at south site ranged 21.10 ± 1.19 to 35 ± 1.33 (mg/l). The maximum value recorded 35 ± 1.33 (mg/l) and coefficient variation was 3.80 per cent was recorded in May; minimum value recorded 21.10 ± 1.19 (mg/l) and coefficient variation was 5.63 per cent was recorded in January.

During the study January-December 2008 seasonal mean and coefficient variation values recorded 31.52 ± 1.20 (mg/l) and 3.81 per cent during summer, 28.15 ± 1.79 (mg/l) and 6.39 per cent during monsoon, 22.30 ± 1.96 (mg/l) and 8.79 (Fig. 3.31). In the second year study January-December 2009 seasonal mean and coefficient variation values recorded 33.45 ± 1.26 (mg/l) and 3.79 per cent during summer, 29.37 ± 2.28 (mg/l) and 7.78 per cent during monsoon, 23.32 ± 2.14 (mg/l) and 9.20 per cent during winter (Table 3.61 and Fig. 3.32).

North Site

In the study January-December 2008 at north site the Chloride ranged 19 ± 1.10 to 32.30 ± 0.91 (mg/l). The maximum value recorded 32.30 ± 0.91 (mg/l) and coefficient variation was 2.81 per cent was recorded in April and minimum value recorded 19 ± 1.10 (mg/l) and coefficient variation was 5.78

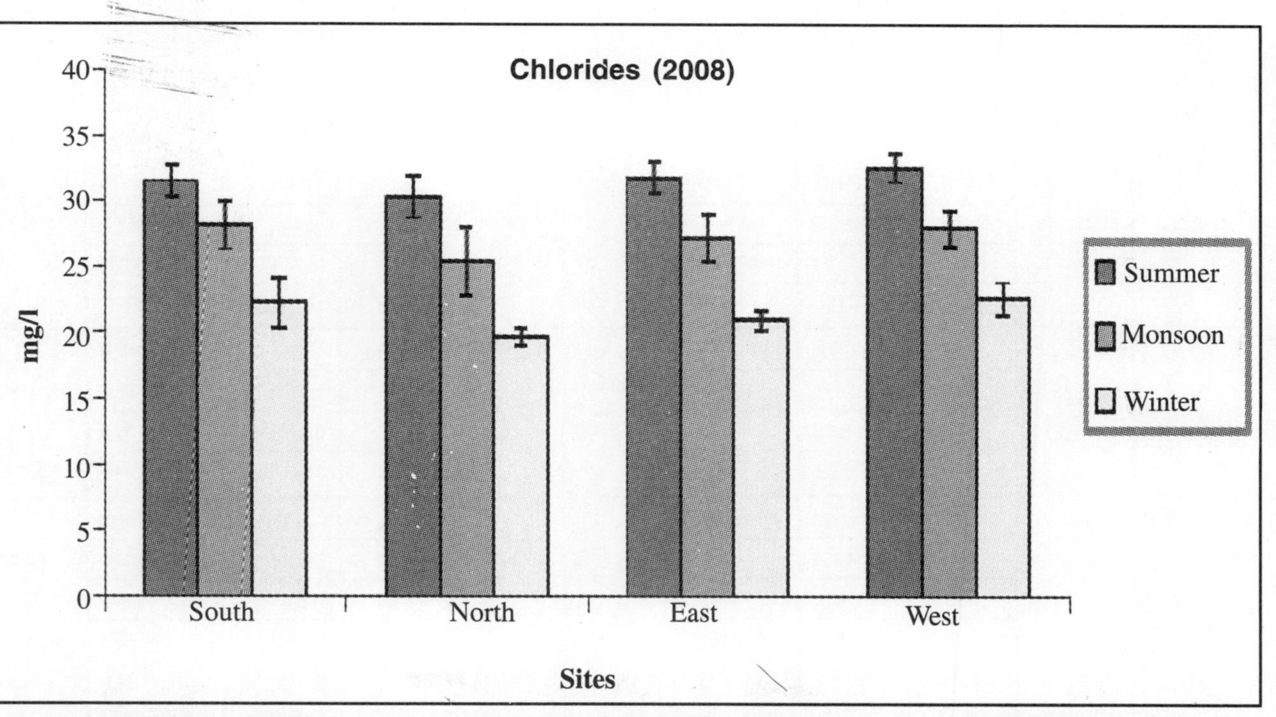

Fig. 3.31: Seasonal Variations in Chlorides (mg/l) at Different Sites of Harsool-Savangi Dam January to December 2008

Table 3.61: Seasonal Variations in Chlorides (mg/l) at South Site, Harsool-Savangi Dam

Season	Months Jan. 2008 - Dec. 2008	Monthly Mean Values	Monthly C.V. (%)	Seasonal Mean Values	Seasonal C.V. (%)	Months Jan. 2009 - Dec. 2009	Monthly Mean Values	Monthly C.V. (%)	Seasonal Mean Values	Seasonal C.V. (%)
Summer	February	30.2±1.10	3.64	31.52±1.20	3.81	February	32±0.75	2.34	33.45±1.26	3.79
	March	31±0.90	2.90			March	33±0.98	2.96		
	April	31.9±0.57	1.78			April	33.8±0.12	0.35		
	May	33±1.97	5.96			May	35±1.33	3.80		
Monsoon	June	30±2.0	6.66	28.15±1.79	6.39	June	32±1.50	4.68	29.37±2.28	7.78
	July	29.2±1.70	5.82			July	30.5±1.10	3.60		
	August	27.4±1.84	6.71			August	28±1.19	4.25		
	September	26±1.09	4.19			September	27±1.10	4.07		
Winter	October	25±0.90	3.60	22.30±1.96	8.79	October	26±0.91	3.50	23.32±2.14	9.20
	November	22±1.19	5.40			November	24±1.27	5.29		
	December	21.9±0.50	2.28			December	22.2±0.79	3.55		
	January	20.3±1.27	6.25			January	21.1±1.19	5.63		

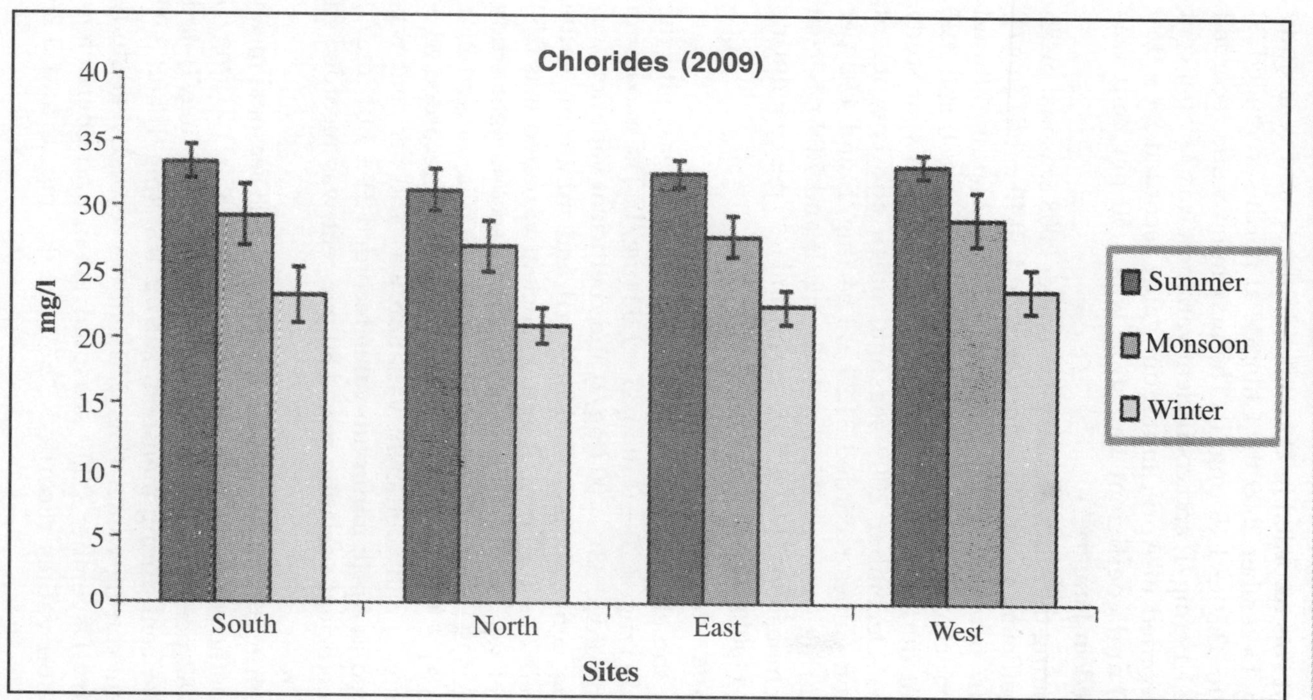

Fig. 3.32: Seasonal Variations in Chlorides (mg/l) at Different Sites of Harsool-Savangi Dam January to December 2009

per cent was recorded in December. In the second year study January-December 2009 the Chloride at north site ranged 20 ± 0.90 to 33.10 ± 1.19 (mg/l). The maximum value recorded 33.10 ± 1.19 (mg/l) and coefficient variation was 3.59 per cent was recorded in April; minimum value recorded 20 ± 0.90 (mg/l) and coefficient variation was 4.50 per cent was recorded in January.

During the study January-December 2008 seasonal mean and coefficient variation values recorded 30.40 ± 1.54 (mg/l) and 5.07 per cent during summer, 25.47 ± 2.60 (mg/l) and 10.21 per cent during monsoon, 19.75 ± 0.64 (mg/l) and 3.26 per cent during winter (Fig. 3.31). In the second year study January-December 2009 seasonal mean and coefficient variation values recorded 31.35 ± 1.54 (mg/l) and 4.93 per cent during summer, 27.07 ± 1.92 (mg/l) and 7.09 per cent during monsoon, 21.07 ± 1.35 (mg/l) and 6.40 per cent during winter (Table 3.62 and Fig. 3.32).

East Site

In the study January-December 2008 at east site the Chloride ranged 20 ± 0.10 to 33 ± 1.00 (mg/l). The maximum value recorded 33 ± 1.00 (mg/l) and coefficient variation was 3.03 per cent was recorded in April and minimum value recorded 20 ± 0.10 (mg/l) and coefficient variation was 0.50 per cent was recorded in January. In the second year study January-December 2009 the Chloride at east site ranged 21 ± 1.01 to 34 ± 1.19 (mg/l). The maximum value recorded 34 ± 1.19 (mg/l) and coefficient variation was 3.50 per cent was recorded in April; minimum value recorded 21 ± 1.01 (mg/l) and coefficient variation was 4.80 per cent was recorded in January.

During the study January-December 2008 seasonal mean and coefficient variation values recorded 31.85 ± 1.21 (mg/l) and 3.82 per cent during summer, 27.22 ± 1.86 (mg/l) and 6.84 per cent during monsoon, 20.97 ± 0.81 (mg/l) and 3.90 per cent during winter (Fig. 3.31). In the second year study January-December 2009 seasonal mean and coefficient variation values recorded 32.62 ± 1.06 (mg/l) and 3.26

Table 3.62: Seasonal Variations in Chlorides (mg/l) at North Site, Harsool-Savangi Dam

Season	Months Jan. 2008 - Dec. 2008	Monthly Mean Values	Monthly C.V. (%)	Seasonal Mean Values	Seasonal C.V. (%)	Months Jan. 2009 - Dec. 2009	Monthly Mean Values	Monthly C.V. (%)	Seasonal Mean Values	Seasonal C.V. (%)
Summer	February	29.3±0.93	3.17	30.40±1.54	5.07	February	30±1.12	3.73	31.35±1.54	4.93
	March	31±1.19	3.83			March	32.2±0.25	0.77		
	April	32.3±0.91	2.81			April	33.1±1.19	3.59		
	May	29±1.01	3.48			May	30.1±0.75	2.49		
Monsoon	June	28.9±0.50	1.73	25.47±2.60	10.21	June	29.8±0.60	2.01	27.07±1.92	7.09
	July	26±1.97	7.57			July	27±1.75	6.48		
	August	24±1.58	6.58			August	26±0.57	2.19		
	September	23±0.91	3.95			September	25.5±1.35	5.29		
Winter	October	20.5±0.51	2.48	19.75±0.64	3.26	October	23±1.0	4.34	21.07±1.35	6.40
	November	20±0.10	0.50			November	21±1.10	5.23		
	December	19±1.10	5.78			December	20.3±0.50	2.46		
	January	19.5±0.30	1.53			January	20±0.90	4.50		

per cent during summer, 27.82 ± 1.60 (mg/l) and 5.78 per cent during monsoon, 22.50 ± 1.29 (mg/l) and 5.73 per cent during winter (Table 3.63 and Fig. 3.32).

West Site

During the study January-December 2008 at west site the Chloride ranged 21.10 ± 0.40 to 33.90 ± 0.51 (mg/l). The maximum value recorded 33.90 ± 0.51 (mg/l) and coefficient variation was 1.50 per cent was recorded in April and minimum value recorded 21.10 ± 0.40 (mg/l) and coefficient variation was 1.89 per cent was recorded in January. In the second year study January-December 2009 the Chloride at west site ranged 22 ± 0.20 to 34 ± 0.02 (mg/l). The maximum value recorded 34 ± 0.02 (mg/l) and coefficient variation was 0.05 per cent was recorded in April; minimum value recorded 22 ± 0.20 (mg/l) and coefficient variation was 0.90 per cent was recorded in January.

In the study January-December 2008 seasonal mean and coefficient variation values recorded 32.60 ± 1.11 (mg/l) and 3.42 per cent during summer, 28.02 ± 1.44 (mg/l) and 5.16 per cent during monsoon, 22.62 ± 1.23 (mg/l) and 5.44 per cent during winter (Fig. 3.31). In the second year study January-December 2009 seasonal mean and coefficient variation values recorded 33.20 ± 0.86 (mg/l) and 2.60 per cent during summer, 29.20 ± 2.04 (mg/l) and 6.99 per cent during monsoon, 23.75 ± 1.70 (mg/l) and 7.19 per cent during winter (Table 3.64 and Fig. 3.32).

In the present study January to December 2008 the maximum chloride was recorded during summer season at west site and minimum values of chloride was recorded during winter season at north site. In the second year study January-December 2009 the maximum chloride was recorded during summer season at south site where as minimum chloride was recorded during winter season at north site (Tables 3.61, 3.62 and 3.64).

Table 3.63: Seasonal Variations in Chlorides (mg/l) at East Site, Harsool-Savangi Dam

Season	Months Jan. 2008 - Dec. 2008	Monthly Mean Values	Monthly C.V. (%)	Seasonal Mean Values	Seasonal C.V. (%)	Months Jan. 2009 - Dec. 2009	Monthly Mean Values	Monthly C.V. (%)	Seasonal Mean Values	Seasonal C.V. (%)
	February	31.3±1.19	3.80			February	32±0.90	2.81		
	March	32.7±1.50	4.58			March	32.9±1.10	3.34		
Summer	April	33±1.0	3.03	31.85±1.21	3.82	April	34±1.19	3.50	32.62±1.06	3.26
	May	30.4±1.10	3.61			May	31.6±0.50	1.58		
	June	29.9±0.50	1.67			June	30±0.45	1.50		
	July	27.1±0.90	3.32			July	28±1.33	4.75		
Monsoon	August	26±2.10	8.07	27.22±1.86	6.84	August	27±2.10	7.77	27.82±1.60	5.78
	September	25.9±2.0	7.72			September	26.3±1.50	5.70		
	October	22±1.09	4.95			October	24±0.40	1.66		
	November	21±0.50	2.38			November	23±0.50	2.17		
Winter	December	20.9±0.40	1.91	20.97±0.81	3.90	December	22±1.19	5.40	22.50±1.29	5.73
	January	20±0.10	0.50			January	21±1.01	4.80		

Table 3.64: Seasonal Variations in Chlorides (mg/l) at West Site, Harsool-Savangi Dam

Season	Months Jan. 2008 - Dec. 2008	Monthly Mean Values	Monthly C.V. (%)	Seasonal Mean Values	Seasonal C.V. (%)	Months Jan. 2009 - Dec. 2009	Monthly Mean Values	Monthly C.V. (%)	Seasonal Mean Values	Seasonal C.V. (%)
	February	32±0.19	0.59			February	33.2±0.01	0.03		
	March	33.1±0.97	2.93			March	33.6±0.10	0.29		
Summer	April	33.9±0.51	1.50	32.60±1.11	3.42	April	34±0.02	0.05	33.20±0.86	2.60
	May	31.4±1.12	3.56			May	32±1.57	4.90		
	June	30±0.88	2.93			June	31.9±0.73	2.28		
	July	28.2±0.23	0.81			July	29.6±0.81	2.73		
Monsoon	August	27.1±1.01	3.72	28.02±1.44	5.16	August	28±1.40	5.00	29.20±2.04	6.99
	September	26.8±0.91	3.39			September	27.3±0.70	2.56		
	October	24±1.10	4.58			October	26±0.11	0.42		
	November	23.1±1.50	6.49			November	24±1.51	6.29		
Winter	December	22.3±0.70	3.13	22.62±1.23	5.44	December	23±0.90	3.91	23.75±1.70	7.19
	January	21.1±0.40	1.89			January	22±0.20	0.90		

During the study January 2008-December 2009 chloride indicating significant positive correlation with water temperature, pH, alkalinity and sulphate and it indicating significant negative correlation with total solid, total dissolved solids and dissolved oxygen (Tables 4.7 and 4.8).

In the present study, the Chloride value was maximum during summer and minimum during winter. Maximum Chloride was recorded during summer and minimum during winter. It can be concluded that there was no definite pattern of chloride fluctuation, lower value during winter could be attributed to dilution effect and renewal of water mass alter summer stagnation and also may be due to high sedimentation rate on relatively stable environmental condition. Maximum value during summer could be due to higher concentration of chloride resulted from evaporation.

Nitrate

Nitrate is the most highly oxidized form of nitrogen compounds commonly present in natural waters, because it is a product of aerobic decomposition of organic nitrogenous matter. Significant sources of nitrate are fertilizers, decayed vegetable and animal matter, domestic and industrial effluents and atmospheric washouts. Unpolluted natural water contain usually only minute amount of nitrate. Excessive concentration in drinking water is considered hazardous for infants because their intestinal tract nitrate is reduced to nitrites, which may cause Methaemoglobinaemia or blue baby syndrome. Nitrate is also an essential nutrient for algal growth and hence when present in high concentration along with phosphates causes eutrophication. Atmospheric nitrogen fixed into nitrate by the nitrogen-fixing organism is also a significant contributor to nitrate in the water (Trivedy and Goel, 1984). Determination of nitrate levels is important as it helps in measuring the pollution status and gives relative picture of availability of decomposable organic matter. The urban water bodies receive excess of nitrate through untreated domestic sewage. Unpolluted natural water contains usually only minute amount of nitrate. High nitrate content in potable water is harmful for children and cause anemia (Methamo-globanaemia) (De, 2002).

South Site

During the study January-December 2008 at south site the nitrate ranged 0.51 ± 0.01 to 2 ± 0.20 (mg/l). The maximum value recorded 2 ± 0.20 (mg/l) and coefficient variation was 10.00 per cent was recorded in September and minimum value recorded 0.51 ± 0.01 (mg/l) and coefficient variation was 2.35 per cent was recorded in May. In the second year study January-December 2009 the nitrate at south site ranged 0.53 ± 0.07 to 2.20 ± 1.10 (mg/l). The maximum value recorded 2.20 ± 1.10 (mg/l) and coefficient variation was 50.00 per cent was recorded in September; minimum value recorded 0.53 ± 0.07 (mg/l) and coefficient variation was 13.39 per cent was recorded in May.

In the study January-December 2008 seasonal mean and coefficient variation values recorded 0.65 ± 0.11 (mg/l) and 18.17 per cent during summer, 1.60 ± 0.42 (mg/l) and 26.51 per cent during monsoon, 0.95 ± 0.23 (mg/l) and 24.24 per cent during winter (Fig. 3.33). In the second year study January-December 2009 seasonal mean and coefficient variation values recorded 0.67 ± 0.11 (mg/l) and 16.95 per cent during summer, 1.67 ± 0.48 (mg/l) and 28.71 per cent during monsoon, 1.01 ± 0.22 (mg/l) and 22.21 per cent during winter (Table 3.65 and Fig. 3.34).

North Site

In the study January-December 2008 at north site the nitrate ranged 0.53 ± 0.019 to 2.10 ± 0.10 (mg/l). The maximum value recorded 2.10 ± 0.10 (mg/l) and coefficient variation was 4.76 per cent was recorded in September and minimum value recorded 0.53 ± 0.01 (mg/l) and coefficient variation was 3.58 per cent was recorded in May. In the second year study January-December 2009 the nitrate at north site ranged 0.58 ± 0.02 to 2.14 ± 1.19 (mg/l). The maximum value recorded 2.14 ± 1.19 (mg/l) and coefficient variation was 55.60 per cent was recorded in September; minimum value recorded 0.58 ± 0.02 (mg/l) and coefficient variation was 5.00 per cent was recorded in May.

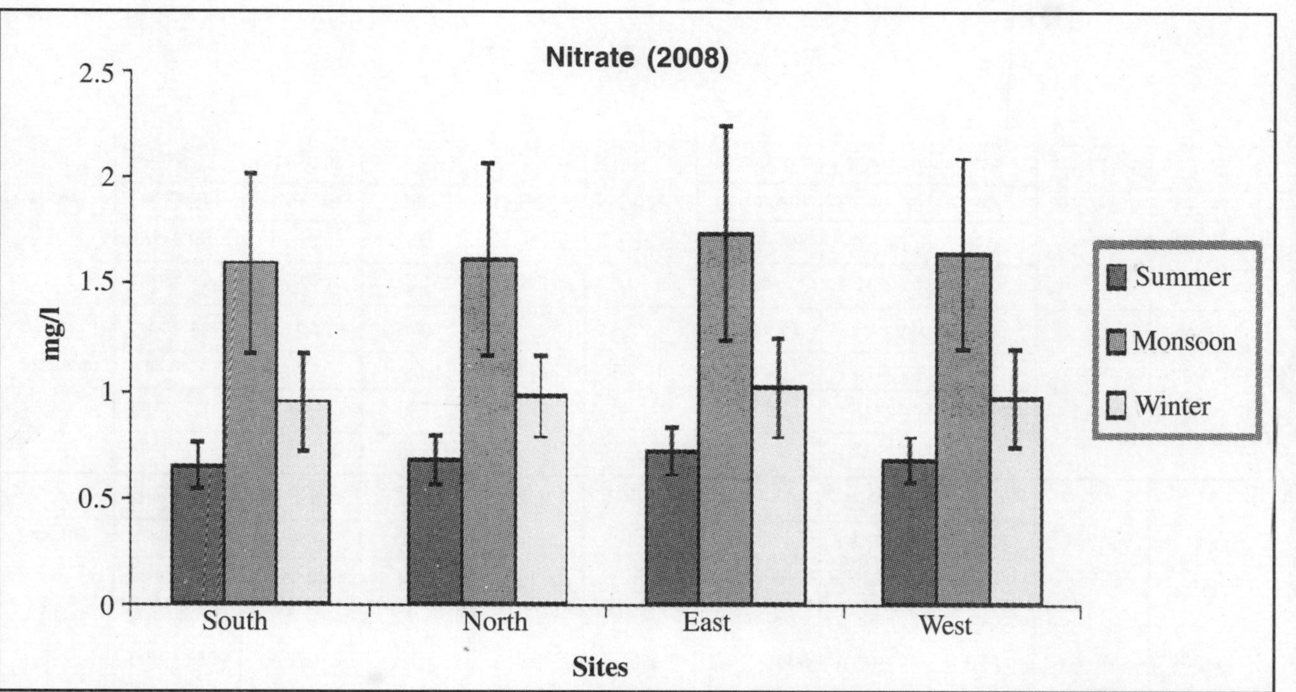

Fig. 3.33:Seasonal Variations in Nitrate (mg/l) at Different Sites of Harsool-Savangi Dam January to December 2008

Table 3.65: Seasonal Variations in Nitrate (mg/l) at South Site, Harsool-Savangi Dam

Season	Months Jan. 2008 - Dec. 2008	Monthly Mean Values	Monthly C.V. (%)	Seasonal Mean Values	Seasonal C.V. (%)	Months Jan. 2009 - Dec. 2009	Monthly Mean Values	Monthly C.V. (%)	Seasonal Mean Values	Seasonal C.V. (%)
	February	0.79±0.091	11.51			February	0.8±0.013	1.62		
	March	0.7±0.09	12.85			March	0.72±0.011	1.52		
Summer	April	0.62±0.021	3.38	0.65±0.11	18.17	April	0.65±0.025	3.84	0.67±0.11	16.95
	May	0.51±0.01	2.35			May	0.53±0.07	13.39		
	June	1.1±0.12	10.90			June	1.14±0.10	8.77		
	July	1.4±0.19	13.57			July	1.42±0.14	9.85		
Monsoon	August	1.9±0.09	4.73	1.60±0.42	26.51	August	1.93±0.19	9.84	1.67±0.48	28.71
	September	2±0.20	10.00			September	2.2±1.10	50.00		
	October	1.3±0.21	16.15			October	1.34±0.90	67.16		
	November	0.9±0.02	2.22			November	1±0.81	81.00		
Winter	December	0.83±0.011	1.32	0.95±0.23	24.24	December	0.9±0.025	2.77	1.01±0.22	22.21
	January	0.8±0.07	8.75			January	0.83±0.019	2.28		

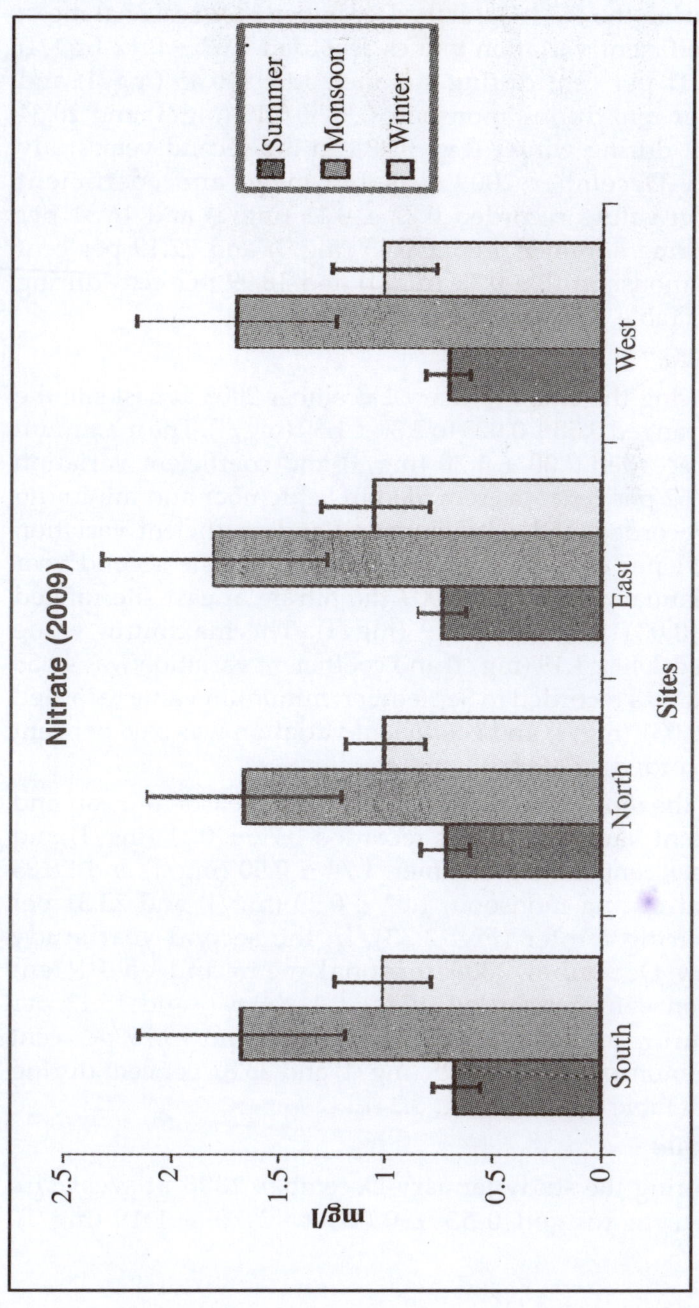

Fig. 3.34: Seasonal Variations in Nitrate (mg/l) at Different Sites of Harsool-Savangi Dam January to December 2009

During the study January-December 2008 seasonal mean and coefficient variation values recorded 0.68 ± 0.12 (mg/l) and 18.11 per cent during summer, 1.62 ± 0.45 (mg/l) and 28.00 per cent during monsoon, 0.98 ± 0.19 (mg/l) and 20.34 per cent during winter (Fig. 3.33). In the second year study January-December 2009 seasonal mean and coefficient variation values recorded 0.72 ± 0.11 (mg/l) and 16.31 per cent during summer, 1.66 ± 0.45 (mg/l) and 27.19 per cent during monsoon, 1 ± 0.19 (mg/l) and 18.99 per cent during winter (Table 3.66 and Fig. 3.34).

East Site

During the study January-December 2008 at east site the nitrate ranged 0.58 ± 0.025 to 2.30 ± 1.30 (mg/l). The maximum value recorded 2.30 ± 1.30 (mg/l) and coefficient variation was 56.52 per cent was recorded in September and minimum value recorded 0.58 ± 0.025 (mg/l) and coefficient variation was 4.31 per cent was recorded in May. In the second year study January-December 2009 the nitrate at east site ranged 0.61 ± 0.031 to 2.40 ± 1.19 (mg/l). The maximum value recorded 2.40 ± 1.19 (mg/l) and coefficient variation was 49.58 per cent was recorded in September; minimum value recorded 0.61 ± 0.031 (mg/l) and coefficient variation was 5.08 per cent was recorded in May.

In the study January-December 2008 seasonal mean and coefficient variation values recorded 0.72 ± 0.11 (mg/l) and 15.83 per cent during summer, 1.74 ± 0.50 (mg/l) and 28.83 per cent during monsoon, 1.02 ± 0.23 (mg/l) and 23.31 per cent during winter (Fig. 3.33). In the second year study January-December 2009 seasonal mean and coefficient variation values recorded 0.74 ± 0.11 (mg/l) and 15.13 per cent during summer, 1.80 ± 0.53 (mg/l) and 29.79 per cent during monsoon, 1.05 ± 0.25 (mg/l) and 23.81 per cent during winter (Table 3.67 and Fig. 3.34).

West Site

During the study January-December 2008 at west site the nitrate ranged 0.53 ± 0.035 to 2.10 ± 1.19 (mg/l).

Table 3.66: Seasonal Variations in Nitrate (mg/l) at North Site, Harsool-Savangi Dam

Season	Months Jan. 2008 - Dec. 2008	Monthly Mean Values	Monthly C.V. (%)	Seasonal Mean Values	Seasonal C.V. (%)	Months Jan. 2009 - Dec. 2009	Monthly Mean Values	Monthly C.V. (%)	Seasonal Mean Values	Seasonal C.V. (%)
Summer	February	0.81±0.02	2.46	0.68±0.12	18.11	February	0.84±0.014	1.66	0.72±0.11	16.31
	March	0.75±0.012	1.60			March	0.79±0.02	2.53		
	April	0.64±0.021	3.28			April	0.67±0.051	7.61		
	May	0.53±0.019	3.58			May	0.58±0.02	5.00		
Monsoon	June	1.10±0.90	81.81	1.62±0.45	28.00	June	1.13±1.20	106.19	1.66±0.45	27.19
	July	1.41±0.97	68.79			July	1.47±1.51	102.72		
	August	1.9±0.20	10.52			August	1.92±1.10	57.29		
	September	2.1±0.10	4.76			September	2.14±1.19	55.60		
Winter	October	1.28±0.19	14.84	0.98±0.19	20.34	October	1.29±1.09	84.49	1.00±0.19	18.99
	November	0.91±0.029	3.18			November	0.96±0.07	7.29		
	December	0.89±0.05	5.61			December	0.9±0.089	9.88		
	January	0.85±0.031	3.64			January	0.88±0.012	1.36		

Table 3.67: Seasonal Variations in Nitrate (mg/l) at East Site, Harsool-Savangi Dam

Season	Months Jan. 2008 - Dec. 2008	Monthly Mean Values	Monthly C.V. (%)	Seasonal Mean Values	Seasonal C.V. (%)	Months Jan. 2009 - Dec. 2009	Monthly Mean Values	Monthly C.V. (%)	Seasonal Mean Values	Seasonal C.V. (%)
Summer	February	0.85±0.01	1.17	0.72±0.11	15.83	February	0.87±0.012	1.37	0.74±0.11	15.13
	March	0.76±0.013	1.71			March	0.79±0.019	2.40		
	April	0.69±0.019	2.75			April	0.7±0.02	2.85		
	May	0.58±0.025	4.31			May	0.61±0.031	5.08		
Monsoon	June	1.18±1.09	92.37	1.74±0.50	28.83	June	1.22±1.02	83.60	1.80±0.53	29.79
	July	1.49±1.21	81.20			July	1.51±1.09	72.18		
	August	2±1.50	75.00			August	2.1±1.10	52.38		
	September	2.3±1.30	56.52			September	2.4±1.19	49.58		
Winter	October	1.38±1.10	79.71	1.02±0.23	23.31	October	1.43±1.01	70.62	1.05±0.25	23.81
	November	0.95±0.07	7.36			November	0.99±0.045	4.54		
	December	0.9±0.003	0.33			December	0.92±0.010	1.08		
	January	0.87±0.019	2.18			January	0.89±0.009	1.01		

The maximum value recorded 2.10 ± 1.19 (mg/l) and coefficient variation was 56.66 per cent was recorded in September and minimum value recorded 0.53 ± 0.035 (mg/l) and coefficient variation was 6.60 per cent was recorded in May. In the second year study January-December 2009 the nitrate at west site ranged 0.58 ± 0.021 to 2.20 ± 1.00 (mg/l). The maximum value recorded 2.20 ± 1.00 (mg/l) and coefficient variation was 45.45 per cent was recorded in September; minimum value recorded 0.58 ± 0.021 (mg/l) and coefficient variation was 3.62 per cent was recorded in May.

In the study January-December 2008 seasonal mean and coefficient variation values recorded 0.68 ± 0.11 (mg/l) and 16.93 per cent during summer, 1.65 ± 0.45 (mg/l) and 27.77 per cent during monsoon, 0.97 ± 0.23 (mg/l) and 24.34 per cent during winter (Fig. 3.33). In the second year study January-December 2009 seasonal mean and coefficient variation values recorded 0.71 ± 0.10 (mg/l) and 14.31 per cent during summer, 1.70 ± 0.47 (mg/l) and 27.65 per cent during monsoon, 1.01 ± 0.24 (mg/l) and 24.37 per cent during winter (Table 3.68 Fig. 3.34).

In the present study January to December 2008 the maximum nitrate was recorded in monsoon season at south site and minimum nitrate was recorded in summer season at south site. In the second year study January-December 2009 the maximum nitrate was recorded in monsoon season at east site where as minimum nitrate was recorded in summer season at south site (Tables 3.65 and 3.67).

During the study January 2008-December 2009 nitrate indicating significant positive correlation with turbidity, electric conductivity, total solid, total dissolved solids, total suspended solids, biochemical oxygen demand, chemical oxygen demand, total hardness and phosphate and it indicating significant negative correlation with transparency and fish (Tables 4.7 and 4.8).

Table 3.68: Seasonal Variations in Nitrate (mg/l) at West Site, Harsool-Savangi Dam

Season	Months Jan. 2008 - Dec. 2008	Monthly Mean Values	Monthly C.V. (%)	Seasonal Mean Values	Seasonal C.V. (%)	Months Jan. 2009 - Dec. 2009	Monthly Mean Values	Monthly C.V. (%)	Seasonal Mean Values	Seasonal C.V. (%)
Summer	February	0.8±0.021	2.62	0.68±0.11	16.93	February	0.82±0.011	1.34	0.71±0.10	14.31
	March	0.73±0.015	2.05			March	0.75±0.015	2.00		
	April	0.66±0.01	1.51			April	0.69±0.01	1.44		
	May	0.53±0.035	6.60			May	0.58±0.021	3.62		
Monsoon	June	1.12±1.01	90.17	1.65±0.45	27.77	June	1.18±1.01	85.59	1.70±0.47	27.65
	July	1.43±1.50	104.89			July	1.45±1.09	75.17		
	August	1.97±1.55	78.68			August	1.99±1.19	59.79		
	September	2.1±1.19	56.66			September	2.2±1.0	45.45		
Winter	October	1.33±0.19	14.28	0.97±0.23	24.34	October	1.38±1.03	74.63	1.01±0.24	24.37
	November	0.91±0.01	1.09			November	0.93±0.073	7.84		
	December	0.85±0.023	2.70			December	0.86±0.053	6.16		
	January	0.82±0.029	3.53			January	0.88±0.019	2.15		

In the present study, a value of nitrate was maximum during monsoon and minimum during summer season. Nitrate levels in surface water often show marked seasonal fluctuations with higher concentrations being found during monsoon months as compared with summer and winter months. During summer months the reduction in nitrate could be due to algal assimilation and other biochemical mechanism and nitrate value high during monsoon may be due to surface run off and domestic sewage and specially washing activities.

Phosphate

Phosphate is a nutrient for plant growth and a fundamental element in the metabolic reaction of plants and animals. It controls algal growth and primary productivity. In most natural waters, phosphorus ranges 0.005 to 0.020 mg/L. Algae require only small amounts of phosphorus. Excess amounts of phosphorus can cause eutrophication leading to excessive algal growth called algal blooms. In natural water phosphates, are present in small quantities. Generally aquatic ecosystems receive excess of this nutrient through untreated domestic sewage and agriculture runoff. Normally phosphate acts as a limiting nutrient in the process of eutrophication and lakes can be aesthetically classified in to good, fair and bad on the basis of per cent phosphates loading. Phosphates and nitrate are the main nutrients responsible for the process of eutrophication that leads to ultimate degradation of an aquatic ecosystem. Phosphate is an essential metabolic element, which normally occurs in low concentration in natural aquatic ecosystem and hence, often acts as a limiting factor for primary production (Rigler, 1956).

South Site

In the study January-December 2008 at south site the phosphate ranged 0.14 ± 0.01 to 0.90 ± 0.027 (mg/l). The maximum value recorded 0.90 ± 0.027 (mg/l) and coefficient variation was 3.00 per cent was recorded in September and minimum value recorded 0.14 ± 0.01 (mg/l) and coefficient variation was 7.14 per cent was recorded in May. In the second year study January-December 2009 the phosphate at south site ranged 0.18 ± 0.011 to 0.92 ± 0.041 (mg/l). The maximum value recorded 0.92 ± 0.041 (mg/l) and coefficient variation was 4.45 per cent was recorded in September; minimum value recorded 0.18 ± 0.011 (mg/l) and coefficient variation was 6.11 per cent was recorded in May.

During the study January-December 2008 seasonal mean and coefficient variation values recorded 0.27 ± 0.12 (mg/l) and 44.98 per cent during summer, 0.78 ± 0.08 (mg/l) and 10.84 per cent during monsoon, 0.63 ± 0.17 (mg/l) and 27.39 per cent during winter (Fig. 3.35). In the second year study January-December 2009 seasonal mean and coefficient variation values recorded 0.29 ± 0.11 (mg/l) and 39.96 per cent during summer, 0.81 ± 0.88 (mg/l) and 10.24 per cent during monsoon, 0.66 ± 0.17 (mg/l) and 26.44 per cent during winter (Table 3.69 and Fig. 3.36).

North Site

During the study January-December 2008 at north site the phosphate ranged 0.17 ± 0.099 to 0.92 ± 0.031 (mg/l). The maximum value recorded 0.92 ± 0.031 (mg/l) and coefficient variation was 3.36 per cent was recorded in September and minimum value recorded 0.17 ± 0.099 (mg/l) and coefficient variation was 58.23 per cent was recorded in May. In the second year study January-December 2009 the phosphate at north site ranged 0.19 ± 0.025 to 0.97 ± 0.029 (mg/l). The maximum value recorded 0.97 ± 0.029 (mg/l) and coefficient variation was 2.98 per cent was recorded in September; minimum value recorded 0.19 ± 0.025 (mg/l) and coefficient variation was 13.15 per cent was recorded in May.

In the study January-December 2008 seasonal mean and coefficient variation values recorded 0.28 ± 0.11 (mg/l) and 39.33 per cent during summer, 0.80 ± 0.08 (mg/l) and 10.80 per cent during monsoon, 0.67 ± 0.19 (mg/l) and 29.77 per cent during winter (Fig. 3.35). In the second year study January-December 2009 seasonal mean and coefficient variation values recorded 0.29 ± 0.10 (mg/l) and 34.42 per cent during summer, 0.84 ± 0.09 (mg/l) and 11.03 per cent during monsoon, 0.70 ± 0.20 (mg/l) and 28.64 per cent during winter (Table 3.70 and Fig. 3.36).

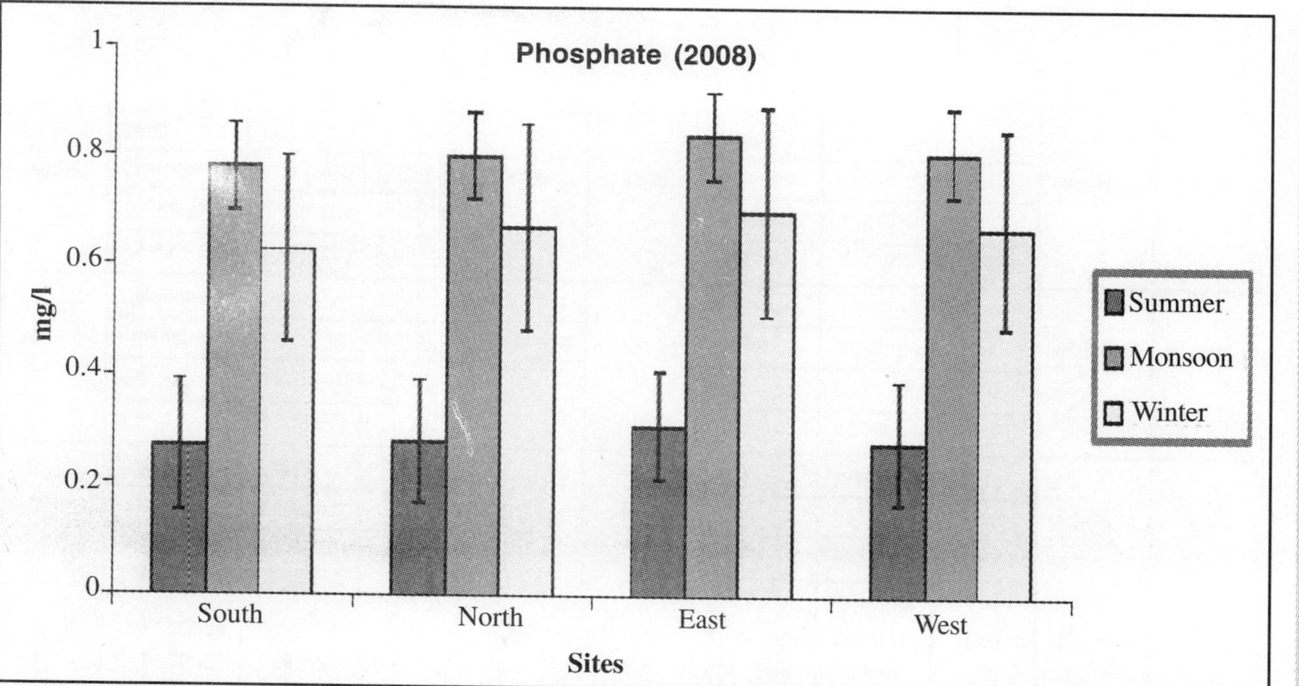

Fig. 3.35: Seasonal Variations in Phosphate (mg/l) at Different Sites of Harsool-Savangi Dam January to December 2008

Table 3.69: Seasonal Variations in Phosphate (mg/l) at South Site, Harsool-Savangi Dam

Season	Months Jan. 2008 - Dec. 2008	Monthly Mean Values	Monthly C.V. (%)	Seasonal Mean Values	Seasonal C.V. (%)	Months Jan. 2009 - Dec. 2009	Monthly Mean Values	Monthly C.V. (%)	Seasonal Mean Values	Seasonal C.V. (%)
Summer	February	0.4±0.021	5.25	0.27±0.12	44.98	February	0.42±0.031	7.38	0.29±0.11	39.96
	March	0.35±0.015	4.28			March	0.37±0.057	15.40		
	April	0.2±0.012	6.00			April	0.21±0.092	43.80		
	May	**0.14±0.01**	7.14			May	**0.18±0.011**	6.11		
Monsoon	June	0.7±0.025	3.57	0.78±0.08	10.84	June	0.73±0.099	13.56	0.81±0.08	10.24
	July	0.75±0.015	2.00			July	0.77±0.001	0.12		
	August	0.8±0.02	2.50			August	0.84±0.029	3.45		
	September	**0.9±0.027**	3.00			September	**0.92±0.041**	4.45		
Winter	October	0.81±0.011	1.35	0.63±0.17	27.39	October	0.84±0.019	2.26	0.66±0.17	26.44
	November	0.73±0.03	4.10			November	0.75±0.010	1.33		
	December	0.6±0.012	2.00			December	0.61±0.029	4.75		
	January	0.41±0.019	4.63			January	0.44±0.057	12.95		

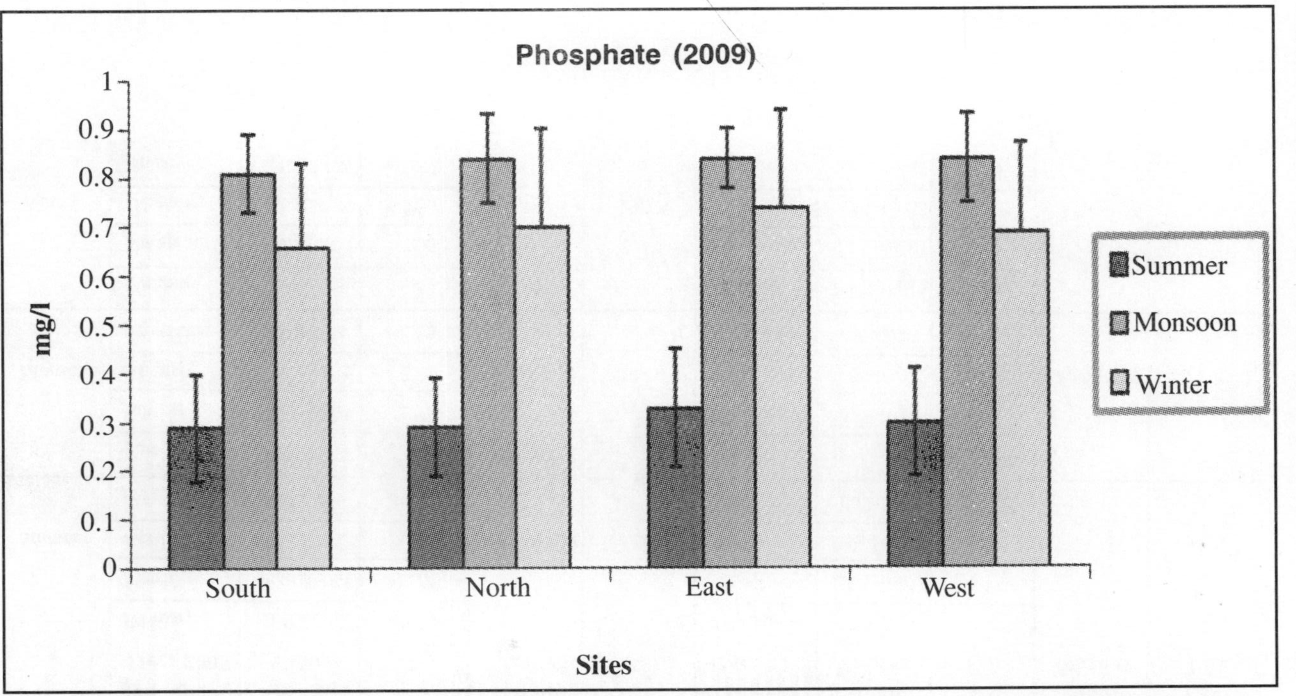

Fig. 3.36: Seasonal Variations in Phosphate (mg/l) at Different Sites of Harsool-Savangi Dam January to December 2009

Table 3.70: Seasonal Variations in Phosphate (mg/l) at North Site, Harsool-Savangi Dam

Season	Months Jan. 2008 - Dec. 2008	Monthly Mean Values	Monthly C.V. (%)	Seasonal Mean Values	Seasonal C.V. (%)	Months Jan. 2009 - Dec. 2009	Monthly Mean Values	Monthly C.V. (%)	Seasonal Mean Values	Seasonal C.V. (%)
	February	0.40±0.02	5.00			February	0.39±0.019	4.87		
	March	0.36±0.041	11.38			March	0.38±0.017	4.47		
Summer	April	0.21±0.057	27.14	0.28±0.11	39.33	April	0.23±0.011	4.78	0.29±0.10	34.42
	May	0.17±0.099	58.23			May	0.19±0.025	13.15		
	June	0.72±0.077	10.69			June	0.76±0.097	12.76		
	July	0.76±0.015	1.97			July	0.79±0.01	1.26		
Monsoon	August	0.82±0.019	2.31	0.80±0.08	10.80	August	0.86±0.022	2.55	0.84±0.09	11.03
	September	0.92±0.031	3.36			September	0.97±0.029	2.98		
	October	0.85±0.08	9.41			October	0.87±0.013	1.49		
	November	0.81±0.011	1.35			November	0.85±0.001	0.11		
Winter	December	0.6±0.021	3.50	0.67±0.19	29.77	December	0.65±0.035	5.38	0.70±0.20	28.64
	January	0.42±0.037	8.80			January	0.44±0.042	9.54		

East Site

In the study January-December 2008 at east site the phosphate ranged 0.19 ± 0.031 to 0.96 ± 0.032 (mg/l). The maximum value recorded 0.96 ± 0.032 (mg/l) and coefficient variation was 3.33 per cent was recorded in September and minimum value recorded 0.19 ± 0.031 (mg/l) and coefficient variation was 16.31 per cent was recorded in May. In the second year study January-December 2009 the phosphate at east site ranged 0.20 ± 0.011 to 0.94 ± 0.017 (mg/l). The maximum value recorded 0.94 ± 0.017 (mg/l) and coefficient variation was 1.80 per cent was recorded in October; minimum value recorded 0.20 ± 0.011 (mg/l) and coefficient variation was 5.50 per cent was recorded in May.

During the study January-December 2008 seasonal mean and coefficient variation values recorded 0.31 ± 0.10 (mg/l) and 34.84 per cent during summer, 0.84 ± 0.08 (mg/l) and 10.21 per cent during monsoon, 0.70 ± 0.19 (mg/l) and 27.19 per cent during winter (Fig. 3.35). In the second year study January-December 2009 seasonal mean and coefficient variation values recorded 0.33 ± 0.12 (mg/l) and 37.35 per cent during summer, 0.84 ± 0.06 (mg/l) and 7.40 per cent during monsoon, 0.74 ± 0.20 (mg/l) and 27.76 per cent during winter (Table 3.71 and Fig. 3.36).

West Site

In the study January-December 2008 at west site the phosphate ranged 0.16 ± 0.062 to 0.92 ± 0.029 (mg/l). The maximum value recorded 0.92 ± 0.029 (mg/l) and coefficient variation was 3.15 per cent was recorded in September and minimum value recorded 0.16 ± 0.062 (mg/l) and coefficient variation was 38.75 per cent was recorded in May. In the second year study January-December 2009 the phosphate at west site ranged 0.18 ± 0.018 to 0.96 ± 0.01 (mg/l). The maximum value recorded 0.96 ± 0.01 (mg/l) and coefficient variation was 1.04 per cent was recorded in September; minimum value recorded 0.18 ± 0.018 (mg/l) and coefficient variation was 10.00 per cent was recorded in May.

Table 3.71: Seasonal Variations in Phosphate (mg/l) at East Site, Harsool-Savangi Dam

Season	Months Jan. 2008 - Dec. 2008	Monthly Mean Values	Monthly C.V. (%)	Seasonal Mean Values	Seasonal C.V. (%)	Months Jan. 2009 - Dec. 2009	Monthly Mean Values	Monthly C.V. (%)	Seasonal Mean Values	Seasonal C.V. (%)
Summer	February	0.42±0.01	2.38	0.31±0.10	34.84	February	0.48±0.02	4.16	0.33±0.12	37.35
	March	0.38±0.029	7.63			March	0.4±0.012	3.00		
	April	0.25±0.025	10.00			April	0.27±0.027	10.00		
	May	0.19±0.031	16.31			May	0.2±0.011	5.50		
Monsoon	June	0.77±0.057	7.40	0.84±0.08	10.21	June	0.78±0.019	2.43	0.84±0.06	7.40
	July	0.79±0.09	11.39			July	0.8±0.097	12.12		
	August	0.87±0.019	2.18			August	0.88±0.061	6.93		
	September	0.96±0.032	3.33			September	0.91±0.069	7.58		
Winter	October	0.89±0.013	1.46	0.70±0.19	27.19	October	0.94±0.017	1.80	0.74±0.20	27.76
	November	0.8±0.005	0.62			November	0.85±0.021	2.47		
	December	0.67±0.04	5.97			December	0.7±0.027	3.85		
	January	0.45±0.015	3.33			January	0.47±0.019	4.04		

Table 3.72: Seasonal Variations in Phosphate (mg/l) at West Site, Harsool-Savangi Dam

Season	Months Jan. 2008 - Dec. 2008	Monthly Mean Values	Monthly C.V. (%)	Seasonal Mean Values	Seasonal C.V. (%)	Months Jan. 2009 - Dec. 2009	Monthly Mean Values	Monthly C.V. (%)	Seasonal Mean Values	Seasonal C.V. (%)
Summer	February	0.41±0.07	17.07	0.28±0.11	40.69	February	0.43±0.019	4.41	0.30±0.11	38.05
	March	0.36±0.072	20.00			March	0.38±0.012	3.15		
	April	0.22±0.082	37.27			April	0.24±0.009	3.75		
	May	0.16±0.062	38.75			May	0.18±0.018	10.00		
Monsoon	June	0.73±0.059	8.08	0.81±0.08	10.16	June	0.75±0.05	6.66	0.84±0.09	10.95
	July	0.77±0.019	2.46			July	0.79±0.021	2.65		
	August	0.83±0.02	2.40			August	0.86±0.037	4.30		
	September	0.92±0.029	3.15			September	0.96±0.01	1.04		
Winter	October	0.85±0.051	6.00	0.67±0.18	27.43	October	0.88±0.015	1.70	0.69±0.18	26.13
	November	0.78±0.01	1.28			November	0.79±0.02	2.53		
	December	0.64±0.012	1.87			December	0.66±0.09	13.63		
	January	0.43±0.09	20.93			January	0.46±0.099	21.52		

During the study January-December 2008 seasonal mean and coefficient variation values recorded 0.28 ± 0.11 (mg/l) and 40.69 per cent during summer, 0.81 ± 0.08 (mg/l) and 10.16 per cent during monsoon, 0.67 ± 0.18 (mg/l) and 27.43 per cent during winter (Fig. 3.35). In the second year study January-December 2009 seasonal mean and coefficient variation values recorded 0.30 ± 0.11 (mg/l) and 38.05 per cent during summer, 0.84 ± 0.09 (mg/l) and 10.95 per cent during monsoon, 0.69 ± 0.18 (mg/l) and 26.13 per cent during winter (Table 3.72 and Fig. 3.36).

In the present study January to December 2008 the maximum phosphate was recorded in monsoon season at east site and minimum phosphate was recorded in summer season at south site. In the second year study January-December 2009 the maximum phosphate was recorded in monsoon season at north site where as minimum phosphate was recorded in summer season at south and west sites (Tables 3.69, 3.70, 3.71 and 3.72).

During the study January 2008-December 2009 phosphate indicating significant positive correlation with turbidity, electric conductivity, total solid, total dissolved solids, total suspended solids, biochemical oxygen demand, chemical oxygen demand, total hardness and nitrate and it indicating significant negative correlation with water temperature, transparency, pH, alkalinity and fish (Tables 4.7 and 4.8).

In the present study, the phosphate values were maximum during monsoon and minimum during summer. Maximum during monsoon might be due to the washing activities, there is an entry of detergents in the water body and less water quantity and during summer season the relatively low level of phosphate have been reported which attributed to abundance of phytoplanktons.

Fish Diversity

Introduction

Ichthyofaunal diversity deals with variety of fish species; depending on context and scale, it could refer to alleles or genotypes within fish population to species of life forms within a fish community and to species or life forms across aqua regimes (Burton *et al.*, 1992). Biodiversity is essential for stabilization of ecosystem protection of overall environmental quality for understanding intrinsic worth of all species on the earth (Ehrlich and Wilson, 1991).

A fresh water perennial tank has got prime importance as a source of drinking water and for aquaculture potential in terms of fish. These water bodies are located in different parts of the country especially in rural areas and are mainly used as a source of drinking water, irrigation and for fish production by the local fishermen communities. However, tropical climate of the region creates an environment helpful for fast growth of fish. Fish is most important bio-product of fresh, marine and brackish water ecosystems contributing an essential and beneficial food item to mankind since ancient time (Pailwan and Muley, 2006). Success of fish culture depends apart from other factors, on selection of suitable species. Secondly the country rich fish diversity of this important group of animals. Further, there is a need of diversity survey different types of habitats all over the country. Indian fisheries are an important component of the global fisheries, India being the sixth largest producer of fish amounting to 5.39 m mt. Playing an important role in fisheries and aquaculture scenario. India produces over 2.44 m mt. from the inland fisheries sector being in the second position in the World. Indian fisheries has rich resources of 1,31,334 km of rivers and canals 2.05 m ha of reservoirs (Sone and Malu, 2000).

Reservoir fishery in India is also important from socio-economic point of view as it has the potential of providing employment to about 2 million people (Khan *et al.*, 1991). According to Sugunan (1995) total area under the reservoir in India is 3:1 million hectores and it is expected to double by 2020. This includes 19,000 small reservoirs, 180 medium and 56 large reservoirs. The Maharashtra is endowed with an area 1,79,430 ha under reservoirs and the state produces 516 tons of fish from this area, the state fisheries corporation was operating in 6,272 ha of reservoirs and marketing the catches (Sreenivasan, 1991).

The total area under ponds and tanks are estimated about 2.2 million hectares and the resources are widely spreading through the length and breadth of the country. Scientific management of such water bodies will assist to enhance the concept of sustainable utilization. Besides, the evaluation of present fishery status and potential for fish production will help in implementation of developmental activities and improvement of fish production of fresh water habitats (Pailwan and Muley, 2006).

Fishes are one of the most important groups of vertebrates, influencing his life in various ways. Millions of human beings suffer from hunger and malnutrition and fishes form a rich source of food and provide a meal to tide over the nutritional difficulties of man. In addition to serving as an important item of food, fishes provide several by-products to us. Fishes have formed an important item of human diet from time immemorial and are primarily caught for this purpose. Fish diet provides proteins, fat and vitamins A and D. A large amount of phosphorous and other elements are also present in it. They have a good taste and are easily digestible. As there is economic importance and scope of fish and fisheries especially in Maharashtra, it is essential to study distribution and the availability of fish from freshwater reservoirs and tanks (Shinde *et al.*, 2009a).

The inland resources are 1.9 million ha of reservoirs and 2.25 million ha of ponds at the production rate of 2.0 tonnes/ha the additional estimated production would be 2.0 million tones of fish. India needs 13.0 million tones of fish to meet the minimum protein requirement for 1 billion people, as 70 per cent Indians eat fish. The annual fish production in 1998 was around 5.4 million tones; this means country has to double its fish production (Dwivedi, 2000). Thus, fresh water tanks and ponds will probably contribute a major role to fulfil the additional requirement of fish to improve the socio-economic status of the fishermen of the rural areas of particular region.

Fisheries of the lakes and reservoirs constitute an important component of the inland fish production in India (Jhingran, 1985). Before popularization of fish culture technology in India, capture fisheries of the Lakes and reservoirs mostly constituted to the inland fish production.

Minor reservoirs which are contributing significantly to the total inland agricultural production, the fisheries potential remains to be fully exploited. Further, attention seems to have been paid towards systematic investigation on either of diversity of ichthyofauna or total catch of fishes from these reservoirs. Thus there is a need to survey fish fauna associated with different fresh water bodies which will help in planning for their effective exploitation of fish production.

The health of environment decides the diversity and productivity of the systems. Therefore, for sustaining the diversity of plankton and fish for sustainable management of the dam, it is important to know the factors controlling the quality of the dam systems. Certain changes in physico-chemical parameters, pesticides and fertilizers from the surrounding crop fields, heavy siltation during heavy rainfall, high density of fingerling stocking to selected culture fishes, poor management of fish culture and fish diseases were found to exert undesirable impacts on plankton diversity, fish diversity and productivity.

Rational management methods by creating public awareness has to be followed for sustaining fish diversity and sustainable fish production in the dam for preventing further rural economic loss. A periodic survey and monitoring of these water bodies is essential to check the water quality and prevent disturbances to these ecosystems. The documentation of fish species distribution in various habitats will assist resource allocation between different user communities who depend on fishing as a livelihood strategy.

This approach captures the key tenets of the ecosystem approach, defined by IUCN as 'a strategy for management of land, water and living resources that promotes conservation and sustainable use in an equitable way' (Smith and Maltby, 2003). Awareness programmes among the locals regarding the importance of preserving the water resources and sensible exploitation of fish resources will immense helpful in sustaining these valuable aquatic resources.

The study of fish and their stability is very important. Fish population of any given aquatic habitat vary significantly year to year. Consequently, it would be necessary for experiment which carried out for several successive years. The stability of fish is profound importance due to urgent need of environmental management to know how much fish population naturally change over time (Korai *et al.*, 2008). Fish biodiversity study contributes a better knowledge of fishes and a tool for conservation planning of aquatic environments. To maintain fish biodiversity has immense importance as it is not always possible to identify individual species critical to sustain aquatic ecosystem (Shinde *et al.*, 2009b).

Keeping in mind this view present study has been undertaken to assess monthly values, standard deviation, total percentage, correlation and annual variations biodiversity indices, i.e. species richness, species diversity, species evenness and correlation coefficient of Harsool-Savangi Dam.

Material and Methods

Fishes were collected from Harsool Savangi Dam. The geographical coordination is 19° 56′ 14.32′ N and 75° 21′ 30.56″ E Aurangabad, (M.S) India, with the help of local fishermen using different type of nets namely; gill nets, cast nets, dragnets and Bhor-jal. Immediately photographs were taken with help of digital camera.

Fishes were brought to laboratory and preserved in four per cent formalin solution in separate specimen jars according to the size of species. Small fishes were directly placed in the four per cent formalin solution. At the same time as large fishes were given an incision in their abdomen and preserved. The meristic and morphometric characters were measured and identified up to the species level, with the help of standard keys (Day, 1994; Talwar and Jhingran, 1991; Jayaram, 1999 and Rahman, 2005) and statistical ecological methods as described by Ludwick and Reynold, (1988). The correlation coefficient was used to examine the relationships among the different environmental variables including fish density. The Correlation model was performed using SPSS 12.0.

Community Structure Analysis

Three indices were used to obtain estimation of species diversity, species richness and species evenness.

1. Shannon and Weaver, (1949) and Simpson, (1949) diversity index values were obtained by using the following equation:

$$H' = -\sum_{i=I}^{S} (P_i \ln P_i) \text{ (Shannon's index)}$$

$$\lambda = -\sum_{i=I}^{S} \frac{n_i(n_i-1)}{n(n-1)} \text{(Simpson index)}$$

Where,

P_i = Proportion of the first species.

The proportions are given P_i=ni/N

2. Species richness (R_1 and R_2) obtained using the following equation:

$$R_1 = \frac{(S-1)}{In(n)}$$ (Margalef, 1958a)

$$R_2 = \frac{S}{\sqrt{n}}$$ (Menhinick, 1964)

Where,

R = Index of species richness

S = Total number of species

N = Total number of individuals

3. Species equitability or evenness was determined by using the following expression.

    1. Evenness index 1 (E_1): (Pielou, 1977)

    $$E_1 = \frac{In(N_1)}{In(N_0)}$$

    2. Evenness index 2 (E_2): (Sheldon, 1969)

    $$E_2 = \frac{N_1}{N_0}$$

    3. Evenness index 3 (E_3): (Heip, 1974)

    $$E_3 = \frac{N_1 - 1}{N_0 - 1}$$

    4. Evenness index 4 (E_4): (Hill, 1973)

    $$E_4 = \frac{N_2}{N_1}$$

    5. Evenness index 5 (E_5): (Alatalo, 1981)

    $$E_5 = \frac{N_2 - 1}{N_1 - 1}$$

Where,

N_0 = Number of species on the sample

N_1 = Number of abundant species in the sample.

Results

In the ichthyofaunal study, 15 species of 12 different genera 4 families and 3 orders were recorded at Harsool-Savangi Dam in number of catches carried out during (January 2008-December 2009). The members of Order Cypriniformes were dominated by 11 species followed by Perciformes 3 species and Siluriformes with one species.

Fifteen fish species representing by 3 orders, Cypriniformes was dominant with 11 species was dominant group in the assemblage composition in which *Catla-catla, Labeo rohita, Cyprinus carpio* and *Rasbora daniconius* were found most abundant. *Hypothalmichthys molitrix* and *Puntius ticto* were found in abundant form. *Puntius stigma, Chela bacaila, Cirrhinus mrigala, Garra lamta* and *Thynnichthys sandkhol* were found less abundant. Followed by Perciformes in which *Channa striatus* was found abundant form *Channa punctatus* and *Oreochromis mossambica* were found less abundant form and Siluriformes in which one species reported that is *Clarias batrachus* found less abundant (Table 4.1).

Family wise population density was as follow:

I. Family

Cyprinidae

During first year January to December 2008 the Cyprinidae population density ranged 1 to 30. The maximum population density of *Rasbora daniconius* recorded 30 in April and minimum population density of *Hypothalmichthys molitrix, Puntius stigma, Chela bacaila, Cirrhinus mrigala, Garra lamta and Thynnichthys sandkhol* recorded 1 in January, June, July, August, October and December. In the second year January-December 2009 the population density of Cyprinidae ranged 1 to 35. The maximum population density of *Rasbora daniconius* recorded 35 in April; minimum population density of *Catla-catla, Labeo-rohita, Cyprinus carpio, Hypothalmichthys molitrix, Puntius ticto, Puntius stigma, Chela bacaila, Cirrhinus mrigala, Garra lamta and Thynnichthys sandkhol* recorded 1 in January, June, July, August, October and November (Tables 4.2 and 4.3).

ICHTHYOFAUNA
CYPRINIDAE

CATLA-CATLA

LABEO ROHITA

CYPRINUS CARPIO

RASBORA DANICONIUS

HYPOTHALMICHTHYS MOLITRIX

PUNTIUS TICTO

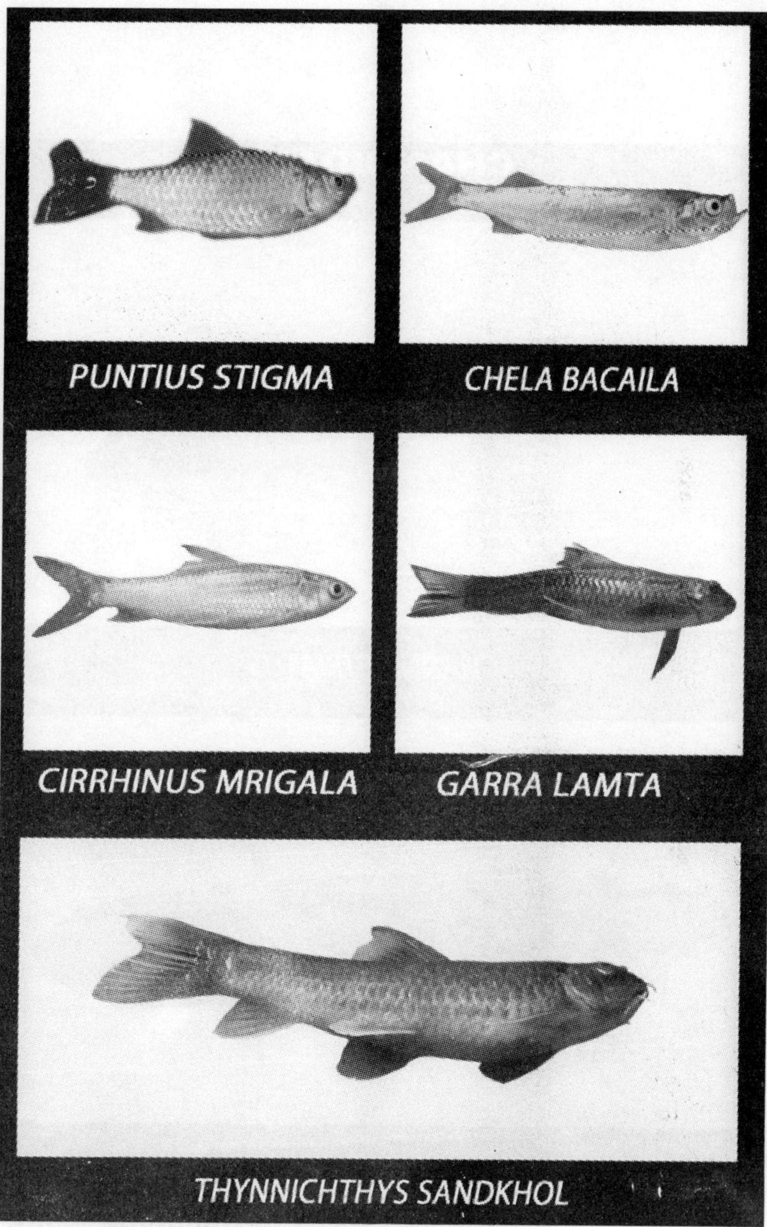
PUNTIUS STIGMA
CHELA BACAILA
CIRRHINUS MRIGALA
GARRA LAMTA
THYNNICHTHYS SANDKHOL

CHANNIDAE
CHANNA STRIATUS
CHANNA PUNCTATUS

CICHLIDAE

OREOCHROMIS MOSSAMBICA

CLARIIDAE

CLARIS BATRACHUS

Table 4.1: The Ichthyofaunal Diversity of Harsool-Savangi Dam (January 2008 - December 2009)

Order	Family	Scientific Name	Common Name	Groups of Food Fish	Economic Value	Fin Formula
1	2	3	4	5	6	7
Cypriniformes Cyprinidae		*Catla-catla* (Hamilton)	Catla	Carps	FD	D iii-iv 14-21; A iii 6-8; P I 12-13; V ii-iii 7-8
		Labeo-rohita (Hamilton)	Rohu	Carps	FD	D. 15-16 (3/12-13); P_1. 16-17; P_2 9; A. 7(2/5)
		Cyprinus carpio (Linneaus)	Common carp	Carps	FD	D. 3-4/18-20, P_1: 1/15, P_2: 1/8, A. 3-5
		Rasbora daniconius (Ham - Buch)	Black line Rasbora	Food fish	LV	D 17; A 15; P 11; V 8
		Hypothalmichthys molitrix (Valenciennes)	Silver carp	Food fish	FD	D 3/7; P_1 1/17; P_2 1/7; A 2-3/12-14
		Puntius ticto (Hamilton)	Ticto	Miscellaneous fishes	BT, LV,WF	D iii-iv 8; A ii-iii 5; P i 12-14; V i 8
		Puntius stigma (Hamilton)	Stigma	Miscellaneous fishes	BT, LV,WF	D. 3-4/8-9, P_1. 1/14-17, P_2. 1/7-8, A. 2-3/7-8
		Chela bacaila (Ham - Buch)	Chela	Food fish	LV	D. 10(2/8); P_1. 12-13; P_2 9; A. 14-15(2/12-13)
		Cirrhinus mrigala (Hamilton)	Mrigala	Carps	FD	D. 16; P1. 17; P2. 9; A. 8

(Contd…)

1	2	3	4	5	6	7
		Garra lamta (Hamilton)	Garra	Food fish	FD	D III 7-8; A II 5 ; Pi 12; Vi 7-8
		Thynnichthys sandkhol(sykes)	Sandkhol carp	Food fish	FD	Diii 9; Aii 5 ; Pi 18; Vi 8
Perciformes	**Channidae**	*Channa striatus* (Bloch)	Banded snake head	Live fish	LV, PF	D. 42-46; P_1. 15-17; P_2 6; A. 24-27
		Channa punctatus (Bloch)	Spotted snake head	Live fish	LV, PF	D. 29-32; P_1. 15-18; P_2 6; A. 20-22
	Cichlidae	*Oreochromis mossambica* (Hamilton)	Tilapia	Food fish	FD	D. XV-XVI 10-12, P_1. 14-15, P_2. I 5 A. III 10-11
Siluriformes	**Clariidae**	*Clarias batrachus* (Linneaus)	mangur/ cat fish	Live fish	LV	D 62 - 76; P 9-12; V 6 ; A 45- 58 ; C 17

1. LV – Larvivous fish.
2. BT – Bait.
3. PF – Predatory Food Fish.
4. WF – Weed Fish.
5. FD – Food Fish.

Table 4.2: Monthly Variation in Ichthyofauna of Harsool-Savangi Dam (January-December 2008)

Family	Scientific Name	Jan.	Feb.	Mar.	Apr.	May	June	July	Aug.	Sep.	Oct.	Nov.	Dec.
Cyprinidae	*Catla-catla*	5	10	8	6	12	4	2	2	5	3	7	5
	Labeo-rohita	6	5	9	11	6	2	3	3	3	5	5	4
	Cyprinus carpio	4	8	8	12	9	5	2	5	3	3	7	4
	Rasbora daniconius	20	25	20	30	28	4	8	3	5	12	16	20
	Hypothalmichthys molitrix	4	6	2	7	10	2	1	1	2	3	2	3
	Puntius ticto	9	15	10	20	15	0	0	0	0	2	0	0
	Puntius stigma	3	2	8	2	5	5	1	0	0	0	0	4
	Chela bacaila	0	2	4	4	5	1	0	0	0	0	2	3
	Cirrhinus mrigala	1	4	2	2	6	0	0	0	0	1	0	0
	Garra lamta	1	6	8	12	4	0	0	0	0	0	0	2
	Thynnichthys sandkhol	3	8	3	10	5	0	0	0	0	0	0	1
Channidae	*Channa striatus*	1	6	10	6	12	3	0	0	0	2	4	4
	Channa punctatus	5	8	3	2	10	1	0	0	0	1	0	0
Cichlidae	*Oreochromis mossambica*	2	3	1	2	3	2	0	0	0	0	0	2
Clariidae	*Clarias batrachus*	0	1	2	0	0	0	0	0	0	0	0	1

Table 4.3: Monthly Variation in Ichthyofauna of Harsool - Savangi Dam (January-December 2009)

Family	Scientific Name	Jan.	Feb.	Mar.	Apr.	May	June	July	Aug.	Sep.	Oct.	Nov.	Dec.
Cyprinidae	*Catla-catla*	3	7	5	5	10	3	1	2	3	5	2	4
	Labeo-rohita	2	4	6	6	12	1	2	2	2	1	3	5
	Cyprinus carpio	1	3	3	10	14	2	1	3	2	4	2	6
	Rasbora daniconius	27	30	22	35	29	8	4	10	3	12	18	23
	Hypothalmichthys molitrix	2	5	6	13	9	2	1	1	3	3	2	4
	Puntius ticto	5	12	7	18	12	5	1	0	0	0	8	10
	Puntius stigma	1	3	5	4	8	2	0	0	0	0	1	3
	Chela bacaila	1	2	4	4	6	1	0	0	0	0	0	3
	Cirrhinus mrigala	0	2	2	8	3	0	0	1	0	0	0	2
	Garra lamta	2	4	7	10	6	3	1	0	0	0	5	2
	Thynnichthys sandkhol	1	5	9	3	11	2	0	0	0	0	1	2
Channidae	*Channa striatus*	2	4	8	15	3	1	0	0	0	2	2	3
	Channa punctatus	0	2	6	2	8	1	0	0	0	0	4	2.
Cichlidae	*Oreochromis mossambica*	0	0	4	5	2	0	0	0	1	0	0	3
Clariidae	*Clarias batrachus*	0	0	2	2	1	0	0	0	0	0	0	0

Channidae

In the first year January to December 2008 the population density of Channidae ranged 1 to 12. The maximum population density of *Channa striatus* recorded 12 in May and minimum population density of *Channa striatus* and *Channa punctatus* recorded 1 in January, June and October. In the second year January-December 2009 the Channidae population density ranged 1 to 15. The maximum population density recorded of *Channa striatus* was 15 in April; minimum population density of *Channa striatus* and *Channa punctatus* recorded 1 in June (Tables 4.2 and 4.3).

Cichlidae

Oreochromis mossambica

During first year January to December 2008 the population density of *Oreochromis mossambica* ranged 1 to 3. The maximum population density recorded 3 in February and May and minimum population density recorded 1 in March. In the second year January-December 2009 the population density of *Oreochromis mossambica* ranged 1 to 5. The maximum population density recorded 5 in April; minimum population density recorded 1 in September (Tables 4.2 and 4.3).

Clariidae

Clarias batrachus

First year January to December 2008 the population density of *Clarias batrachus* ranged 1 to 2. The maximum population density recorded 2 in March and minimum population density recorded 1 in February and December. In the second year January-December 2009 the population density of *Clarias batrachus* ranged 1 to 2. The maximum population density recorded 2 in March and April; minimum population density recorded 1 in May (Tables 4.2 and 4.3).

In the January-December 2008 the maximum population density of Fishes recorded during summer season and minimum population density of Fishes recorded during monsoon season. In the second year January-December 2009 the maximum population density of Fishes recorded during summer season and minimum population density of Fishes recorded during monsoon season (Table 4.4).

During first year January to December 2008 orderwise seasonal variations and seasonal total population density of Ichthyofaunal diversity at Harsool-Savangi Dam of Maximum Cyprinidae recorded 8.95 ± 6.74 and 394 during summer, minimum Cyprinidae 1.63 ± 2.02 and 72 during monsoon and grand total 636. Maximum Channidae recorded 7.12 ± 3.52 and 57 during summer, minimum Channidae 0.5 ± 1.06 and 4 during monsoon and grand total 78. Maximum Cichlidae recorded 2.25 ± 0.95 and 9 during summer, minimum Cichlidae 0.5 ± 1 and 2 during monsoon and grand total 15. Maximum Clariidae recorded 0.75 ± 0.95 and 3 during summer, minimum Clariidae 0 ± 0 and 0 during monsoon and grand total is 4. In the second year January-December 2009 orderwise seasonal variations and seasonal population density of Ichthyofaunal diversity at Harsool-Savangi Dam, Maximum Cyprinidae recorded 8.84 ± 7.52 and 389 during summer, minimum Cyprinidae 1.63 ± 2.08 and 72 during monsoon and grand total 637. Maximum Channidae recorded 6 ± 4.37 and 48 during summer, minimum Channidae 0.25 ± 0.46 and 2 during monsoon and grand total 65. Maximum Cichlidae recorded 2.75 ± 2.21 and 11 during summer, minimum Cichlidae 0.25 ± 0.5 and 1 during monsoon and grand total 15. Maximum Clariidae recorded 1.25 ± 0.95 and 5 during summer, minimum Clariidae 0 ± 0 and 0 during monsoon and grand total 5 (Table 4.4 Figs. 4.1 and 4.2).

During first year January to December 2008 total number of Ichthyofaunal diversity recorded 733 in Harsool-Savangi Dam and total percentage of fishes recorded at Harsool-Savangi Dam were 86.76 per cent in Cyprinidae, 10.84 per cent in Channidae, 2.04 per cent in Cichlidae and 0.54 per cent in Clariidae. In the second year January - December 2009 total number of Ichthyofaunal diversity recorded 722 at Harsool-Savangi Dam and total percentage of fishes recorded at Harsool-Savangi Dam were 88.22 per cent in Cyprinidae, 9 per cent in Channidae, 2.07 per cent in Cichlidae and 0.69 per cent in Clariidae (Table 4.5, Figs. 4.3 and 4.4).

Table 4.4: Seasonal Groupwise Total Population and Seasonal Variation of Total Population in Ichthyofauna of Harsool-Savangi Dam (January 2008 – December 2009)

		2008				2009			
	Family	Summer	Monsoon	Winter	Total	Summer	Monsoon	Winter	Total
Total Population	Cyprinidae	394	72	170	636	389	72	176	637
	Channidae	57	4	17	78	48	2	15	65
	Cichlidae	9	2	4	15	11	1	3	15
	Clariidae	3	0	1	4	5	0	0	5
Seasonal variation in total population	Cyprinidae	8.95±6.74	1.63±2.02	3.86±4.87		8.84±7.52	1.63±2.08	4±5.82	
	Channidae	7.12±3.52	0.5±1.06	2.12±1.95		6±4.37	0.25±0.46	1.87±1.5	
	Cichlidae	2.25±0.95	0.5±1	1±1.15		2.75±2.21	0.25±0.5	0.75±1.5	
	Clariidae	0.75±0.95	0±0	0.25±0.5		1.25±0.95	0±0	0±0	

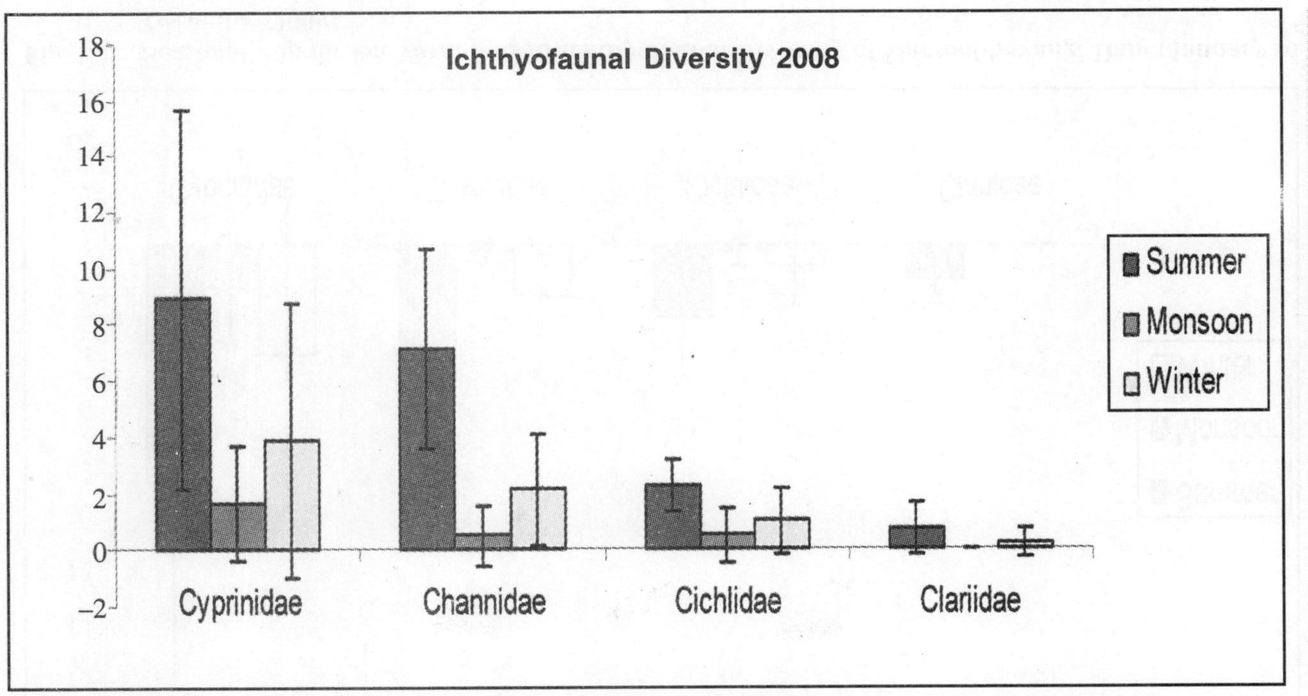

Fig. 4.1: Seasonal Population Variations in Ichthyofaunal Diversity of Harsool-Savangi Dam (January to December 2008)

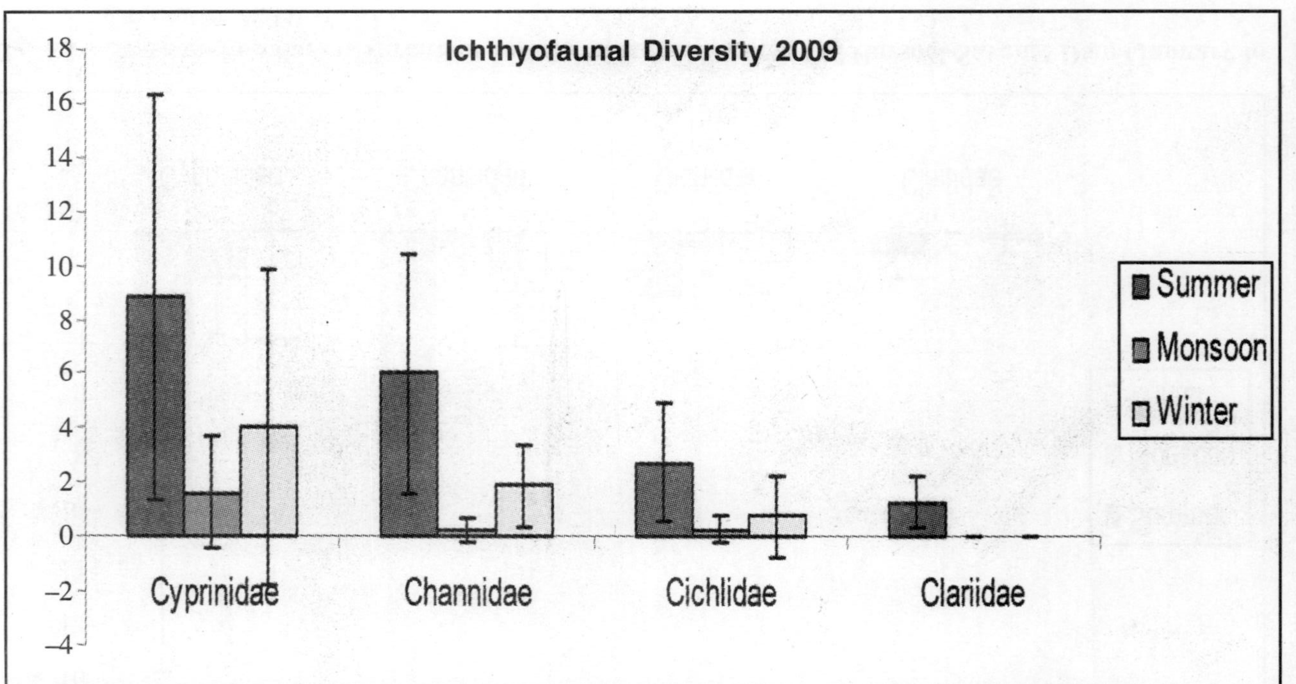

Fig 4.2: Seasonal Population Variations in Ichthyofaunal Diversity of Harsool-Savangi Dam (January to December 2009)

Table 4.5: Total Number and Familywise Total Percentage in Ichthyofauna of Harsool-Savangi Dam (January 2008 – December 2009)

Year	2008		2009	
Family	Total Fish	Total percentage %	Total Fish	Total percentage %
Cyprinidae	733	86.76	722	88.22
Channidae		10.84		9.00
Cichlidae		2.04		2.07
Clariidae		0.54		0.69

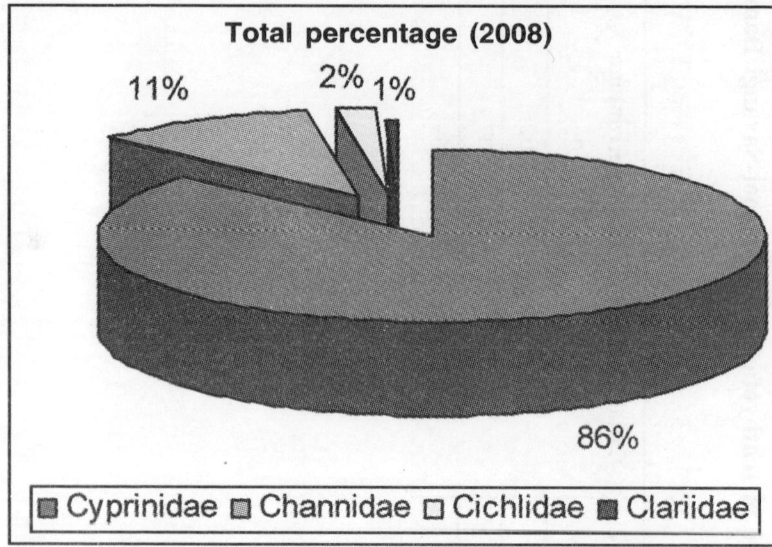

Fig. 4.3: Annual Familywise Percentage Population Density of Ichthyofaunal Diversity Harsool-Savangi Dam (January to December 2008)

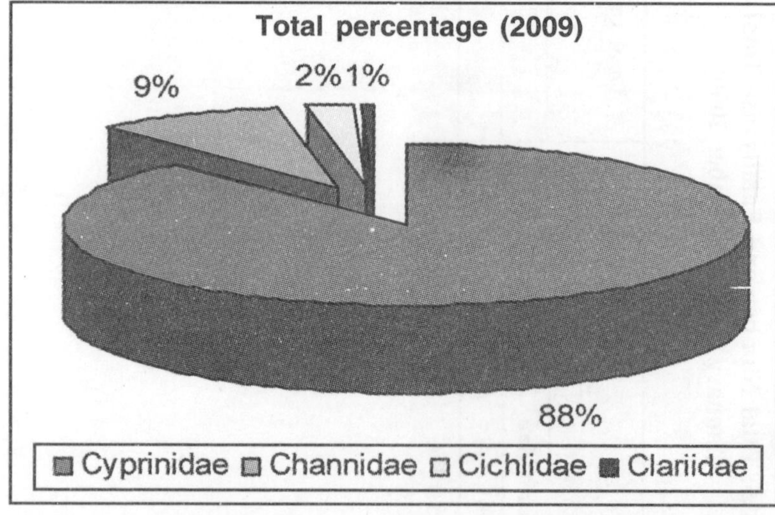

Fig. 4.4: Annual Familywise Percentage Population Density of Ichthyofaunal Diversity Harsool-Savangi Dam (January to December 2009)

In first year January to December 2008 annual variations in Ichthyofaunal diversity indices of Harsool-Savangi Dam at species richness 15 in total number of species (N_0), 2.12 in Margalef's index (R_1) and 0.55 in Menhinick index (R_2). Species diversity were 0.76 in Simpson index (l), 0.42 in Shannon-Weiner index (H'), 1.52 in abundant species (N_1) and 1.31 in very abundant species (N_2). Species evenness was 0.15 in (E_1), 0.10 in (E_2), 0.03 in (E_3), 0.86 in (E_4) and 0.34 in (E_5). In the second year January-December 2009 annual variations in Ichthyofaunal diversity indices of Harsool-Savangi Dam at species richness were 15 in total number of species (N_0), 2.12 in Margalef's index (R_1) and 0.55 in Menhinick index (R_2). Species diversity were 0.78 in Simpson index (l), 0.42 in Shannon-Weiner index (H'), 1.52 in abundant species (N_1) and 1.28 in very abundant species (N_2). Species evenness was 0.15 in (E_1), 0.10 in (E_2), 0.03 in (E_3), 0.84 in (E_4) and 0.37 in (E_5) (Table 4.6).

In the study January 2008-December 2009 fish populations indicating significant positive correlation with water temperature, transparency and pH and it indicating significant negative correlation with turbidity, electric conductivity, total solid, total dissolved solids, total suspended solids, dissolved oxygen, biochemical oxygen demand, chemical oxygen demand, alkalinity, total hardness, sulphate, nitrate and phosphate (Tables 4.7 and 4.8).

Fishing operations carried out throughout year with low catches in monsoon as compared higher in summer and winter seasons. It is suggested that the fishery authorities should notice and practice the proper exploitation and management of inland fishery resources according to ecological principals. They should recommend and determine the stocking standards and reasonable introduction according to potential of fish productivity and characteristics of this water body. Scientific fishing standard and fishing quotas should be worked out; which will play an important role in protection of the reservoir and its biodiversity. Thus, it is necessary for every individual to play an active role regarding sustainable fishery development and hand over the resources in healthy conditions to the future generations.

Table 4.6: Annual Variation in Ichthyofaunal Diversity Indices of Harsool–Savangi Dam (January 2008 - December 2009)

Year		2008	2009
Indices	Index	Ichthyofaunal Diversity	Ichthyofaunal Diversity
Species Richness	(N_0)	15.00	15.00
	(R_1)	2.12	2.12
	(R_2)	0.55	0.55
Species Diversity	(λ)	0.76	0.78
	(H′)	0.42	0.42
	(N_1)	1.52	1.52
	(N_2)	1.31	1.28
Species Evenness	(E_1)	0.15	0.15
	(E_2)	0.10	0.10
	(E_3)	0.03	0.03
	(E_4)	0.86	0.84
	(E_5)	0.34	0.37

(R_1): Margalef's index
(R_2): Menhinick index
(λ): Simpson's index
(H′): Shannon – Weiner index
(N_0): No. of all species
(N_1): No. of abundant species
(N_2): No. of very abundant species
(E_1): Evenness index
(E_2): Evenness index
(E_3): Evenness index
(E_4): Evenness index
(E_5): Evenness index

In the present study, fishes have been studied under four family viz., Cyprinidae, Channidae, Cichlidae and Clariidae. Cyprinidae showed its dominance in Harsool-Savangi Dam followed by Channidae, Cichlidae and Clariidae.

In present study species richness recorded same in both years. In species diversity maximum Simpson index recorded in first year and minimum in next year. Shannon-Weiner index recorded same in both years. Species evenness recorded same in both years.

During present study, Fish Species Diversity Index (FSDI), Simpson's index (l) which varied 0 to 1, gives the probability that two individuals drawn at random from a population belong to the same species. Simply stated, if the probability was high that both individuals belong to the same species, then the diversity of the community sample was low. Shannon's Index (H'), combines species richness and spices evenness components as one overall index of diversity. The higher values of Shannon's Index (H'), indicated the greater species diversity. The greater species diversity means large food chain and more of inter-specific interactions and greater possibilities for negative feedback control which reduced oscillations and hence increases the stability of the community.

According to May (1975) the Shannon-Weaver diversity index was related to both the total number of species and their relative abundances and can be designated as a positive function of total number of species. This diversity index indicates that the ponds under study have a well balanced Fish community that enjoyed an even representation of several species indicating the dynamic nature of this aquatic ecosystem. However, remedial measures should be undertaken to minimize the impact of pollution load as revealed by the ecological indicators. Equitability (evenness) was relatively high during the rainy season indicating a reduction in the plankton diversity at this period (Adesalu and Nwankwo, 2008).

Peet (1974) has reported that species diversity implies both richness and evenness in the number of species and equitability for the distribution of individual among the species. Evenness indices indicate whether all species in a sample are equally abundant. This means that species evenness decreased with increasing size of the fish's population. The indices E_1, E_2 and E_3 are also sensitive to species richness while E_4 and E_5 are relatively unaffected by species richness.

The present study reveals the occurrence of total 15 fish species belonging to 3 orders, 4 families and 12 genera.

Table 4.7: Values of Correlation Coefficient Among Physico-chemical Parameters, Phytoplanktons, Zooplanktons and Fishes Density of Harsool-Savangi Dam during January to December 2008

Parameters	W.T (0°C)	Turbidity (NTU)	Tra. (cm)	pH	E.C (μmhos/cm)	T.S (mg/l)	TDS (mg/l)	TSS (mg/l)	DO (mg/l)
W.T(0°C)	1								
Turbidity (NTU)	-0.17	1							
Transperancy (cm)	0.68*	-0.83**	1						
pH	0.99**	-0.16	0.67*	1					
E.C(μmhos /cm)	-0.69*	0.83**	-0.99**	-0.68*	1				
TS(mg/l)	-0.87**	0.63*	-0.95**	-0.86**	0.95**	1			
TDS(mg/l)	-0.88**	0.61*	-0.94**	-0.88**	0.94**	0.99**	1		
TSS(mg/l)	-0.50	0.93**	-0.97**	-0.49	0.97**	0.86**	0.84**	1	
DO(mg/l)	-0.98**	0.003	-0.54	-0.98**	0.55	0.77**	0.79**	0.34	1
BOD(mg/l)	-0.68*	0.83**	-0.99**	-0.68*	0.99**	0.95**	0.94**	0.97**	0.55
COD(mg/l)	-0.69*	0.83**	-0.99**	-0.68*	0.99**	0.95**	0.94**	0.97**	0.55
Alkalinity (mg/l)	0.99**	-0.23	0.72**	0.99**	-0.73**	-0.90**	-0.91**	-0.55	-0.97**
Total Hardns. (mg/l)	-0.35	0.98**	-0.92**	-0.35	0.92**	0.76**	0.75**	0.98**	0.19
Sulphate (mg/l)	0.92**	0.22	0.34	0.92**	-0.35	-0.61*	-0.63*	-0.13	-0.97**
Chloride (mg/l)	0.98**	-0.01	0.55	0.98**	-0.56	-0.77**	-0.79**	-0.35	-0.99**
Nitrate(mg/l)	-0.38	0.97**	-0.93**	-0.37	0.93**	0.78**	0.76**	0.99**	0.21
Phosphate (mg/l)	-0.76**	0.76**	-0.99**	-0.75**	0.99**	0.98**	0.97**	0.94**	0.64*
Fish	0.74**	-0.78**	0.99**	0.73**	-0.99**	-0.97**	-0.96**	-0.95**	-0.61*

(Contd...)

Parameters	BOD (mg/l)	COD (mg/l)	Alkalinity (mg/l)	T.H (mg/l)	Sulphate (mg/l)	Chloride (mg/l)	Nitrate (mg/l)	Phosphate (mg/l)	Fish
W.T(0°C)									
Turbidity (NTU)									
Transperancy (cm)									
pH									
E.C (μmhos/cm)									
TS(mg/l)									
TDS(mg/l)									
TSS(mg/l)									
DO (mg/l)									
BOD (mg/l)	1								
COD (mg/l)	0.99**	1							
Alkalinity (mg/l)	-0.73**	-0.73**	1						
T.H(mg/l)	0.92**	0.92**	-0.41	1					
Sulphate (mg/l)	-0.35	-0.35	0.89**	0.03	1				
Chloride (mg/l)	-0.56	-0.56	0.97**	-0.20	0.97**	1			
Nitrate(mg/l)	0.93**	0.93**	-0.43	0.99**	0.007	-0.22	1		
Phosphate (mg/l)	-0.99**	0.99**	0.80**	0.87**	-0.45	-0.64*	0.88**	1	
Fish	-0.99**	-0.99**	0.78**	-0.89**	0.42	0.62*	-0.90**	-0.99**	1

** significant at $p < 0.01$, * significant at $p < 0.05$, W.T = Water temperature, Tra. = Transparency, E.C = Electrical conductivity, T.S = Total solids, T.D.S = Total Dissolved Solids, T.S.S. = Total Suspended Solids, DO= Dissolved Oxygen, BOD= Biochemical Oxygen Demand, COD= Chemical Oxygen Demand, T.H = Total Hardness.

Table 4.8: Values of Correlation Coefficient Among Physico-chemical Parameters, Phytoplanktons, Zooplanktons and Fishes Density of Harsool-Savangi Dam during January to December 2009

Parameter	W.T (0°C)	Turbidity (NTU)	Tra. (cm)	pH	E.C (μmhos/cm)	T.S (mg/l)	TDS (mg/l)	TSS (mg/l)	DO (mg/l)
W.T(0°C)	1								
Turbidity (NTU)	-0.38	1							
Transparency (cm)	0.64*	-0.95**	1						
pH	0.98**	-0.52	0.76**	1					
E.C (μmhos /cm)	-0.65*	0.94**	-0.99**	-0.77**	1				
TS(mg/l)	-0.81**	0.84**	-0.96**	-0.89**	0.97**	1			
TDS(mg/l)	-0.82**	0.83**	-0.96**	-0.90**	0.96**	0.99**	1		
TSS(mg/l)	-0.56	0.97**	-0.99**	-0.68*	0.99**	0.93**	0.93**	1	
DO(mg/l)	-0.98**	0.22	-0.51	-0.94**	0.52	0.70*	0.72**	0.42	1
BOD(mg/l)	-0.64*	0.95**	-0.99**	-0.76**	0.99**	0.97**	0.96**	0.99**	0.51
COD(mg/l)	-0.65*	0.94**	-0.99**	-0.76**	0.99**	0.97**	0.96**	0.99**	0.52
Alkalinity (mg/l)	0.97**	-0.16	0.45	0.92**	-0.46	-0.65*	-0.67*	-0.35	-0.99**
Total Hardns. (mg/l)	-0.32	0.99**	-0.93**	-0.47	0.92**	0.81**	0.80**	0.96**	0.17
Sulphate(mg/l)	0.98**	-0.19	0.48	0.93**	-0.50	-0.68*	-0.69*	-0.39	-0.99**
Chloride(mg/l)	0.99**	-0.28	0.55	0.96**	-0.57	-0.74**	-0.75**	-0.46	-0.99**
Nitrate(mg/l)	-0.31	0.99**	-0.92**	-0.46	0.92**	0.80**	0.79**	0.96**	0.15
Phosphate (mg/l)	-0.72**	0.91**	-0.99**	-0.83**	0.99**	0.99**	0.98**	0.97**	0.60*
Fish	0.68*	-0.93**	0.99**	0.79**	-0.99**	-0.99**	-0.98**	-0.97**	-0.98**

(Contd...)

Parameter	BOD (mg/l)	COD (mg/l)	Alkalinity (mg/l)	T.H (mg/l)	Sulphate (mg/l)	Chloride (mg/l)	Nitrate (mg/l)	Phosphate (mg/l)	Fish
W.T(0°C)									
Turbidity (NTU)									
Tra.(cm)									
pH									
E.C(μmhos /cm)									
TS(mg/l)									
TDS(mg/l)									
TSS(mg/l)									
DO(mg/l)									
BOD(mg/l)	1								
COD(mg/l)	0.99**	1							
Alkalinity (mg/l)	-0.45	-0.46	1						
T.H(mg/l)	0.93**	0.92**	-0.10	1					
Sulphate(mg/l)	-0.48	-0.49	0.99**	-0.13	1				
Chloride(mg/l)	-0.56	-0.56	0.99**	-0.22	0.99**	1			
Nitrate(mg/l)	0.92**	0.92**	-0.08	0.99**	-0.12	-0.20	1		
Phosphate (mg/l)	0.99**	0.99**	-0.55	0.88**	-0.58	-0.65*	0.87**	1	
Fish	-0.56	-0.99**	0.99**	0.50	-0.90**	0.53	-0.60*	-0.90**	1

**significant at $p < 0.01$, *significant at $p < 0.05$, **W.T = Water temperature, Tra. = Transparency, E.C = Electrical conductivity, T.S = Total solids, T.D.S = Total Dissolved Solids, T.S.S. = Total Suspended Solids, DO= Dissolved Oxygen, BOD= Biochemical Oxygen Demand, COD= Chemical Oxygen Demand, T.H = Total Hardness.

The order Cypriniformes found dominant with 11 species, followed by Perciformes 3 species and Siluriformes with one species. Seasonally, fishes showed its dominance during summer season followed by winter and monsoon season.

During summer, the rise in temperature enhances the rate of decomposition due to which the water becomes nutrient rich similarly due to concentration followed by evaporation in summer season the nutrient concentration increases and abundant food present in form of Phytoplanktons, zooplanktons and micro-organism to fish that's why high fish population density during the summer season could be related to stable hydrological factors and low water level due to high catch, while low density during the monsoon season is attributed to heavy flood and fresh water inflow. They are resumed again in monsoon due to dilution and high water level due to low catch.

Conclusion

1. The present study thus indicates seasonal fluctuation of physico-chemical parameters and ichthyofaunal.
2. The water of present reservoir is useful for irrigation as well as fish culture.
3. The water parameters indicate that the reservoir is rich in nutrients.
4. Total hardness was found beyond the permissible limit in monsoon season according to WHO and ISI standards for drinking purpose.
5. Physico-chemical parameters increased in second year compared with first year study.
6. Ichthyofaunal population density increased in first year compared with second year study.
7. The presence of species will depend on its environmental tolerance, but the resources available will determine its abundance. If competition or predation is reduced or the food supply or suitable habitat increased, the species will become more abundant.
8. In the present study basic information of fish distribution and abundance form a useful tool for further ecological assessment and monitoring of ecosystems at Harsool-Savangi dam.

9. Fish were characterized by higher diversity, lower dominance and higher evenness with indefinite patterns of annual variations.
10. According to Shannon index values 0 > 1 at north site i.e. shows the habitat is under stress polluted; 1 < 3 at south, east and west sites i.e. shows not highly polluted and above 3 i.e. show healty habitat.
11. According to biodiversity indices values show year by year pollution increase in dam and under going stress pollution conditions.
12. To improve water quality ichthyofaunal diversity of dam should be continuous monitoring of pollution level.
13. To maintain the favourable conditions essential for fish survival, growth and reproduction in Harsool-Savangi Dam Aurangabad (M.S) India.
14. It concludes that further studies may carry out in connection with developed techniques regarding fish culturing. The use of illegal methods of catch fish should be banned in this area to prevent further depletion of freshwater fish resources.
15. The fisherman's should make aware of fishing, scientific training and facilities made available to the fish farmers fishing of the spawn, larval fish and immature fish should be avoided and subsidies loan facility may be provided on large scales may help for high yield of fish production in the Harsool-Savangi Dam.
16. Maintain diversity has immense importance as it is not always possible to identify individual species but critical to sustain aquatic ecosystem.
17. The present work will provide future strategies for development and biodiversity conservation of Harsool-Savangi Dam.

Bibliography

Adesalu, T.A. and Nwankwo, D.I. (2008): Effect of Water Quality Indices on Phytoplankton of a Sluggish Tidal Creek in Lagos, Nigeria. *Pakistan J. Biol. Sci.*, 11: 836-844.

Alatalo, R.V. (1981): Problems in the Measurement of Evenness in Ecology. *Oikos*. 37: 199-204.

Anitha, G. (2002): "Hydrography in Relation to Benthic Macro-invertebrates in Mir-Alam Lake Hyderabad Andhra Pradesh, India". Ph.D. Thesis submitted to Osmania University. Hyderabad.

APHA (2005): *Standard Methods for the Examination of Water and Waste Waters*, 21st Edn., Washington, DC. USA.

Bhatt, S.D. and Negi, U. (1985): Physico-chemical Features and Phytoplanktons Population in a Subtropical Pond. Comp. *Physiol. Ecol.*, 10(2): 85-88.

Boyd, C.E. and Tucker, C.S. (1998): Pond Aquaculture and *Water Quality Management*. Kluwer Academic Pub., London, 44-8.

Burton, P.J; Balisky, A.E; Coward, L.P; Cumming, S.G. and Kneshwaw, D.D. (1992): The Value of Managing Biodiversity. *The Forestry Chronicle* 68 (2); 225-237.

Chhatawal, G.R. (1998): Encyclopedia of Environmental Biology. Vol. 2, 287-301. *Anmol Pub. Pvt. Ltd.*, New Delhi, India.

CIFE (1998): *Training Mannual of Central Institute of Fisheries Education*, Vorsoa Mumbai.

Day, F.S. (1994): *The Fishes of India, being a Natural History of the Fishes Known to Inhabit the Seas & Freshwaters of India, Burma & Ceylon*, Fourth Indian Reprint. Vols. I & II. Jagmander Book Agency, New Delhi.

Deshmukh, J.U. and Ambore, N.E. (2006): Seasonal Variationss in Physical Aspects of Pollution in Godavari River at Nanded. Maharashtra, India. *J. Aqua. Biol.*, Vol. 21(2), 93-96.

De, A.K. (2002): *Environmental Chemistry*. 4th ed., New Age International Publication, New Delhi, 231-232.

Devi Rama, T. (2007): Study of Some Aspects of Hydrobiology of Alisagar Dam Water, Ph.D. Thesis submitted, S.R.T. University, Nanded.

Dwivedi, S.N. (2000): S&T Approach for Exponential Growth in Fish Production (In: Souvenir, *The Fifth Indian Fisheries Forum, CIFA*, pp. 14-18.

Ehrlich, P.R. and Wilson, E.O. (1991): Biodiversity Studies Science and Policy. *Science* 253: 758-762.

Gonzalves, E.A. and Joshi, D.B. (1946): Fresh Water Algae Near Bombay. I. The Seasonal Succession of the Algae in a Tank of Bandra. *J. Bomb. Nat. Hist. Soc.* 46: 154-176.

Heip, C. (1974): A New Index Measuring Evenness, *Journal of Marine Biological Association*. 54: 555-557.

Hill, M.O. (1973): Diversity and Evenness; A Unifying Notation and its Consequences, *Ecology*. 54: 427-432.

Holmes, J.W. and Talsma, T. (1981): *Land and Stream Salinity*. Ellsevier Scentific Publishing Co., Amsterdam.

Hulyal, S.B. and Kaliwal, B.B. (2008): Water Quality Assessment of Almatti Reservoir of Bijapur (Karnataka State, India) With Special Reference to Zooplanktons. *Environ. Monit. Assess.* Vol. 139: 299-306.

IAAB (1998): *Methodology for Water Analysis*.

Iwama, G.K., Vijayan, M.M. and Morgan, J.D. (2000): Stress *Response in Fish. Ichthyology, Recent Research Advances*. Oxford and IBH pub. Co. Ltd, New Delhi. 453.

Jayabhaye, U.M., Pentewar, M. S. and Hiware, C.J. (2008): A Study on Physico-chemical Parameters of a Minor Reservoir, Sawana, Hingoli District, Maharashtra. *J. Aqua. Biol.*, Vol 23 (2): 56-60.

Jayaram, K.C. (1999): *The Freshwater Fishes of the Indian Region*, Narendra Publication House, New Delhi; India XVIII.

Jhingran, V.G. (1977): *Fish and Fisheries of India*. Hindustan Publishing Corporation, India.

Joshi, P.K. and Sakhare, S.V. (2003): Physico-chemical Limnology of Papnas: A Minor Wetland in Tuljapur Town, Maharashtra. India. *J. Aqua. Biol, Vol.*, 18 (2): 87-91.

Kaliya Murthy, M. (1973): Observations on the Transparency of the Waters of the Pulicat Lake with Particular Reference to Plankton Population. *Hydrobiologia* 41: 3-11.

Kant, S. and Raina, A.K. (1990): Limnological Studies of Two Ponds in Jammu II Physiological parameters. *J. Env. Biol.* 11 (2): 137.

Kaven, N. and Bell, R.C. (1965): Primary Productivity and Energy Relationship in Artificial Streams. *Limnol. and Oceanogr*. 10 (1): 74-87.

Khan, A.A., Kartha, K.N., Percy Dawson and George V.C. (1991): Fish Harvesting Systems in Indian Reservoirs. *Proc of Nat. Workshop on Low Energy Fishing*, 8-9.

Khan Atiya and Zafar, A.R. (1983): Inter-relationship Amongst Biomass Parameters of Phytoplanktons and Filamentous Algal Community. *J. Aqua. Biol.* 1 (1): 17-18.

Khabade, S.K., Mule, M.B. and Sathe, S.S. (2002): Studies on Physico-chemical Parameters of Iodhe Water Reservoir from Tasgaon Teshil (Maharastra): Indian. *J. Environ and Ecoplan.*, 6 (2): 301-304.

Kim, B., Ju-Hyun Park., Gilson Hwang., Man-Sig Jun and Kwangsoon Choi (2001): Eutrophication of Reservoirs in South Korea. *Limnology*. 2: 223-229.

Korai, A.L., Sahato, G.A. and Lashari, K.H. (2008): Fish Diversity in Relation to Physico-chemical Properties of Keenjhar Lake (District, Thatta), Sindh, Pakistan. *Res. J. Fish. & Hydrobiol.,* 3(1): 1-10.

Kudari, V.A., Kadadevaru, G.G. and Kanamadi, R.D. (2006): Characterisation of Selected Lentic Habitates of Dharwad, Haveri and Uttar Kannada districts of Karnataka State, India. *Environmental Monitoring and Assessment* 120: 387-405.

Lal, B. (1981): "Ecology of Bhainsa Tiba pond, Amabala, Haryana". M.Phil Thesis, Panjab Univeristy, Chandigarh (India). 126.

Lepoid, L.B. (1968): Hydrology for Urban Land Planning. A Guide Book on the Hydrologic Effects of Urban Land Use. US. *Geol. Surv. Cric.* 554-18.

Lloyd, R. (1992): Pollution and Fresh Water Fish, *Fishing News Books*.

Lovley, D.R. and Klug, M.J. (1983): Sulphate Reducers Competed Mehanogens at Fresh Water Sulphate Concentrations. *Appl. Environ. Microbiol.* 45: 187-192.

Ludwik, J.A. and Reynolds, J.F. (1998): *Statistical Ecology a Primer on Methods and Computing*. A Wiley-Interscience Publication. New York. pp. 1-337.

Margalef, R. (1958): Information Theory in Ecology, *General Systematic,* 3: 36-71.

May, R.M. (1975): *Patterns of Species Abundance and Diversity in Ecology and Evolution of Communities* (Eds.: M.L. Cody and J.M. Diamond), The Belknap Pres of Harvard Univers ity Pres, Cambridge, Massachusetts. pp. 81-120.

Menhinick, E.P. (1964): A Comparison of Some Species - Individuals Diversity Indices Applied to Samples of Field Insects. *Ecol.,* 45: 859-881.

Pailwan, I.F. and Muley, D.V. (2006): Limnology and Fishery Status of a Fresh Water Perennial Tank at Kaneriwadi Near Kolhapur, (M.S.), India. *J. Aqua. Biol.,* Vol. (212), 72-76.

Pawar, B.A. and Mane, U.H. (2006): Hydrography of a Sadatpur Lake Near Pravaranagar, Ahmednagar District, Maharashtra. *J. Aqua. Biol.* Vol. 21 (1): 101-104.

Peet, R.K. (1974): The Measurement of Species Diversity. *Ann. Rev. Ecol. Systematic*, 5: 285-307.

Pielou, E.C. (1977): *Mathematical Ecology*, Wiley, New York.

Piska, R.S. (2000): *Concepts of Aquaculture*, Lahari Publications Hyderabad.

Prasad, S.C., Singh, J.P., Yadav, P.K., Singh, S. (1999): BOD Contamination in Kali River at Sadnu Ashram in Aligarh. *Indian J. Env. Port.* 11(5): 325-326.

Rahman, A.K.A. (2005): *Freshwater Fishes of Bangladesh*. The Zoological Society of Bangladesh, Dhaka.

Rao, Y.N.R. and Valsaraj, C.P. (1984): Hydrological Studies in the Inshore Waters of the Bay of Bengal. *J. Mar. Biol. Ass. India*, 26 (1&2): 58-65.

Rigler, F.H. (1956): A Trace Study of the Phosphorous Cycle in Lake Water. *Ecology*, 37: 550-562.

Salaskar Pramod (1998): "*Some Environmental Aspects of Powai Lake*", Ph.D. Thesis University of Mumbai.

Shashikant and Raina, A.K. (1990): "Limnological Studies of Two Ponds in Jammu". *J. Env. Bio.* Vol. 11 (2): 137-144.

Saxsena, M.M. (1987): *Environmental Analysis of Water, Soil and Air*. Agro-botanical Publishers, India: 1-176.

Shinde, S.E., Pathan, T.S., Bhandare, R.Y. and Sonawane, D.L. (2009 a): Ichthyofaunal Diversity of Harsool-Savangi Dam, District Aurangabad, (M. S.) India. *World J. Fish & Marine sci.*, 1(3): 141-143.

Shinde, S.E., Pathan, T.S., Raut, K.S., Bhandare, R.Y. and Sonawane, D.L. (2009 b): Fish biodiversity of Pravara River, in Devgad Dist. Ahamadnagar, (M. S) India. *World J. Zool.*, 4 ([illegible]): 176-179.

Singh, T.S. (1984): "Ecology of Zooplanktons in the Lower Lake", Ph.D. Thesis Bhopal University, Bhopal.

Smith, R.D. and Maltby, E. (2003): Using the Ecosystem Approach to Implement the Convention on Biological Diversity: Key Issues and Case Studies. *IUCN, Gland, Switzerland and Cambridge*, U.K. p. 118.

Sone, A.A. and Malu, R.A. (2000): Fish Diversity in Relation to Aquaculture in Ekburgii Reservoir, Washim, Maharashtra. *J. Aqua. Biol.* Vol. 15 (1 & 2): 40-42.

Sreenivasan, A. (1991): Integrated Development of Reservoir Fisheries of India; Production to Marketing; *Fishing Chimes*. April issue: 60-63.

Sugunan V.V. (1995): *Reservoir Fisheries of India. FAO fisheries Tech.* Paper No. 345 FAO Rome: 1-424 Ps.

Talwar, P.K. and Jhingran, A.G. (1991): *Inland Fishes of India and Adjacent Countries*. Oxford and IBH Publishing Co. Pvt. Ltd., New Delhi. 1-322.

Trivedy, R.K. and Goel, P.K. (1984): *Chemical and Biological Methods for Water Pollution Studies*, Environmental Publications, Karad, India. 122.

Verma, S.R. and Dalela (1975): Studies on the Pollution of Kalinadi by Industrial Waste Near Mansupur Part-I, Hydrometric and Physico-chemical Characteristic of the Wastes and River Water. *Hydrobiol.* 3 (3): 230-257.

Verma, S.R., Tyagi, A.K. and Dalella, R.C. (1978): Pollution Studies of a Few Rivers of Western Uttar Pradesh With Reference to Biological Indices. *Proc. Ind. Acad. Sci. B.* 87 (6): 123-131.

Vernberg, G.G. and Liaknoich, V.P. (1965): Udobrenie Prudov (Fertilization of Fish Pond). Moscow. Ladatel Stovo Pischcherai Promyshelennost. *Fish Res. F Canada. Sv. No.* 1339: pp. 484 [INT].

Voznaya, N.F. (1981): Chemistry of Water and Microbiology (Trans. A. Rosinkin) MIR Publ. Moscow.

Watson Susan, B. and John Lawrence (2003): Overview Drinking Water Quality and Sustainability. *Water Qual. Res. Jour. Canada.* 38 (1): 3-13.

Welch, P.S. (1952): *Limnology Municipal Corporation*. Graw-Hill Book Co., New York: 538.

Wetzel, R.G. (1975): *Limnology* (Ed): W.B.S. Saunders Company, Philadelphia, 743.

Yadav, Y.S., Sing, R.K., Choudhary, M. and Kalekar, V. (1987): Limnology and Productivity of Dilghali Bhel (Assam), India. *Trop. Ecol.* Vol (28): 137-147.

Index